A
THOUSAND
SCREAMING
MONKEYS

One Man's Journey
To Peace Through
Addiction, Alcoholism
and Recovery

Kevin Arthur Hart

FOR THE JOURNEY

Cover design by Rhonda Dicksion, Indigo Dog Design

Formatting by Rory Briski, Briski Consulting, LLC

ISBN-13: 978-0-9860914-6-9

Published by Merkabah Press
(www.merkabahpress.com)

This book is dedicated to all who love the great mystery of human existence.

I owe a debt of gratitude to many others besides my patient editor, J.R. Nakken, who has helped me immeasurably. Throughout our lifetimes many people intersect our paths to help us. Oftentimes, the ones that seem to cause us the greatest stress instead turn out to offer the most profound opportunity. Some stick around, others soon disappear.

Many have helped forge this story and many more helped in the writing process. To all who have impacted not only my own story but also those who gave their time, encouragement, resources, and stood by my side to see this book and journey through to completion, for whatever purposes it may serve, please accept my deepest gratitude.

You know who you are.

Thank You

Prologue

You hold in your hands a true story of my life. It was not easy to write and no easier to bring it through to completion, mostly due to the raw nature and sharing at such an intimate level with any who might read. But it is for a purpose; part of that purpose is to be helpful to those who struggle with similar issues or find their lives affected by those who do. This snapshot of a specific time in my life, with glimpses of a whole life's overview, is much an exercise in radical self-awareness. The story does get ugly in its candor, but the price had to be paid. If you can remain steadfast, it should be of benefit.

I could never have done this alone. A series of seemingly strange events occurred along the way, one after the other, usually just when I was confused or unsure or ready to give up. As these events occurred, it felt much like being used by something beautiful and wonderful. Why was life so agonizing before? Some of the reasons deep suffering occurs in the lives of human beings have come to my awareness. The focus of this story stays on me as I learned of them.

The first chapter takes place in the misty, marvelous, mushroom-filled Pacific Northwest just north of Seattle, in 2006. *Welcome Home* was written at the place the book was born *(Mosswood Hollow, Duvall, Washington)* in 2011 as an epilogue. It somehow found its way to the first pages instead. My spirit guides often lead me in this manner, in ways that seem strange but always reveal a greater purpose than I may have initially been aware. This is also how it came to be that the story is told in the third person rather than the first.

This was a simple choice, seemingly arbitrary at the time. But over the years the process took, the reasons became more and more apparent. It allowed me distance from what I once was; the Kevin I wrote about here is not who I am now. Telling the tale in the third person brought freedom to share not only who I was at that time and how the lessons came, but also to offer the benefit of hindsight and much that I've learned since that time. It also allowed me to tell the story without fear that I might sanitize some of the uglier truths. As is often said in the circles in which I now roam: *You can't save your ass and your face at the same time.*

Well, here we are.

When human beings set out to truly find their purpose, to find the 'belonging' for which we all long, the entire universe soon shifts and moves to bring us everything we need. Offering this book now helps me fulfill my own purpose. My greatest wish is that it be of service, somehow, to you.

Table of Contents

Welcome Home

Does everyone wonder of their purpose? How many live in the loneliness and long for another way?

Today is unlike any other day, and March has brought a gift. A snow covered porch is a worthy perch from which to view the white-laden cedar boughs drooping from the unlikely storm. One lone trail showing the only trace of terra firma leads down to a warm yurt where a group of writers had just spent the last several days.

Much has transpired. Tea steams in a green-speckled mug on a cold, solid wood table. Long gazes over the landscape take in Mother Nature's masterpiece. Puffs of cool air breathe the panorama deep into happier lungs, hands gently clasped upon the small of the back. The huge cabin attached to the porch is surrounded by a living forest now covered in ivory splendor. Only a day ago the waking green canopy had been washed in brilliant orange sunlight. Sober eyes absorb each nuance. Although others are nearby, in this moment it is only …

How can any of this be? Certainly it must come from the depth of possibility, that sea of pure potential upon which certain beings somehow stumble. Anyone can find it. What is it that brings awakening, especially from such a low place?

Surely this moment is the cusp of massive transformation into the unknown. Life will weave as unpredictably as this March's bringing of a fine crystal blanket, this filter which has changed everything, if only in perception and experience. Living proof of two vastly different lives in one human body drank in the contemplations.

Someone along the way spoke it. "You can become anything you desire." And so it is, for the things authored and released had come now. But do they not always? We really can fly. We become what we believe. It is what brings this moment.

This life was not possible before the magnificent surrender. The long journey is worth every step. Free of the once constant companion, fear, a humble smile came upon the day. One cedar branch sprang back up and waved as its soggy burden slipped, fell to the ground.

So many had helped thus far, how many more would now? In the Heart they live forever. Living dreams is for those that dare the courage to believe. The new found strength did not come from where it had always been sought. Being used by it, a new world rose up and came alive. But did the old hell have any purpose?

Can entire lifetimes be realized right now? Are all things made only from Imagination, our divine workshop, where all is given? Perhaps the price of admission is only willingness and faith. Surely it is for something. But, how does it work? Figuring it all out was the candy of lesser gods. Enjoying it is enough, sharing the inheritance. Here is peace. Control and domination had been traded in for Love and Gratitude. Where must this path lead?

Little hummingbird appeared suddenly, near a contraption hanging off the overhang. She hovered back and forth with her message. A long time seemed to have passed as the two beings observed each other in the stillness - but it was only a few moments, a handful of breaths. The precious creature darted to each port on the feeder, wings nearly invisible. Then, just as quickly was it gone.

Life sure had become simple. In the stillness are the golden threads revealed. Freedom is for any who allow it. A hidden passageway uncovered, Treasure filled the once great emptiness.

But, it had not always been this way ...

~ Chapter 1 ~

The Access Point

The world was as dark as it had ever been. A shell of a man, a lost ghost, approached the bleak little shack. Light, here, was unpleasant and unwelcome. An old, foul and hideous fog lingered, thickening with each step. Walking with any kind of purpose other than this, this meager existence; what would that even feel like? Living a greater purpose – surely there was no way. Kevin had given up on anything remotely resembling it. The old dwelling, this tired dungeon of mind and thought - danger lurked in every shadow and every crack. It was inescapable. What he was about to do only perpetuated it. He entered the shack, anyway. It was small and cluttered, used up, and about to be condemned.

Must be at least six, maybe seven others scattered about the place, shifty and loaded. It seemed like they were watching from around every corner. The scourge ran deep in these circles. Kevin was certainly among the afflicted, wired and paranoid as always, and well beyond tired from not sleeping for too many days, too often - exhausted, and just couldn't care anymore. A zombie, the living dead, with only one thing on a tired, swollen mind: Staying polluted.

I don't belong here! The intimation persisted, raging, from a hazy mess of convoluted thoughts, mouth dry and eyes cocaine wide. *They're hiding in every room! Why do they want to kill me? Do they want to kill me? Am I imagining it?*

Agony.

Desperation.

Life had become a city after a bad earthquake – destroyed and wasted. He had no skills with which to clean it up, any of it, and being trapped beneath the debris left almost no breathable air. What was happening in his head was just too much to bear.

Just one more, then I'll go ...

The man was tall, skinny, and sketched out big time as well as being the tyrant with the goods and a shotgun to protect it. Moving choppy and fast - erratic, the way smoking that shit makes a person move. The uneasiness crawled along his flesh, pushed out from the center of his bones, through every nerve. A disgusting cigarette hung out of pursed, cracked lips, pulsing veins coursed down emaciated arms through a fading tattoo of a skull inside a Celtic cross.

Constant paranoia ran through Kevin, telltale eyes darting this way and that way. Each tweaker, addict and drunk was a possible cop or narc, and with so much delusion at any given time, each was accused of it. Since he was "different" and they were always talking about him, there was a sense, a gross feeling: *They must think I'm out to get them!*

Fear and anxiety plagued every foreboding thought. What if they really found out how scared he was? What if the things left in the attic were found out? What if he admitted the sheer level of desperation that came with the never ending need for that damn hit of dope, the bottles of vodka and the plethora of narcotics - that relief he was sure he needed? It had become such a high price to pay, every time. In fact, time: Time was straight running out. And somewhere in the recesses, he knew it.

But he was out to get himself, though he would be the last to know that. There was something else, beckoning from another place, only he would not look there, couldn't, not now - only one thing was he concerned with. Just one more hit. *God I need it!* The ever present nagging lingered like rotting food, old and festering.

Fifty lousy bucks, that's all he had left, welfare money he'd conned the state out of ... he'd use it to get more if there was more, and if he could avoid the freaks around every corner trying to get over on him. It was no good idea sitting with your back to any doorway or window, and it always seemed like they were trying to make him do just that. If it meant another rock he would go anywhere, though. Nervous, he flipped around in the chair, teeth grinding, expecting an axe to the back of the skull at any moment - strange, why would he not just leave? He would; but first, *just one more ...*

Something else loomed, as well, the same way most cogitation bounced around now - distorted, tainted and painful. *Tomorrow I'm supposed to go to rehab.* He winced around a clenched jaw, knowing he would fail again. He could not make it. This demon had him bad, but he just did not care. Just one more hit and he might do something about it this time, just one more would bring the courage to do *something* about it, although it never did. It was always *just one more and then I'll do it,* and all one more ever did was get you stuck again and again. So tired, so lost.

Nope, he was a fraud and always had been, powerless over life. Despair so great it was ten tons of loose gravel showering down, a falling dark sky – No. If he did not stay high he was going to have to face life and what he had become, feel that gut wrenching horror again and it was just too much.

No!

Loud music blared from the stinking, tiny kitchen, thick in the air … not enough drugs for everyone, and when it got like this, it got weird, man. *Dangerous.*

Kevin began insisting –

"C'mon man, just one more!"

Begging. Desperate. *Pleading –*

"Just sell me a little and I'll be out of here!"

But these guys were not like him, not sheltered with Mommy always giving them everything like his had done. These people would happily kill him. And the man who held the gun and the last of the dope had just gotten out of prison for yet another violent crime. Kevin was in grievous territory and knocking at death's door once again, asking the grim reaper himself for just "one more," imploring him even, taunting him …

"C'MON!"

This man that was literally holding the bag was freaking him out. Kevin was not stupid - just stoned, coming down, and impetuous. Yet, he recognized the energy of someone looking for a fight, looking to share a shotgun blast with any willing participant.

He knew deep rage and could feel it in this man.

Inevitably, the gun was going to be used, maybe even by accident with all the confusion.

And yet, somehow he wanted it - *c'mon, end my suffering, please.* How had his best thinking come to this?

"Come on, dude! Just give me ONE MORE," Kevin implored, like he had been every night, every lonely night, seeking solace in that which only brought more emptiness with every coming down.

Up it came in a fiery instant, aimed at him right between the eyes. Third eye center, to be exact.

"FUCK YOU!" the man blasted with defiant rage, dirty stinking shaking hands cocking the weapon, loving the power, hating life.

Reality itself shifted - Kevin went outside himself.

Time slowed into nothing and everything, some cosmic blur where the walls between realms seemed to melt and fade into each other.

He became a witness, watching the sordid movie, floating above now. In this morbid scene, he and the man now became viewable from above, from all angles, all at once.

What was happening, and how?

He saw from both up close and afar the man's erratic movements, crazy high eyes and finger trembling the trigger … knew the gun was loaded and ready. So ready to perform its function.

A sacrificial ceremony of sorts and he was to be the sacrificed. In the moments that followed, it was as though thousands of lifetimes were revealed. Like some giant expansion of mind, in one instant this strange awareness was available, transcending all previous limitations. It became fractal as he engaged it and viewed from every angle at once his own impaired, pain-ridden body standing there, helpless. A more human part of him thought about what it was going to feel like to be blown to bits like that, could almost feel the tiny pellets separating his brain into fragments, shredding bone and skin.

He invited it.

It was the great instant of retribution. *Here it comes - Death, and it's not so bad.*

In this moment, through the exhaustion of the whole last few years, maybe a whole lifetime of dis-ease culminating in one timeless instant, he even welcomed it.

When suddenly …

A surreal whisper carried him into a safe, ethereal zone. Something greater than the body took over and allowed vision past the double-barrels and directly into this man, through the drug-hazed, angry and desperate eyes of this shotgun-wielding demon, past his mind and into his very depths, into a place where he and Kevin were not separate beings.

In this imperceptible place, their souls struck a silent bargain. He both witnessed and was a part of it all from beyond the scene, suspended in and out of time and space like some docile cherub. It was a gentle and peaceful moment of pure being.

The gun lowered, the entire scene dissipated, and Kevin, back in his body, realized it was a good time to leave and found the strength, somehow, to go.

He left the little shack, slipped out the back door and into his car. Sheba was waiting.

***

Just the sight of her triggered a hundred ugly memories and feelings all at once … and there were no diversions to smoke.

That poor dog, he never was too good with them, always getting angry and losing his temper and often beating them while in his care. Perhaps he was only trying to beat his own demons; he could not even take care of himself. The frustration often boiled over and projected onto a dog or anything else close. There were disgusting things about certain animals, - about people, for that matter - if only reflections of his own need for a loving master and to be taken care of. Maybe this was it; maybe the way a dog relies on the one taking care of it sent him into rage. He sought this, also - someone that would show up and be there, to provide nourishment and love. This is why he never had a dog for too long, just could not be that for anyone or anything.

Just a few days ago it had happened in the car after a long run of using …

He didn't even want to eat, but days without food can be persuasive. Sheba was hungry, also. Part Rottweiler, she was black and tan. The only thing that indicated she was mixed Australian Shepherd was her intelligence, and full-grown size - only 50 pounds. Her brown, begging eyes and head cocked just enough in a gesture of asking for some would have been adorable to anyone else. Instead of appearing cute, it only set him off, and that poor dog – yelping and howling as he hit her over and over with a tight, angry fist. Just like the week before, only that time she retaliated and ripped open his swinging fist. The blood and pain stopped him. He deserved much worse.

Each time he tried to make up, holding her, sobbing. It was killing someone slowly and apologizing as they slipped away in increments. Each time Sheba went colder; she let him weep and hug her, squeeze her shaking body tight even though reeling in the residue of violence. He felt so ashamed and barren afterwards. The hole in his soul just kept growing, a giant vacuum sucking only more emptiness. Sheba felt unsafe, and every movement from her spoke it. *You will only hurt me again. I do not trust you.*

She forgave him, but her confidence in being cared for had slipped yet another notch, and he knew it. This always happened - he knew he could not help himself, and yet still attempted to hold up some miserable two-hundred-ton façade that it was some other way.

How lost and alone and desperate he was!

This memory and so many more like it, the date for treatment tomorrow that he knew he would miss, and a thousand other screaming monkeys closed in as he crawled back in the car, nearly defeated.

What to do. The same answer kept popping up, the one this confused mind had always gone to – more drugs, more booze. *Feed us*, the monkeys insisted, like hairy chomping mental zombies.

He knew another dealer dude and would head there now. *Must be around midnight*, he figured. This guy would be able to hook him up. In the back of a tattered mind that damn bed date the very next day at the treatment center *nagged*. His mom had chosen the place, had done so much trying to help him out of this abyss. She researched places for hours, for days, seeking just the right place that might help her broken son.

But this would mean dealing with the wreckage he had been causing like a shit tornado for these last few years, probably his whole life. *Anyone I touch gets it all over them.*

Already had there been four other dates set up for rehab - always somehow missed. Mom said this would be the last chance, the last time the family would be willing to help. He sure didn't have the damn money for it and his brother had reluctantly agreed to pay the bill on the condition it was paid back, even though he would likely never see that money again. Everyone had all but lost faith in Kevin's ability to pull himself out of the hell that he had made out of life. But still, Brother was willing to help out his lost sibling, and very likely for the last time.

Another hit just sounded way more appealing - just one more, then he could think about going, then he might do something about it. Just a little bit more.

Sheba gave a long, lost look - *what now?* Her brown eyes traced back and forth, scanning for even a semblance of sanity.

He ignored it - got business to do. The cell phone had been long since shut off, along with everything else. He headed towards a grocery store that was open and had a free courtesy phone anyone could use. Such a mess! Why could he not just stop? At this particular store they always looked on him "that way," like they knew something was up. Maybe he just imagined it, or maybe it was that internal, uncomfortable knowing. Something *was* up. Not to mention the scratches from head to toe …

On many occasions, being high and driving around aimlessly, the woods would call, beckoning to his wounded soul, drawing him in. And he was compelled to go into them, always tormented and strangely intrigued by what felt like someone watching, shimmering even, *taunting* – Something, anyway. Always it seemed there was a presence around, in and yet through the bushes and trees, the soil and rocks … *the water.* He just wanted some peace, to be left alone, to get high and escape. Often, as if invisible hands pushed and cajoled, he would flail the drugs on the ground where the leaves would disappear them, swallow them up.

Poof

Gone, like they had fallen into a tiny portal that opened only for that instant.

?

Just days ago it happened. Kevin was traipsing through the woods, on an early afternoon, otherwise beautiful spring day, so delusional that crawling through heavy sticker bushes somehow seemed like a good idea. *How pathetic,* he thought, hanging there on thick green stalks of razor sharp thorns, fumbling for the pipe and lighter… and then, upon inhaling a giant toke of the crap that was wrecking him, a huge fly implanted itself directly inside his ear!

Foooompt!

It crawled right inside, probably the biggest fly in the world, at least eight hairy gross legs bouncing around inside his ear canal, its fuzzy body palpable as it went *deeper*. It felt like this thing took a hundred steps a second, each one creepy crawly - *Oh my god, this is so unbelievably nasty!* The agony came even through the cloud of thick buzz from taking the oversized hit of rock cocaine. They called them bell-ringers and man, was this one of them.

But was this bug even real? Or was the work of some damn trickster going on in his cranium? He pounded on the side of his head to try and pop the thing out. "Aggghhhh!" Even in the midst of such a travesty were thoughts of how he had failed in life, at life, and as a human being.

It was as if the Spirit of the Woods had sent that bug in there, a winged demon sent to do a particular job. "Oh my god!" He began screaming, but then muffled it so no one would call the cops … the torment was unbearable.

Get it out! The fly, or whatever it was, found his sinus cavity - the damn thing was going to crawl out his nose. He could almost taste it in his throat now, wanted to cough it up and spit it out like a giant loogey.

"Jesus Christ. How did I get here?" *How did I get here!*

Is this really happening? Still reeling from the massive hit of dope, head spinning, bell ringing. Is a fly *really* walking around in his head while crawling prostrate through sticker bushes? Really?

How he longed to be normal, to simply enjoy a day. To be his old self again …

Am I hallucinating? What the HELL is happening? It was sheer agony. The voices of children and various people came. Were *they* real? He kept trying to get the damn thing *out*. He might have screamed for help if a clear thought had even come. For twenty minutes this went on, then thirty, trying to figure out if there was in fact a bug inside his head (Honestly, what are the chances?) or just another perfidious hallucination. Still, he kept taking *more* hits of the damn dope, as if more would help.

He had already been to the hospital once before, swearing there were bugs crawling all over his body. Locking the door of the exam room, he inhaled snorts off the counter in the few minutes before the doc came in and barely, through paranoid delusion, escaped a mental evaluation by the state. But that was over 15 years ago. How had it come to this, again?

Finally, whatever it was died, or at least quit moving - but it was still in there, wasn't it?

No! He could feel it. Something was going on, some thing in there, just … so … confused. He crawled out of the bushes, which took more than an hour. They were so thick, thick like the crazed dementia. Stickers and bramble scratched him to bleeding: Face, arms, legs, hands, all over. It was as if his mind could not work. God how he wanted it all to *please stop.*

The next day, telling Mom about this odd insect incident, she was disgusted. Of course the story was altered to pad the depravity of events. How he must have appeared, sunken in from days, weeks, months of using, not sleeping, barely eating, paranoid and falling fast. Scratched all to high heaven, and with a maybe dead bug lodged in his head - and still trying to act as if he had it all together! The look of disgust his mother gave him along with her tone should have been an indicator for him of his true condition and need for help. But, the delusion inside of which he chose to live was much more powerful, and he maintained: Everything was just *fine.*

She talked him into going to the doctor; after all, part of being on welfare is that you have great medical coverage. So he went – besides, might get some painkillers out of the deal. And, when seeing his condition, they too had gazed upon him "that way." Deep in his ear, however, they tweezed out the exoskeleton of a huge fly. It really had happened. *God I hate my life right now.*

***

2:00 a.m. Calling dude again and again from the store's phone, no answer … damn. Looks like beer would have to do. *Maybe best, anyway, been up for days … so damn tired. No food, either.* A few beers might take the edge off and something to eat might help. There would still be enough money to get some dope - somehow he always figured out how to get more. But the waiting was *agonizing.* With each coming down, the terrifying prospect of having to face all the wreckage he was in the midst of came rushing closer. When reality closed in, he needed his escape route.

Up and down each aisle of the store at least ten times, he finally settled on three giant, potent, cheap, crappy beers, a buck-twenty-nine each, and some ice cream. *Try dude again.* No answer. *Try again in a bit.* Slithering into the driver's seat, he forced down a few tasteless bites of the disgusting ice cream. A starved and neglected body then devoured the whole half gallon. Needing food was so inconvenient.

I'll just drive over there, it's not so far. Dude will be there, I know it.

For some unknown reason, he did not drink any of the beer, not yet. They just lay there on the seat, Band-Aids for later. He hit the highway heading south, glancing in the back at Sheba peering at him. Dogs can reflect human condition quite accurately. Mistrust beamed from her every cell as she shifted back and forth, panting with an uncomfortable whine. Kevin was unsafe and invoking nothing but trouble; he recognized her look, her body language. It was how he felt about himself, and if he had been willing to catch his reflection in the mirror even once, he would have seen it. That's probably why he avoided mirrors – except, of course, for snorting lines.

He did not even feel himself begin to nod off.

Once the food settled in his belly, the body took over and basically began shutting down. Drifting off, he went into a sort of reverie, half in and half out, asleep yet somehow aware in the thick and distorted fog, of what was happening. Abruptly navigating due east toward the curb, amazingly avoiding hitting anything or anyone, going god knows how fast, he began grinding the right front wheel alongside the curb while insisting over and over in a loud voice: "We can do whatever we want!" Cackling like a madman, "Haa-ha!"

Maybe it was to Sheba, or to himself, that he offered such spiel. Who knows? He surely did not, but was losing it, no matter how you slice it.

"Ha-ha-haaaaa! We can do anything!"

On he went, holding the wheel into the curb, then scattering back to the road, back and again, the aluminum from the rim grinding away, shearing off in all directions. He had gone beyond any state of rational awareness and fallen into detached, partial reality and stark delusion. He could have killed any pedestrian, smashed any number of things, driven through a house - but somehow avoided hurting anyone. The vehicle came to a stop, finally, along the curb of this major highway, as he passed out into an exhausted and tormented slumber. A makeshift crack pipe made of a hollow screwdriver shaft was between his legs, where it had landed following an attempt to extract the last residue out of it after finishing the pathetic dinner.

Hours had gone by, passed out on the side of the road, against the curb. No one had seemed to even notice him there, when a loud noise disrupted the otherwise quiet interior of the Ford Explorer. "Knock knock. KNOCK KNOCK KNOCK."

Kevin began to come to. "What? ... Where? ... "

Where the hell am I? A hazed mind finally worked enough to see through the passenger door glass. It was a police officer banging on it.

"You a' right, what happened?" the cop asked. These were good questions.

What had happened? He went back through the events and thought about the store. But how had he gotten *here*? He recognized through burnt eyes the general location; he had driven this highway for decades, but how now, what, even? A foggy glance in the back at Sheba as if maybe she could shed some light on just what had happened only found disgusted canine eyes. They said: "You're on your own, dumbass."

Then he remembered the pipe and that's not cool with cops, a one-way ticket … he quickly got his legs together just in case it could be seen. Immediately he went into crisis management and the standard operating procedure of manipulator-liar mode - except for one thing, when the cop inquired again. "What happened?"

He answered honestly: "I don't know."

He did not have any damn idea what in hell had actually happened.

A twenty second pause heard only cars going north and south. "I'm off duty and on my way home, but I'm going to call in an officer from this jurisdiction to come down and handle this. Hang tight in your car." The cop looked confused, and besides that, like he just wanted to be on his way. Kevin tried to put it together, but couldn't. And *where* was that damn pipe? Even if he found it, where could he stash it?

A black-and-white whipped in behind the Explorer after only a few minutes, then another one right behind it. Great. Two fresher-faced cops were on him in seconds. "You been drinking?" The taller one demanded. The other was scrutinizing the backseat and its contents, as well as Kevin. Three beers sat silent in the passenger seat, in full view.

"No" - he hadn't. Not in the last half a day, anyway.

After running his name they learned that he was on probation and no drugs or alcohol allowed in his possession was one of the stipulations, and those three oversized brews that practically had eyeballs now, were a violation. But he was a seasoned liar, and without a single hesitation he told them they were for the employees of his business, neither of which he had anymore. They bought it, sort of.

"K, well, step out of the car please, we'd like you to do a field sobriety test." The door creaked open. Kevin squinted as the full bright morning sky hit his eyes. It caused him to lift his arm to shelter his face. How was he going to pass this damn thing?

He stood on one leg, he walked the line. He touched his nose while leaning back, recited his ABC's. And none of it very well, either.

Both the officers had puzzled looks. "Give us a minute, wait here – don't move," instructed the one with a chiseled, cleanly shaven jaw, pointing to the rear bumper of the Ford. Would he pass or fail? What if he failed?

The other officer found the makeshift pipe and was scrutinizing it. *Dammit.* Kevin stayed quiet; the less you say the better. The shorter and rounder cop with a moustache said there seemed to be something in it. "People use stuff like this for smoking drugs."

Kevin just shrugged. "Don't know," he said. "Not me." An older Chevy with only half a muffler whooshed by, going too fast. What would it feel like to have a morning without problems such as these?

It had been several hours since he'd had any drugs, and thank god he had not drank since … when? Maybe 12 hours? 20? He'd been up for days and knew he was in bad shape. And, he needed a hit of something, bad. If he could get out of this mess, that was next.

A world of thoughts flew through shot nerves … *what now?* He hated what his life had come to, standing here on the side of the road with the sun rising up, vehicle messed up, nowhere to go, except … *How did I get here?*

Treatment is not going to work, I already know that, he thought, scared and confused. But how could he know? He'd never even been there. *No one could forgive what I have done. Everyone has watched me fall into this* mess *… they are all so disgusted with me.*

He could feel the cold cement slab in the booking cell already. He was going to cry, but would not let himself. He was simply too cowardly to kill himself any expeditious way - and he knew it - so the notion was dismissed quick as it came. And it always came.

A little bewildered, the two officers seemed to have reached an impasse. "We're not going to give you a DUI but can't let you drive, either. Got anyone that can come get you?"

He did not. "Nope," he said with the old game-on voice; now his mind began devising again. "Can you take me back to my work and I'll find someone to help me come get it?"

The Explorer had thrashed against the curb enough to waste the tire and wheel, but that would be easy to replace and get moving again. "I can pull it up here on the curb, out of the way. Be right back to grab it, maybe two hours." He knew there was a perfectly good spare in the back, but that would waylay the real plan.

"Yeah, that's OK. But no more than two hours, or we'll have it towed. And don't *you* drive it."

Man, we're good. Got out of it again, the mischievous monkeys sneered.

The men stood there only two miles from his mom's house and four miles from the drug house where he had nearly lost his life. A little con-man silver-tongue slickness coerced the taller one into a ride to "work," but instead he'd have the cop drop him close to the drug house. He will go and see if their supply was now replenished. No simple little near-shotgun-blast-to-the-head could deter him. Minor details.

This was the plan, and it sounded good to him. Only 40 bucks left to his name, but that was enough to get high for a little while, anyway. Screw everything else, again. He locked his sights on the next crack hit like Luke Skywalker locking onto the Death Star.

***

As they drove, he began to think about everything. What a mess was life! *So tired of running.* What did sleep free of restlessness even feel like? *Must be around 7:00 a.m.* He was supposed to meet his sister at Mom's house at nine. Of course, he had not been in touch with them for days. Surely they figured he had chosen not to go once more, and in so many ways was this true. His gut sank. If he let any tears come they might never stop.

About this time, the cruiser cruised right past Mom's. In this fleeting moment was the awful realization of how convoluted it all was. He longed to be different. *I'm a horrible person. No one, NO ONE likes me, let alone loves me. I've gone too far. I've got nothing left, nowhere to go. I think I'll die tonight, I want to die. I would rather be anywhere but in this broken body, rather be anywhere but face all those judging eyes.* The last chance about to slip away, but - *God, I need to get high right now.*

There was still time, maybe …

The morning sun had now come over the horizon; how he wanted to like it. Living in the dark was empty and lonely, but the sunlight hurt his toxic skin. Everything hurt, but had he not gone too far down now to allow any help? Had he ever let anyone help? Or had he only lived inside a prison of his own making? *I can see no other way.* Monkeys screamed inside his head, echoing in the chasm of confusion.

Still, there came a whisper, just through the din …

An omniscient voice spoke to him, through him, right there in the back of the cruiser:

It is possible to change

Where had it come from! What was it?

Weak and depleted, it had not come from anything he thought he was. Still, it came from within.

Maybe it is possible … it's not too late, I could call my sister and ask her to please, please help me.

But the drugs - only two miles away now.

In flashes came lonely thoughts of the road the drugs and booze would take him down, and then the frightening aspect of facing his family, his ruined life, and actually going to treatment – of accepting help. They were now about to pass the same store he had left only hours ago. *Last chance.*

A moment of surrender. Some hidden power broke through. It spoke to the officer. "Stop here, please. Let me out. I'll figure it out from here." And so, the officer pulled over, and the beaten and exhausted Kevin went into the store and used the free phone - this time to call his sister. No answer. His stomach dropped – there was still time to go back to the drug house, walk there.

No! He did not want that. Shaking sweaty hands dial again. She answers. "What do you want?"

Begging and pleading with her, he grovels. "Please take me to treatment, I am lost and alone … afraid … I don't know what to do. Please. Please help me."

This was more truth than he would even let himself realize. Speaking it, acknowledging it, was so valuable. He stood there, trembling, in uncharted territory, admitting that he was underwater and drowning. Using anyone to stay above water even if *they* drown was the only way he really knew.

She was cautious. "I will only do it if Kristi Ann will come with me. I am afraid of you. I don't know what you might do." She is afraid of him, and doesn't mind letting him know. Minutes of sheer agony go by while she checks with the family friend, Kristi Ann. Kevin teeters on the edge of insanity while selfish thoughts play see-saw: *Go back to the place I nearly got blown away, maybe let 'em finish the job? Take a leap of faith into the damn unknown?* Trembling, he picks up the phone – Kristi Ann is willing. "OK, we'll do it."

"Thank you. Thank you so much!" He is plagued with thick butterflies and so much anxiety he is going to throw up at any moment.

"I'll be there as soon as I can," she says, her voice guarded and doubtful.

Facing Up

Mom's is just a one-agonizing-mile walk away. The large recliner-chair in the front room provides a momentary respite. It has been another long run, and when Mom finally wakes she is disgusted, just like his sister, just like everyone - just like him.

"What are you doing here," Mom queries, voice full of resentment and ridden with frustration.

"I'm going to treatment," Kevin replies, choking back the breaking point.

"I seriously doubt your sister will take you now; she is not happy with you. No one is." She is rigid, firm.

"I talked to her. She said she will … but only if Kristi Ann would go, and so they are going to be here soon." His voice is frightened, shaky, on the verge of flooding the living room with tears.

Something had allowed the strength to get out of the police car and not go back to the drug house. Something.

Here he was again. Trying to convince Mom the way he always could how this time it was going to be different. But now, too much has happened and the hollow promises fall on worn-out ears. Too many times has he proven otherwise.

Sis shows up with *two* friends. Were it not for these three, this story may have never been told. They agree to go down to the Explorer that still sits sadly on the side of the road. 11:00 a.m. now, already two hours late for the bed date. Being on time never was a strong point. Putting the spare on in his condition is an extraordinary feat of sheer will, the late-spring morning sun agonizing upon him after so long in the cave of darkness. Limping the rig back to Mom's, Kevin begins to realize - *this is it.* This is standing at the turning point.

I am not good enough to do this.

No clean clothes to bring and nothing decent to even pack the dirty, threadbare ones in. *God I feel like shit.* Desperately fighting the guilt and shame is too much – the weight of it all. Then it came, the inevitable, spoiled:

"Fuck it! I am not going!"

It is only a cry for love, for help, which fills the space between the words. Anyone could hear it.

No one knows what to do. He crumples, defeated and crushed, slumped over in the old recliner. Decades of getting his way must stop for the next step to be taken. One, two, three, four, five sullen minutes pass. Sis hands him the phone. It is Brother's wife, whose family is paying for the treatment center. She sounds different than he has ever heard her, her voice calm and powerful, as if she is channeling some divine source; she is able to say the exact words that resonate like an access code to something in another place within him. It simply works.

"Now gather whatever you *do* have that you need and get in the car. That is all." She speaks with the authority of a benevolent Queen.

"OK," is the mousy and defeated reply, "I'll do it." An attempt is made again to get together what few pathetic necessities he has left, rummaging through the mess and disarray of his doings over these last months. Crap everywhere, what a mess … and how symbolic. And what about Sheebs? He glances at her lying innocently on the living room floor. *She'll be better off with anyone but me.*

To have just one sober breath

What would that even feel like? He did not know, and surely never would. *How can I possibly live life without the only escape I know?? Without drinking and drugging? It is who I am. It is how I cope, how I find any comfort at all inside of this god damn world I hate!*

No, this isn't going to work, I have tried everything within my power to live life and it has come to this. The best I could do got me right here: Body scratched all to hell, mind a jumbled mess of crap, everything I have ever worked for destroyed. I am so lost. God I need some dope! Just need to get high again. Can't take these screaming voices in my head. Why won't it STOP? I can't stand it!

Crying from the inside out, he looked in every thought for some kind of relief, some way of stopping the insanity that crashed into every part of him. But there was only more of what was killing him. It was all stabbing daggers - every foul move he had ever pulled just trying to survive *begged* to be let go, but no! He could not let go, *would not* - he would fight.

But, his innermost being knew he was broken. He could not stand on his own any longer. Always taking from everyone, and too much was never enough. Anything the people had given, never good enough. All he ever wanted was just to be OK. And now, these people had been used up. His bullshit had run out, quit working on them, and he knew it. No, in here, inside of who he thought he was, there were no more answers.

Desperate. Frantic. Trying to gather *something* of value from the *damn* Explorer for the long trip to this *damnable* place. Anything. "I have nothing," Kevin whispers. Just then - what's this?

Three giant, glorious, un-finely crafted beers! Darting eyes found no witnesses. *Everyone's inside waiting for me to get my crap together.* Even though it was warm, he pounded one. So easily did it slide down. *Ohhh, finally. Some relief.* He grabbed at a few clothes and tried to organize them, looking over his shoulder … *Anyone coming?* Pounding another, the foamy buzz began to come over him, numbing just enough, quieting the damn screaming monkeys *just* enough. The temporary solution would have to do until he could figure out how to get out of this mess and get back to what he really needed to do. But that never …

He guzzled the last one. It gave just enough lying liquid courage to walk back in that house and face the judging eyes of his family and the trip that lay ahead.

***

The ruby-red Dodge Caravan's backseat was cozy enough. Fortunately, a tip-out rear window provided enough fresh air for Kevin not to puke everywhere as the van hit the highway. Even more comforting was this odd soul, Steven, a mentally disabled twenty-something fellow who sat in the back next to Kevin. Sis sat in the front passenger seat next to her friend, the driver who saved the day. Kristi Ann was a caretaker, and since she was watching Steven today, and Sis would only make the trip if she came, they all four embarked on the three-hour journey toward Eastern Washington. It was even hotter there in the summer. He hated the heat. No clean clothes - and no shorts.

Such a mess: Reeking. Broken. *Tired.* Buzzed. In and out of restless, selfish nodding off. As they drove, he tried to have a conversation, to actually connect with Steven, and strangely, it worked; this young man calmed him. It took him by surprise. He always wanted to like people, all people, but just could not get there. Through a foggy mind and fading buzz he longed to connect where he never could, just be together enough to interact without thinking of himself, where the next drink or hit was coming from ... to actually be interested in others, in life.

These longings did he ponder, if only in dismembered thoughts. Such comfort did this kind, pleasant, mentally disabled and carefree young man bring, but why? Clearly Steven had more to offer the world than did Kevin. And he passed out in the easiness of the boy's presence, as the Caravan cruised into the unknown.

Half in and half out the whole way, it came again, from somewhere, unfamiliar:

It is possible to change

What is this voice? He searched ... It felt like a gentle female voice, but whose? Maybe it was possible, though he couldn't see how. In fact, it was unlikely he would ever pull out of this nosedive. He recalled the time just a few months ago when he had quit breathing and they were barely able to bring him back and how ungrateful he had been for their efforts. Perhaps more resentful than anything that they *had*, for that matter. It always felt like war inside of him.

Marie was the one that had to endure the brunt of his anger. The things he had said and done to her. And without her help that night he would be dead, for she had breathed for him and manually operated his own heart when it had given out. How cruel he was to his girlfriend for too many years. How she must hate him, surely as much as he hated himself - and both rightfully so.

There was also Selena, another failed relationship. And a plethora of countless others his constant storm had poured upon.

How would he ever clean up any of this horrible mess? Broken and alone, surely no one would ever impart forgiveness. Surely, forgiving himself was unattainable, unwelcome and implausible.

It is possible to change

It came again! Listening to it felt much better than thinking about all the wreckage and damage. The intimation provided just enough relief to calm down and get a little restless sleep.

The voice must have ... done something. He drifted into an unlikely dream. Native American Elders came to him. They visited from afar and spoke, soft yet firm. He answered them, out loud and witnessed by the others. Sis would remind him of this later, and he would remember. This piece of the puzzle would take some time to reveal its purpose - but it was, along with the sweet whispering voice, just enough to begin a new journey.

First Day

"Here it is," they yelled from the front. "The treatment center!"

His gut rippled as his head popped up, stiff now with the absence of any buzz, replaced instead by a nasty hangover. Sun-drenched mountains surrounded the valley below as the Caravan descended the last hill. Warm air blew in through the little-opened window.

God, we are in the middle of nowhere, he thought to himself. *Just need sleep, some real rest.* Exhausted every way a human can be, Kevin was used up emotionally, physically and mentally bankrupt, and depleted in ways well beyond these, *all at once.* He managed a reluctant sideways grimace out the window.

Rooftops and pathways of a beautifully landscaped ranch came into view, set between rolling hills. Manicured bright-green lawns underneath giant blue skies surrounded several buildings; sprinklers shooting water made rainbows in the open air. But he could only see ugliness in the day. He did *feel something,* though. What was it? *Just need rest, so tired.*

Crossing the threshold of the place, lush green grass on either side held the long, winding black-top driveway in place. Lamp posts ran along one side, perfectly placed little greeters. Each lamp pole bore a small sign with just one word on it. He looked around in pure curious dread while the girls began to read each one as they went by:

"Today ... Is ... The ... First ... Day ... Of ... The ... Rest ... Of ... Your ... Life. "

This caused mixed feelings. One part, the worn-out hung-over "him," thought, with a groan and eyes rolling, *fuck you, ridiculous.*

But, just a little more perceptible now, it came, again:

It is possible to change

Appearing as hell itself and probably not realizing just how close to the end of this life he had come, or how fortunate he was to actually be here, Kevin said goodbye to his sister.

"Thanks. Please take care of Sheba." She had agreed, reluctantly, to that much anyway.

"I will, don't worry about that – just get better."

"Bye Kristi Ann, and, thank you."

On the heat-soaked cement of the parking lot, he takes one more selfish gaze upon Steven, longing to have such innocence. Marie had called him an energy vampire more than once. He would have taken anything he could from Steven, the drowning man trying to survive. Only, Steven gave it all willingly. The source of it was omnipotent. It could not be contained or used up. Lost, humiliated, and on the verge of tears, Kevin was not yet able to realize just how much compassion they had shown.

He also was not aware of Sis being pregnant with her first child, nor did he see her salute him with just one finger on her way out.

Not realizing a whole world outside of the same-old. But that was all about to change.

"How humiliating," he whispered under his breath. The front office was claustrophobic, and he wanted to bolt already. After he abashedly signed a few forms for admission, some worker picked up Kevin's light brown faux-suede duffel bag he'd stolen from some drug house along the way.

"Your temporary room is just over here a ways." Kevin followed, but didn't even give a bloodshot glance up. The man toting his bag could have been twenty or eighty, black or white.

The employee set the duffel bag on the bed. "Your counselor would like to see you ASAP. Here's a map of the place. Her room is highlighted here, #103."

***

"Come in." Her steady gaze sized him up, but not in a judgmental way. Instead, large accepting brown eyes offered some kind of respite. "Hello, I'm Sarah," she said, looking kind and concerned. She couldn't be more than a few years older than him. Her sandy-blonde shoulder-length hair and unimposing presence was comforting. "Have a seat." Her face was not without evidence of having once lived a harder life.

"Uh …. Hello." He had already begun concocting a thin plan to some way tweak the situation to best accommodate his needs. An escape route of lies began to formulate - standard operating procedure. Sitting in that chair, though, broken down, the weight of a lifetime of abuse was heavy upon his shoulders. Wrecked and exhausted, something came over him.

What if I just told the freakin' truth?

The unlikely thought crept in, only the cadence wasn't his – or so it seemed.

It was so much pressure *being* all this crap, and after all, there was that quiet soothing voice … maybe it was possible to change. He just could not see how. Not from inside *this* current paradigm, from inside what always has been – not from inside a life to which he had somehow been condemned could he see any other way.

Sarah spoke kindly, with a voice that offered solace. "We're going to do an intake interview. It's best if you are completely honest … can you do that?"

A surge of longing shot through him when she asked. Kevin had lied successfully on several such interviews and even passed some UA drug and alcohol tests with his sly maneuverings. This was his plan here. One assessment a few years back he even conned the counselor into saying he had "no significant problem." What a joke that was, he thought at the time, on his way to get a drink after leaving that place at 3:30 p.m. - he was so good at manipulating these fools. They were all idiots, anyway. Why didn't they just leave him alone?

But, a long overdue volcano of molten lava was brewing underneath, near threshold. "I'll try," Kevin said. The corners of his mouth curled under as his throat clenched tight.

"What age were you when you first tried drugs or alcohol?" Sarah asked, holding a pen in her right hand over a small pile of papers, ready to mark the answer.

"I don't know." His childhood flashed through his mind like a swampy bog. "13, maybe 14, I guess."

"How did it make you feel?" He'd never been asked such a question, and thought long on it. Something needed to give; his throat began to hurt from holding so tight, tattered eyes ready to burst. It all burned.

"Like I belonged, I guess. I never felt like I belonged anywhere ... or fit in. Still don't ... especially not now." A great sob followed the answer and Kevin began to cry. Sarah just let him. It went on for a good minute as he tried to speak more but could not. He wiped away some drooling snot as Sarah handed over several tissues.

"When you drink, how often? Once a week, three times, once a day?" The pen was ready.

"Every day! I drink every day, I have to." He leaned forward with a cheek in each palm, scorching tears now free-falling.

"And how many drinks per day? One to two? Two to five? Five to ten? Or more than ten?"

"More than ten dammit! OK? More, much more, always! I drink a ton, and take massive pills and snort and smoke tons of cocaine!" Oh, it felt good to get some of it out, but, "God dammit!"

"We'll get to all that. I know you're upset. This honesty stuff is difficult. I know it's hard, believe me. I've been there. Let's just keep going; please just answer the questions as they come." She was so soothing but equally aggravating.

"You've been here? What do you mean? How could you know?" He had never spoken with anyone that understood this hidden horror, not that he was aware of anyway. Not like this.

"I'm in recovery, too. Been there, done that with the drugs and booze. I've run over people's lives to get what I want and lived inside the awful emptiness that I know you feel right now." Her eyes peered right into his with full disclosure. In this moment he knew he could trust her.

And so right here did he set aside the lies and deceit, in this strange place where he now found himself. He answered the rest of the questions honestly. Over the next hour something happened that surprised and shook him to the core - the truth bubbled up, oozing from a boiling, rotten cauldron. Much of the wretched filth that spewed forth had been buried so long it was nearly new to him.

He had always felt like some kind of an alien, alone in the world. Barfing it all up, Sarah was there for him, holding his proverbial head above the proverbial toilet. One soul helping another …

She took the shivering responses calmly. Always, he had taken every precaution never to have anything in writing of his true use so no one could have incriminating evidence to prove he was an "addict" or "alcoholic," because then they might try to stop him, take away the only possible solution. But here, now, he disclosed it - all of it.

Worlds crashed down. Guilt and shame for every selfish move ever made began to surface.

"We're almost done. You're doing great." Relief from voicing some of the torment came as she briefly reviewed the pages. The beginning wave of a great purging was finished. He slumped over now in the chair, sobbing, broken and depleted.

The first step had been taken and he did not even realize it. Something had kicked in, something he had not known was there. A state of shock now presided through a pounding headache, with dismay that these things had been spoken.

"You are a late stage alcoholic and severe drug addict," she finally said - or at least this is what he heard.

Tell me something I don't know, he thought, but only nodded in defeat, acknowledging agreement.

"Get some rest, as much as you need, and then come to Group."

Oh god, a group. Here we go… what I have diligently avoided my whole life, facing others, and worse, myself. It was like spiders crawling all over his skin just thinking about it.

And so, Kevin walked down the long hallway and across the grounds, still oblivious to the beautiful day. He found his room, his bed, and passed out. But he had made it through this, the first day of the rest of his life.

~ Chapter 2 ~

The Work Begins

Time was an ominous black cloud, and too much was so unclear. It may have been a whole day Kevin slept, maybe more. Upon awakening came an unfamiliar relief, a beginning and an end, at the same time. The room was too warm, sun beat the curtains from outside, and that damn decades-long, clammy sweaty hangover was still there. His mind searched for something to control, but he had never been in any kind of situation like this; never had he crossed the entrance of any treatment center.

Along with the hangover, a thousand unanswered questions. He was surrounded by an uncomfortable safety, but still reeling from all that had transpired. At least he was not on the run anymore, for now.

He slowly came to and drug his weary, useless bones to the coffee room. His head was a mess of cobwebs and his mouth tasted like some random passer-by creature had used it for a toilet in the middle of the night. He choked down some of the innocuous liquid and gagged on the first gulp.

Here he was, in this place.

What even was this place? Who was he? It was like being split in two. Half of him wanted to try and figure out how to get out of here, get back to what he had come to know as his life, horrid as it had become. Another part of him, difficult to recognize, wanted to give something else a chance, something unknown - or so it seemed.

The fragile and desperate moment, the great fork in the road, came with no answers. One way led only to oblivion. The other: God only knows. Just how close to death he had come had not yet registered. Morbid portraits danced on every blank wall. He was tormented by the thousand screaming monkeys in his head. They pulled his face apart. Confused. Taunted. Played with him. *Screaming.*

You can't do it. You never have been and never will be good enough. You always fuck everything up. You are a worthless piece of shit.

God how he hated this.

And in addition he could not get high, not right now anyway. The solution he had always known was out of reach at the moment. This did not help matters, and the coffee just wasn't cutting it.

Then the monkeys flipped the script. *But you can connive your way out of this. There is always a way to get what we want! We'll figure it out, just like always. They don't know just who they are dealing with, how smart we are.* Which was it? Why won't they just *stop screaming?*

* * *

A young woman knocked on the door, half his age and clear-eyed. A plastic badge dangled from her bronze-skinned neck, half way down her chest along with her shiny black hair. "How you doing?" she asked.

"Ummm….OK, I guess." It was a lie but he wanted to look as good as he could - even though he was scraped up from head to toe, his head felt like a washy pounding mess, he was emaciated and on the verge of tears, again.

"Gonna go to Group? Your counselor would like you to."

"Yeah," he replied meekly, getting "it" together as best he could and then heading towards where the interview was done.

Twisting the brass knob and opening the heavy wood door, the room was much lighter now. Maybe it was the long sleep, the time of day, or maybe it was the exchange that occurred here with Sarah that brought such an odd relief.

Everyone stared.

He hated this, too. But, acting as pleasant as possible, installed his best "I got it all under control" look. Sarah introduced him and each man greeted him, saying their names in the circle that had a spot reserved for Kevin. He could feel their eyes burning into him, sizing him up, as he took his dreaded place in Group.

The work commenced. They talked about things that caused two conflicting feelings: Fear and Fascination.

Talking about addiction and about life and living, in an open way, was not something he *ever* did. This scared him. But at the same time, the odd fascination was present, like some hidden yearning. Just what was this whole thing about? It was an uncomfortable feeling. Yet it was enticing.

The only female in the room was Sarah, who had now become a different person. She was much more confrontational than during the compassionate interview, harder. How long had it been since then? 24 hours? More? Much had changed in just that small amount of time.

~ 22 ~

He was not loaded - although still a toxic wasteland. As the session went on that day, he slumped down like a lump of clay, feeling horrible, shameful. The hangover was one thing – but knowing he was about to embark on this journey into the unpleasant, mixed feelings plagued him. Some part was still trying to figure out how to get out of this mess and back to … back to what?

God! Was he going to puke on his shoes? What would happen if he did? He tried to focus his attention on Sarah to quell the sinking feeling in his stomach. She explained details of the recovery process. It was almost like a foreign language. Not interested in much of it, he listened with the same old tired ears that were already always listening. There was, however, a small part of his being that wanted to believe in something else for once. But what? It just seemed so far away.

Oceanic swells of internal discord, he was a seasick sailor on a shipwreck of once-agonies that never had found any good hiding place and were now closing in for the kill. What was happening?

"Please turn in a journal entry each day before breakfast," Sarah said as she handed out a small spiral notebook to each of them. "Write whatever you like." She gave Kevin a yellow one. "It will help, and it is a requirement."

In addition to daily Group, counselors shared their stories in a room that was much like a theater. Appropriate movies were shown here and several types of meetings had; they would be spending a lot of time in this space. A gymnasium as well as outdoor activities would provide plenty of exercise. Three meals a day were at set times in the cafeteria. Down the hall was a break room with coffee, hot chocolate, several kinds of juices, and a few vending machines. Tables and chairs sat near large windows which offered a view into a courtyard with well-groomed grass. People were sitting and talking. Even they were intimidating.

So much to take in. He was a horrible mess and just wanted to sleep, and even heard Sarah refer to him under her breath as "that poor guy" during Group. Compassion flickered in her eyes as she whispered, rarely to be seen again. It would be replaced with a rugged determination for their success which he would mistake for callousness.

Kevin made it through the day. He crashed hard again, and the next day woke up only a little less sick.

He felt safe, something he had not felt in a very long time … had he ever? So confused, though. What was happening? How could he figure it out and control it? The monkeys thrashed around in his head this way and that way - his ruined life, how would he ever fix that? It was beyond repair, and too much to think about right now. Anyway, Group happened after breakfast for a little respite from the cacophony in his head.

Breakfast! He was a ghost, yes, but a hungry ghost. It sounded so wonderful he almost let out a drool. He was an insect buzzing down the hallway, an ant in an ant farm, a sheep in a dust-bowl flock, a scratching chicken with empty claws. The other patients passed him, ten, twenty, maybe a hundred and seventy-five. Too many to count.

Inpatient treatment, he thought. *How did I get here? Aren't I too good for this? Not good enough?* It was certainly one or the other. Then, the aroma of sizzling bacon danced out of a huge double-door down the hallway, swirling invisible Fibonacci Fairies that found his nostrils and filled them. His eyes opened wide as if they could taste it. The unmistakable wafting of pancakes and toast followed, and he was sure there'd be plenty of maple syrup. It felt good to be hungry again.

Two dozen or so large round tables with some eight seats around each were nearly half-full. A line of even more people waited with plates in hand, before a stainless-steel slide-along in front of a Plexiglas-protected kitchen full of cooks, servers, and pans of tummy-pleasing chow. Eggs and French toast, sausage and grits, and there it was - a whole tray of crisp bacon. Oatmeal and cereal decorated another table. It was all a most welcome diversion. With two heaping plates of food he found his guys, along a back-window table. "Hey, Kevin. Saved you a seat."

The nourishment was manna from heaven. The boys shared their little take on things; some had good attitudes and others, not so much. Kevin was not sure yet, and just put on as good a front as he could, as per uze.

They were to go to the meeting hall after breakfast. His body seemed happier: One, for not saturating it with toxicity today (though the monkeys were restless and pissed), and for properly feeding it. A sickened memory crept in: *How close this body came to giving up for good.*

After the last crumb, it was on to the big room to learn about the nature of addiction and alcoholism. A warm interest came. Was it curiosity? The hint of change whispered of another way.

~ Chapter 3 ~

Locked up

What if it was all only an illusion? Could it be the visible world does not exist? What if it were only manufactured by some unseen function? The cause of being in a prison, what we let ourselves believe? Being behind bars, only one more effect? What if the unreal source could be forgiven and undone?

During his darkest times, up for too many days and exhausted, he would show up at his girlfriend Marie's house, wasted. One day, he scared her so bad she put a full-on no-contact-order on him, forbidding contact for *50 years*. He violated it over and over, continuing to go there. Each time, another charge. Whacked out on drugs and on the way *down*, it scared the family so much that they would just call 911. He went to jail every time unless he eluded the boys in blue, which he did on several occasions. This only found him on the run. He was becoming downright dangerous.

Over the course of this year that preceded his arrival at the treatment center, jail had been about the only place where he could get any rest, the only place that was safe. Winding up there was usually the result of missing a court date, or if he did appear, he was obviously torn-up and worn out and had not done anything the courts had asked of him. Without need of a second thought the judge would easily pound the gavel and, Bang! Throw him back in jail for a day or two or five. Marie did care about him and wanted to help, but the choices he was making made that impossible. Kevin just needed … *Something.*

He thought she could and *should* provide this something. In every intimate relationship with women he always put this pressure on them: *Save me, take care of me!* If beauty equaled power, then Marie was powerful. Six feet of dangerous curves, she was an ex-model with seductress hazel eyes and long waves of red hair, an exotic Amazon beauty. With her caring, charming personality and outgoing way, Marie attracted people. This threatened Kevin, while at the same time, drew him to her. She loved her family and took good care of them, and Kevin had become a part of that family. Why would she not help him now? It enraged him! But he could not see himself.

All this insanity. Repeating the same tired offenses and behaviors over and over, the inevitable day came when the police caught up with him. He had racked up several charges and warrants, was now behind bars and facing several months in the county jail. Every day until this point he had managed to stay loaded, grasping and clawing frantically at as much drugs and booze as could be gotten and consumed. Everyday use at this level had caused a massive addiction, and relentless craving and withdrawal came in only hours without feeding it. Not to mention every thought was riddled with obsession of how to cure the allergy that caused his crawling skin to feel like it was boiling and blistering.

In custody, the monkeys thrashed and cajoled and ripped him to pieces. The agony was too great to handle. Every molecule cried out for some kind of relief from this damned place. Waiting to be let into the cell block, he fell to the floor, reduced to a sobbing pile of quivering flesh and bone. A handful of inmates and a guard stood over him, not knowing what to do. No one said a word.

Inside Kevin was a great void of burning torment. He only knew what he had now become – a demanding leech, only capable of taking and using. He wanted to die, have it be over. Looking back, he would realize this to be the high point of his life, his greatest achievement. It certainly did not seem so at the time. In this moment came a primordial cry:

"PLEASE HELP ME"

Over and over he said it, curled up in the fetal position, writhing, clenching, groaning and gasping the words, begging. Broken and drooling, his face and matted long hair lay on cold concrete in a pool of snot and tears.

"Pleeeaase. Help Me." Begging the very ether itself - he was not talking to the inmates or the guard or Marie or his mom or anyone else standing around him or anywhere else. He was only pleading with some unnamed presence.

The bunk bed in the cell was a relief to find. An Asian man of about 30 greeted him. "Herro, my name Yang," he said with an ear-to-ear smile. Something about Yang's soft gaze from compassionate eyes showed he was a kind man. Kevin was desperate and barely able to hold his head up. It was tragically obvious. Yang searched for something to help him, something to console him, something to offer or say, *feeling* Kevin's suffering. This broken man could not make words between the sobs to even answer. Finally, Yang handed to him a book. "Here, Bible! You take Bible. Help you." Yang spoke with a nervous yet hopeful smile. It helped, maybe the kindness the most, and the sobs began to subside. *Curious.*

Kevin never had been religious. His stepfather, who came into his life when he was a young boy, tried to raise him as a Catholic - but he was rebellious and bored in this church that never took. Something about the whole religion thing seemed ... off. Even though he didn't have much direction, he did have a strong drive inside, a sense of some greater purpose he never could quite find or identify or align with.

Yes, a fire burned inside for a connection to something, but what?

The Bible provided just enough relief, and Kevin began to read. But he was so tired, and it was difficult to focus.

He knew what was coming. He would fall off into a cold, clammy, restless sleep, and that would be the best part. But then, he would have to wake and face life without any buffer, awaken right into an ongoing nightmare. It is such a feeling of loss, this inevitable coming down, mind and body a shivering mess, nerves shot all to hell. The horror, like always, would be there for many days to come. Too many times had he endured it, each time more severe than the last. Kevin could see no way out.

This incarceration occurred some five months before arriving at the treatment center. The diversions of life as a hostage seemed to help. Kevin met some nice guys, got some rest and nourishment, and almost began to get some thoughts together.

There were events going on in jail that an inmate could attend, like church. You could also request to meet with a pastor. Neither of these would Kevin usually have considered, but he was so desperate he did request one. Pastor Dick was a tall and slender man of fifty or so, with a firm, warm handshake. His smile was inviting and authentic, his bald head with just a shadow of white fuzz on each side was as charming as it was shiny. Kevin immediately felt safe, but as they walked toward a private meeting room, he had no idea what to say or what to do.

Inside the small room with a desk and several chairs as their witnesses, they just talked for a while. The cement walls were painted white and the place felt a little sterile. There was evidence that many meetings happened here. Kevin told Pastor Dick about some of the things that were going on. It felt good to dump and get these things off his chest, to expose himself if only a little, even if he was on the verge of more tears. Pastor Dick listened. After a short time, he asked, "Would you care to pray together?" Kevin agreed, even though he had never prayed like this before. But there was something about this man, a permeating kindness and sense of trust. In his large warm hands the pastor took Kevin's, and led them in prayer.

Maybe the warmth in his hands and in his voice was compassion. "Kevin, please. Pray with me. Allow yourself to be open."

Something stirred within he had not remembered feeling. In the prayer, Pastor Dick asked for healing and for help. Kevin let something inside his depths move. It did feel like some suppressed part of him, a deep-seated longing. Kevin accepted the pastor's words as his own. Now they were joined and praying as one. The room completely changed, becoming some sort of chamber of solace and goodness. They asked for a Higher Power to come into Kevin's heart and help open it, help him heal. His whole chest burned. Maybe this is why he cried; he needed help so much and simply did not know how to ask for it, never had. In all the ways he had ever learned, the best he could do, he could never figure out how to just be OK – even with taking, taking and more taking. All that seeking on the outside only led to imprisonment within. As Pastor Dick kept praying, tears ran full down Kevin's cheeks. It was the first time in a long time he could actually feel his heart.

Kevin was shocked. Whatever happened that day remains a mystery. He had felt so much better. Continuing to pray this way, asking for help, he did experience some peace, although torment still ruled. Reading the bible helped, even if it was confusing. He developed a slight case of jailhouse religion, but that was better than being out there high, strung-out, and running from the cops.

After being locked up for several weeks, Kevin went to court and was released. He attempted to continue the newfound religion, even going to church, wanting to repair all the damage and get his life together.

For these few months Kevin experienced living without putting toxins into his body. Staying at Mom's (still on the teat at 38) was stagnating. But, there was a peaceful place nearby. Sheba often followed while he rollerbladed along the paved trail. Marie had introduced him to the inline skates. It took over a year and many bumps and bruises to learn how to do it even half-properly. They had skated together all the time. He loved cruising along the soothing Sammamish River. The breeze caressing his skin, thriving plants and grass and trees against a crisp blue sky, were all gentle reminders of a simpler world, a world where the monkeys could be quieted. Eagles often floated overhead in twos and threes. Herons soared low along the water, majestic diversions gliding to a halt along the river's banks.

Going there was what worked for these few months of "sobriety." It was good. But during this time of not using anything, he was only bone dry. It was acute torment, living in worse denial than when guzzling as much booze as possible and taking massive quantities of pharmaceuticals, in addition to all the cocaine.

It was an attempt to do it on his own, though he lacked the tools to achieve any real sobriety or relief. Old patterns were simply too burned in place and too powerful. It is here that the fine line between dimensions was ethereally drawn. In one realm was the stuff that bounced around in his head, the destruction he had done, all the lies and deceit which *he* perpetuated. The wreckage that he had caused, the people he'd hurt, the things he had done to himself, the sheer delusion and despair that had been a constant, unwelcome companion. It was his best attempt to try and survive and live in a world that seemed pointless and hopeless.

The drugs and the booze were like glue, the glue that kept these agonies and atrocities in their proper place.

Those atrocities, that delusion, who and what he thought he was, lay on the one side of that line between dimensions: The familiar, frantic, time-worn side.

On the other side loomed the unknown. From inside the problem, it seemed too great a risk to embark upon such a task as a journey into the unknown.

He had learned at an early age that "being right" was of primary importance, so to admit he did not know - this option was simply not available. And, he was certain that to cross that line would mean taking a look at the hideous creature that he had always known himself to be, yet hidden from. His little-big ego just was not having it - and it, in the crafty and proven methods Ego uses, had convinced him time and again that the old way was the only way.

Desperately holding on and using every ounce of his own will power had sufficed to stay dry during this time, but sobriety and not using are two very different things.

Without the glue, he began to unravel.

Underneath he was writhing, gritting teeth, knuckles glowing white from holding on so tight. Monkeys screamed and insisted. *You want to feel good again. You can handle it just this once. This time will be different. Relief is close. Do it. Do it! How nice will one little high feel? Remember the ecstasy?*

There was one way he knew to assuage them. The old solution danced constantly in the back of his mind, patiently waiting for the opportunity to come to the rescue. Of course, one day it did.

A hundred justifications always came for why getting loaded was the way and the remedy. Any combination of them always sufficed. It seemed like he had this addiction thing licked, just by keeping busy. He was crafty enough anyway - he *thought* - to continue bullshitting everyone into thinking that he was clean forever, even cured.

Skating along, now oblivious to the natural beauty that surrounded him, Kevin was hijacked by impulse. *Just one quick high - then I'll go right back to clean again.* Out came the phone and a call to the dealer, naturally. On the surface he was excited for the escape, the expensive diversion. *Here I go again ... oh well. It'll just be this once.*

He had hurried back to the car with tunnel vision. Ignoring Sheba's *uh-oh* face, he desperately drove to get the crap that had been wrecking him - the glue, without which he was coming apart. Was it really the drugs causing the wreckage, the torment? It sure *seemed* so.

Just a couple hits, that's all; then I'll deal with it. A last dangling thought as he frantically entered into the worst bender ever, its ugliness and torment unparalleled. This run culminated in staring down the barrel of that shotgun in the little run down shack, a ride in a police cruiser, and asking for help.

There is another way

~ Chapter 4 ~

New Beginnings

Now the process of being spin dried at some treatment center was underway. Coming down again, but at least this time, there was some action toward doing something about the real problem. The first several days were a mixture of hope, despair, and possibility. Without a clue how to live life, Kevin was now becoming aware of and admitting defeat. In all the best attempts he always made such a mess of it. Whatever it was he *thought* he was, along with any reputation, had been all but totally destroyed. Thoughts of salvaging any of it felt sad and empty. Even if it could be done, how could he ever face anyone again?

Confusion filled the space between every thought.

And with the confusion came a small staph outbreak right below the belt line, just below the navel and off to one side. Even though it was only a little white pimple at first, it was painful. Combined with being absolutely toxic in every way, the summer heat of Eastern Washington forcing out bullets of uncomfortable sweat, the impact of a shattered life all simultaneously coming down at once, the little outbreak was a most welcome diversion. At treatment, staph is no joke, so they brought him to the hospital. Old habits die hard. Convincing the doctor just how much pain he was in, Kevin coerced him into prescribing narcotic painkillers, along with the antibiotic. Addictive behavior still ruled.

The driver from the treatment center waited outside, ignorant of the situation, as the in-hospital pharmacy filled the prescription. "Take one every four hours as needed for pain," the pharmacist said to him. *Yeah, right.* Knowing from experience and with a tolerance that could make a full-grown grizzly bear envious, he connived how to take as much as possible without getting caught. But this was a joke. Such things would not fly.

He went through all the possible scenarios: How many he could eat and what he could use as an excuse as to why there was not the proper amount in the bottle. The center said any prescriptions with a doctor's order were OK, but had to be turned in and *they* would dispense them as prescribed. There were plenty of people in treatment on many different kinds of medication. Each one had to do this. But *him* – Kevin; he was special.

He convinced himself that telling treatment the hospital must have screwed up on putting the correct amount in the bottle would be a sufficient scam, and settled on the thin alibi. They would probably just conclude it was an honest mistake anyway, and not even say anything - this was Kevin's chosen delusion while pounding four of them at the nearest drinking fountain. It was, after all, life and death at this point, convincing himself that the pain from this tiny pimple was excruciating. *You just couldn't possibly know how bad I hurt,* he thought to tell them, as he found the car. He handed the sack which contained the two pill bottles to the driver, Glenn.

He had even talked his counselor into letting him and Glenn stop at the local clothing store. He had no shorts, and it was over a hundred degrees outside on any given day. They stopped, and using some of those last few bucks, got the new clothes. Stoned again. He was grateful for the shorts, and the drugs, temporary as the high was going to be. *Pain-killer-monster:* After only an hour he began to itch and become restless, needing more already. The itty-bitty-shitty-committee ramped up:

You'll never make it here! There's only one thing you're good at anymore. Let's just get the hell out of here and get back to doing what we do. We can find a way to make it. This place is lame and you don't belong here!

He finished out the day, thinking some scam had been pulled off once again, but nervous about it nonetheless. And coming down, again. It rather reminded him of stealing Mom's painkillers. Even though she hid them from him, he always found them - and then replaced what he took with regular aspirin. Who did he think he was fooling? Who cares if she is in pain, what about me? The selfishness and self-centeredness he could never see past, kicking up the self-loathing another notch. He would wait it out just like always - then, it would seem to pass. Shove another thing away. They would not say anything, just like she never did.

But they knew every scam. Early the next morning, turning in the journal before breakfast, Kevin came eye to eye with Sarah. Her face was so sad, mad and disappointed all at once. "They want to see you in the director's office, right away!" The words were one thing, but the subtext brought a thousand other intimations. Guilt and shame, those two constant and unwelcome demons he walked with every day of his life, landed like a two-by-four to his head.

"What happened," the director, Anthony, wanted to know. More of a statement than a question – *what* happened. Here it was, sitting in the office of the one that had the final say. Sarah, with her long face, sat next to Kevin, her look telegraphing an impending execution … and in a way, it was. Next to her sat the head counselor, Jesse. All three burning looks right through him as he sat there feeling like a tiny piece of crap, pill-hung over, toxic and scared, not having a clue what to do, how to even begin to answer, let alone be OK. He wanted to just sink through the floor. He wanted another pill, or ten. Squirming sea monkeys swam through his sopped brain.

"What?" Kevin acted surprised, like the jackass he was, attempting the concocted scam. Disgusted, Anthony laid it out, just like you do for a kid that ate the cookies; you know he knows but just for clarity you lay out the scenario, step by step. "There were supposed to be 20 Vicodin and there were only 16. What happened to the other four? You know you were supposed to give them *all* to the driver and let us dispense them to you; we told you that."

"I didn't … they must have … ummmm … uhhh, not put the right amount in there … ?"

Silence. Dead stares. Tension so thick it was a wet blanket. They let him stew in that bullshit for a good while. One of them said "Come on," but he couldn't tell who, with his face to the ground. He thought, reached. His mind was a tattered go-kart banging into one wall after another. It did sound tragically stupid. They told him they had seen it all, they had all done the deal he was doing right now. Anthony finally said, "Here's where it's at - you are about out of here. The only thing that can even come close to saving your ass right now is honesty, and even if you do come clean, I can't promise you we can even let you continue, now."

With a giant *fuck it* he came clean, told them exactly what happened, and even said those words, "You couldn't possibly know how bad I hurt." But, they did. Something else was present in that room, along with the anguish and what he perceived as disgust and upset toward him. It was compassion, among the first times he had realized it. He felt them looking past all the crap to something deeper within him, into the soul that was under it all, the true him that was seeking to emerge and could not, not through the thick muck and walls and defenses he had been reinforcing since forever. The honesty he sought with the one small store of courage remaining began another tiny crack in those very walls, and they witnessed it. In fact, they acted as a sort of conduit for access to it.

They told him this: "You don't have much of a chance. If we can find a way to let you stay, which may not happen, that smidgeon of hope is all you've got."

Anxiety ruled the day. They let him go to Group and said they would be discussing what they would have to do. At Group, it was horrible. Sarah, with the same thick upset, came right out with, "Do you have something you want to share with the group?"

Writhing silence, again. *Ugh.* Fighting back tears, looking up at the faces staring back at him in the circle, again he knew he had to come clean. God, he needed another dose of something right now, to run away. Another pill, another hit - and simply was not going to get it. There was only one thing left to do. Tell the truth. And, for the next hour he heard from *each one* how his behavior and actions affected them. How they wanted to use, also, the way they always had. And now even at treatment and in their supposedly safe group, someone lied and cheated and used. He let them all down, and they told him so.

The day went on, sweating bullets from all the heat coming from all ways, smarting from the hurt in Group. *What a loser I am.* He had let everyone down. They were all talking about him, surely. But something else happened. Several of the guys came to him and offered support, commended the honesty, said if he needed anything they were available to hang out, walk, talk. This was different. It helped ease the pain – which was now much more from letting everyone down and facing expulsion. The compassion from the people helped in ways the pills never could.

After lunch they called him back into the office.

"Here's the deal," Anthony said. "We talked to your family, and they are not willing to help anymore."

Thick butterflies.

His brother had been kind enough to pay for treatment even though Kevin had missed five prior bed dates because he could not stop running and using. It was a miracle he was even here, and now this.

I am such a worthless fuck-up.

Anthony went on. "You can only stay if we extend you, which means at least another week."

"Some are sicker than others." Sarah interjected while her expression turned from disgust to pity.

"A week costs $1100, and your family is not willing to pay it. They say if we have to cut you loose, then so be it. They've done all they're willing to do." Anthony was matter-of-fact as he delivered the bitter news.

Tough love, wow ... what did it all mean? He certainly did not have the money, and his life-long enablers were cutting the cord. *Oh well, back to the little shack. It's OK, at least I'll be super-high soon.*

"It's not about the money for us," Anthony said. Kevin somehow believed him, could sense it. Their core intention truly was helping people. Didn't matter, he was out of here anyway.

"We want to see you succeed, and we know how it is, many of us have been there and we know what you're going through." Anthony's tone was shifting. "But you hafta pay this, it's the only way you can stay."

"What are my options?" Kevin gulped, on the verge of more hopeful tears now, wanting to stay. *Truly* wanting to stay! They were good at this. He had nothing else, no other hope that led anywhere good.

"You can agree to pay it off. We have options with no interest. If you make monthly payments, in any amount, we'll give you time to pay it back while you get on your feet."

"Yes. Thank you!" Kevin was overcome with emotion at the chance, so relieved he was going to get to stay. From this day his attitude underwent a drastic change. From this moment, he saw these people, the ones that almost let him go, *all* the workers, everyone in Group, as if they were there not to make him do something he did not want to do, but to help. He had seen and felt first hand this great truth. And he chose right here to accept it. He would listen to them, trust them, instead of what had always run the show and crashed the bus.

Yes, the people here had an odd intrigue; he saw right away that the counselors offered something beneficent, so different from the people he had always seemed to find himself around. They *wanted* to give all they had to these suffering people. He saw lots of suffering, but also, he saw enough caring for all of it. He felt safe. Maybe no one would hurt him here. A kind of nurturing was present that soothed him immediately, but felt awkward to accept. His head pounded - he hovered between the two worlds. One part was still trying to figure out how to get back to the life of the same-old. Another part teetered, dangling on a rickety precipice. Ready to let go and give something else a try, take a chance on something he did not understand at all. A glimpse of this something had been felt, praying those few times in great despair. Yet somehow here, it was different. It was as if *everything* was saying: "It's OK, we will help you."

He saw this in the counselors and the other patients, in the eagles and the clouds, felt it in the sun and mountains. He was surrounded by love, and couldn't quite believe it was true – it was just so unfamiliar. He did not deserve real love, not him. The monkeys still screamed, loud as ever, but for once in his life, he became aware of a more subtle nudge and the glimmer of hope.

It IS possible to change.

The reeling intake session on that first day, that fateful moment of divulging some of the most hidden secrets, had been freeing. But the things he had done, and now even using at treatment. It all felt so heavy and spongy, how could he get any relief from the weight of it? Would the horror of living without alcohol and drugs ever subside? The choice had been made: *I will give it a chance. I will let these people help me.* Sarah knew it, and even he was beginning to realize the benefits. Kevin was hearing things here, in the group sessions, in all the sharing. The new ideas scared him, yet touched his beginning new self through the fear. One day early on, the group was invited to try on three things that were said to be of great importance on their healing journey:

Willingness, Honesty, and Openness.

It sure did sound scary after a lifetime of lies and deceit.

Friendships began to form, especially with the men in his circle. He saw and heard first-hand the stories of suffering and could totally relate. He kept hearing "this is a safe place" to reveal such things, what was really going on. Becoming willing to be open and honest about his true feelings, the ones always hidden from everyone, - most of all himself - they began to be revealed. It was an unfamiliar road, both wonderful and frightening. Sharing these diseased emotions and atrophied feelings seemed such an arduous task - they had always been kept so locked away. It was tortuous, and he wept and shook at the stream of anguish that poured out of him at these times. But he was committed to trying; it provided a respite from the lonely and stagnant old place in which he had dwelled so long.

The First Layer

A scrawny man wearing another badge knocked on the door just after 6:00 a.m. "Way too early," Kevin scoffed as he opened the door, peering at the guy out of one crusty eye, creaking out a "Yes?"

"You're being moved to a room in the regular inpatient area today, so make sure you get all your stuff," the man said. A little too bright and cheery for this early, it seemed to Kevin.

He liked the move. Room 410r was ample-sized with a sliding glass door that looked out over neatly trimmed grass and endless mountains. Two beds were separated by a shared bathroom in the middle. Marcus, a gray-haired older guy from Group, was his new roommate. Marcus seemed like a pretty cool dude.

Upon a little brown bed table next to a reading lamp, they had provided some books, mostly daily readings. Coffee and a little reading before breakfast became the norm as he got used to rising early. The readings were comforting and offered new perspectives on living. Ideas he had never considered came to life from the pages: Letting go and trying not to control, listening, wishing the best for others and looking for it in them, trusting life, accepting others and situations *as they are*.

These contemplations began to inspire him. He found himself looking forward to getting together with people at the breakfast table and at Group, as well as anticipation of the counselor's sharing sessions in the big-room. They were funny, honest, and caring. Many of them had been where he was right now - they knew their stuff and he admired that, especially since he was so lost. It was nice to be somewhere people had something going on, something positive, and for him, fresh and exciting.

He began writing in the afternoon, making the journal entry. Oddly, he liked it very much. At first, it seemed like a ridiculous request, but soon he was writing a couple times a day. About the seventh day, Sarah pulled him aside. "Kevin, please. Four pages? There's no way I can keep up with that much reading."

She handed him a virgin notebook. "This one's for you, just a page or so for me, OK?"

The purple-covered spiral notebook turned out to be a profound gift. Writing throughout the day found great comfort, something to look forward to. He wrote about everything: What he felt, what he saw, what inspired him, and what scared him. It was a hodge-podge of emotion: Hope, despair, anxiety, hate, fear, rage, longing. The daily readings influenced him and helped him find new ideas and pathways that he'd never considered. He wrote about them. He wrote of the epithets the monkeys were screaming, but the stuff just beyond them was way more interesting and inspiring. He got to see, in the writing, what was going on between the ears. Mostly he welcomed it to come, even if it was toxic. Sometimes it was unbelievable how twisted it came out, but it got the stuff out of his head and onto the paper so it didn't have to fly around in there like angry bees stinging pissed off monkeys. He began to feel real relief.

Just after the proposition to become honest, willing and open, it had been suggested to begin to seek a Higher Power of your own understanding. With no point of reference for such a thing, and having misguided *himself* on more than one attempt, he asked one of the guys during a walk. "How do you do it?"

Christian answered, "Sarah says: 'Fake it 'til you make it'."

"You mean, pray as if?" Kevin replied, enjoying the possibility of it all. In jail he'd prayed to an old god that did not work. Why was that? Surely it worked somehow, for he was here now. Maybe something was missing. *So, pray as if what?*

"Yeah, something like that," Christian postulated.

"Maybe this god can fulfill all my deepest desires, then?" Kevin smiled, trying to be over the top but then wondering if such a thing could ever be true.

"Hey, it's worked for a lot of people. I've heard people really do get sober with this program thing and have awesome lives. I'm giving it a shot." Christian smiled, looking like a GQ model. He was tall and brown-skinned, a slender six-foot-two runner.

"Cool, me too." Kevin said, and tried to keep up as Christian broke into a jog. Soon, they slowed back to a walk and were silent for the rest of the way. Kevin was thinking about what a new god might feel like.

Along the east side of his temporary home ran a railroad track, a simple white fence separating the two. Myriad evergreen and deciduous trees decorated the mountains. Various other trees and bushes dotted the hillsides, stood quietly about the grounds. Some lofty and thin, some short and stout. It was amongst a gathering of them, along this white fence, that a spot called to Kevin.

Somewhere it had been suggested that getting on your knees to pray may help one with humility. It sounded like a good idea - besides, he had made the agreement with himself to try anything, especially the things that seemed ridiculous. So, onto the knees he went, to pray in this way.

"Please help me. I do not even know who I am ... or what you are. My life is a failure ... I don't know what to do. I am so lost." Distraught, he revealed the truth. "God, I am so alone ... I'm sick, what do I do?"

But to what? Who? He didn't know; he just did not know.

It was beyond remorse, this whatever-it-was that began happening as he prayed. All he did was pray what he *really* felt. Reaching into the very depths of himself and admitting he had no idea what to do, he asked again and again for help. Huge tears welled up and poured from his eyes, rolled hot down his cheeks as he burned with remorse - he could hear them landing, little bombs of despair in the dusty June dirt.

Those tears are the ice around your heart melting

Each morning was an opportunity to enter the strange relief. This little nook amidst the trees, did he choose this place? Did it choose him? Either way, he felt safe here.

Soon, he looked forward to getting up just for the daily readings and to pray. There were always these birds that came and greeted him at the little spot, singing praises from nearby trees. Accompanying his prayers, they sang straight through his heart, with a message just for him - and he took that message as acknowledgement that he was on a true path.

Just keep doing what you are doing, stay the course

He found himself returning to this spot many times throughout the day, and each time with greater comfort and belonging. The beginning of trusting *Something* beyond the screaming monkeys began to develop. When spinning in the head, he would just come and do this handing it over thing. It was not always easy, but each time it worked. More and more, he went to the spot. If going there was not available, he would say a prayer anyway, wherever he was. It began working, all of it.

One day, the desperation of untreated disease was overwhelming. *I'm a failure. No one will ever want some used up old addict around. It's useless … just* then he cried out, "Please help me!"

To his surprise it brought instant relief, and he began to say this simple mantra many times, often desperately, throughout the day. *Please help me.* His only job, it seemed, was to let go of *it*, whatever it was. And this was the first time in his life he had become willing to do that.

Now the writing became of particular use for real relief from the insatiable monkeys. Starved and relentless, they would stop at nothing to get what they wanted. What had always before seemed to work to quiet them only ever proved but a temporary fix; they always came back with a vengeance. No matter how much diversion, it was never enough. His whole life he had battled the chaos in his head and was always defeated, only putting on the front that he had it all under control.

What if there really was another way? What if Christian was right? No knowledge he held ever worked to find any peace. Something was always missing.

The Ghost Writes

The third journal entry of the day in the second week of treatment was done in the late afternoon heat. It was a flashback to younger years and running wild. It had been a good life in those days – what happened? The realization came and he spoke it to the sun, "I never belonged *anywhere*."

Too high and then too low, up and then down. He did not fit in his own skin and never had:

I was always let run free with no real discipline. And right now I just feel so out of place. I always have. Warren was my step dad, maybe you know that and maybe you don't, whoever you are. Who are you, anyway?

~ 39 ~

Warren was a little rough on us, but still he took pretty good care of the family. He bought us that big house and just wanted us to be good little Catholic children, but there was no way. The hell we put him through - only to watch him die with that horrible cancer that ate him up.

I barely even remember Dad being a part of the family before the divorce. How old even was I? Three? It's like there's a block there, from feeling anything, from remembering. We all know he was an alcoholic back then and probably violent, from some of the stories I've heard. Just like me. But did I *see* any of that? Could that be a part of the reason I'm this way? After Dad got sober he became my best friend, and helped a lot of people. He sure wasn't violent then.

I always remember hearing "you need to: blah blah blah" and all that I was supposed to do, but the chaos in my head was too loud to ever accomplish anything without … without what? So much anxiety and confusion. When I took that first drink, that was my answer, I remember that much. Fuck everything else. God! I can see it now. Ever since that day I have sought my answers in the booze and the drugs. How old was I? 13? 14? They've always been the main focus. Nearly every friend I had was into the same thing, even the crowds I hung with. It was fun, yes it was, but always I felt lost, unless I was loaded. Wow, I've never been willing to admit that. I feel so empty right now!

Maybe I should have stuck with school. Maybe failing that one last damn class that stopped me from graduating was a good thing. It got me to the community college to take those couple credits and get my GED. I was always stoned in the back of the room then, too. But I remember how much I liked the learning when I started going for my two year AA degree. Maybe I'll go back to school. That one math teacher told me I could be a great scientist or physicist. Is it too late?

What messed that up? Oh yeah! Those drums … Mom always got me whatever I wanted. I remember sucking so bad on them and she'd always encourage me to just stick with it. Me and Mom are both dreamers, always have been. Then at school I met the girl that knew that band searching for a drummer … how that changed my life. Quitting school was easy, to be a rock star.

Since Warren had left us with plenty of cash, I always got what I wanted, and had so much fun, not having to worry about bills or responsibility. Maybe this made me miss something important. An occasional tongue-lashing from Mom caused loud yelling matches between us, but I could always appease her and get what I wanted. But I always want more! The more always came alright, but at the expense of others, like the rest of my family. She totally let us have the whole downstairs for the band room and parties and even the guys living there half the time. Terrorizing the neighborhood with keggers and full service bar parties into all hours of the night with the band rocking it. It was the place to be. She loved the parties as much as we did. Ma Bone Child.

And what a time to be in a hot rock band. The early 90's Seattle music scene, when all the big ones were hitting. How awesome it all was, and my band, Stoney Bone Child was playing all the hot clubs, packing them out even. Me and Shackey and the boys were flirting with major record deals as bands were getting signed left and right. I thought for sure we'd be famous any minute. Drinking just seemed so fun then. It was fun! Will such fun days ever be again? Where did it go wrong? Where did I lose control so badly? Every time I came down the low was lower. And now ... now I am a ship with no rudder, a lost child in the dark. I can't drink again or use drugs, but I can't not, either. Can I? How can I? Oh, god, help me. Show me what to do.

That band ended when I got Kara pregnant. How was I going to be a Dad? I can't even take care of myself. What a precious little girl she was. I was so angry and crushed when Kara left just months after she was born. Who could blame her though? Then a couple years later, of course I would let her and her new husband raise my daughter - I sure couldn't. My own demons were taking me over. I think about that little girl often, wonder if I'll ever see her again, ever become able to really show up for anyone. Dammit! Why did I need to drink so much all the time, always get messed up and stuck on the drugs? I remember so many nights isolating after the party or the bar, with whatever I could get a hold of, and then the sun coming up, and feeling so out of place. Or sometimes, I'd walk in the front door of that huge house at sunrise after a long night out and, often, some frivolous, promiscuous encounter. Often times, the morning rays would soar over the panoramic Cascade Mountains, flooding in through the east-facing windows, but I could only try and figure out some way to come down so I could sleep and hide from it – all of it. Stealing mom's booze to come down, then I'd sleep half the day away, trying again to just feel normal. Somehow, to belong, somehow. How I longed to be a part of life, of a simple sunrise, instead of afraid of it. I have always felt so lost and alone, with no direction, like a wayward drifter, and an angry one! Yeah, I remember being lost and alone, but feeling like I needed to pretend to have it all together. Will you help me?

**

Anything Kevin received or achieved was obfuscated by a growing emptiness in the center of him. It was a hole in the soul, and it became increasingly difficult to attempt to fill this emptiness. In fact, the more he took, the bigger it seemed to become. And Mom had her own life to live, her own dreams and desires and longings and humanness and all that comes with being alive. Always he had taken her for granted, taken everything and everyone for granted.

Being loaded was the *solution* to the emptiness, the discomfort. But that solution brought a whole other world of problems. And now there were problems within problems, and those problems came with yet more, indeed. Often in fits of rage, unable to control severe anger, he would lash out at anyone close to him. Always trying to control others to do what he wanted them to do; sometimes it even seemed to work.

But wasn't he just having a good time? In months of elation, lots of stuff would get done, working very hard on music and cars and relationships, and even delving into business. He learned the world of commerce - get rich quick schemes were always fascinating. In many ways, on the outside, it was a good life, especially when loaded. Then it all would be buried in depression, not even able to get out of bed, so lonely and life so not worthwhile. For months it would drag on. The vacillation had always been there. The doctors had said he was manic-depressive and hyper-active. Later the names of these things changed, but always he was a yo-yo: Up and down, high and low, could only pay attention for fleeting moments at a time.

They prescribed psychotropic drugs to try and help but he never remembered to take them regularly. The only ones he *could* remember to take were the painkillers, and always in great excess.

He confused love with sex, and with control. If a girl loved him she would do just what he wanted, and of course they never did; who could live up to such insane demands? "Why are you wearing that? You look like a slut! You're *not* wearing that. Who are you talking to? Why didn't you answer the phone? Be home early. Don't talk to guys. Why are you looking at him? What did you talk about? Why are you friends with her? I don't like your friends. Who called you today? Why were you late? You're acting funny … is something up? Are you seeing someone else? Why wouldn't you have sex with me again last night? Why won't you right now! No, I didn't check your phone. How dare you even ask! OK, I did … what's this number here? And that one! Who are you talking to?" It was a barrage of useless interrogation with no possible sane end.

Their inability to respond "properly" proved they did not love him. But perhaps it was instead his own self-estimation that found him unable to accept real love. Relationships became about his setting impossible demands upon others and becoming enraged when they were not met, and then blaming those others for his pain and for his life's shortcomings. Every relationship was engaged in this manner: Projecting his worst fears onto others and blaming them for his life's frustrations – while himself, perpetrating nearly every accusation. *If they would just do what I want, I'd be happy.* And he chastised them for not acquiescing, to the point of mental and even physical abuse. They always tried their best - and it was never enough, not ever. Nothing *ever* was.

And now, here he was at inpatient treatment, looking back at the mess his life had been and what it had become. Out of ideas and schemes, sick and tired of his own game - sick to death. Surely the world's biggest loser, surely this life was over. Still, the intimation came again:

It is possible to change ...

~ Chapter 5 ~

Writing and Trains

Transferring thoughts from the cluttered thinking mind onto paper created space and relieved pressure. Right there in black and white was visible what was really running the show, what was driving the machine he thought he was. Writing his thoughts and feelings honestly (yet thick with delusion) provided an opportunity to slow them down just enough to bring them under scrutiny. He could see just how crazy it all was. Just how toxic was this thinking. He began to question it, when before he was only a slave to it. Through others came new solutions to old problems. It often seemed unlikely coincidence; someone would share about *the same thing* upon which he was stuck.

Journal writing was good, but it was unguided, so it was easy to run amok. Writing with some guidance and direction was required in the step work. Honesty was of paramount importance, even if it was very difficult and painful to face these things he had worked so hard to make sure no one ever found out. This new work entailed looking with a microscope, digging way down - and he was, for he had made the choice. Here, there was the help of the counselors and the group, who could not be conned. Takes one to know one, apparently.

Oversized tears often fell upon the written pages, smearing the ink – "I can't do this!"

Just keep writing, keep on the path

Then in Group, Sarah would inquire and the tears often came again. Embarrassing, but cleansing, and worth any amount of "looking bad" he might be going through. He was taking chances with honesty he had never even considered before, and it was paying off - big time. An unfamiliar relief and comfort came.

This relief grew as a relationship developed with this whatever-it-was that was inside of him - or was it outside? Was it both? Some kind of listening was beyond him, comforting and helping.

The writing always gave clues: "I must conquer this disease," and, "Must fight this!" It was what he had always known, the so-called winning of battles and other delusions of domination. Only, they were battles where every seeming victory only brought more emptiness and loss. Seeking power from this place felt hollow and lonely. Fighting it only made it come with greater force.

True power doesn't come from you, it comes through you

He found himself writing to this someone or something, and over and over he would acknowledge it, even though he had no idea what it was - by way of comparison. Maybe it was God, unstigmatized. Maybe it was even Marie, or some future partner. But maybe it was whatever was trapped underneath all the insanity, the best part of him, another possible Kevin. Journal entries often began with tormented and twisted thoughts:

"How will I ever find any relief from this agony? The work here is just too hard. She wants me to talk about shit I *hate!* I don't want to share about my *feelings*, or have people staring at me. Fuck it all, I just want to die, and I don't care if I do."

Though, as the days went on, he began to write of the mountains and hills, how they came to form a "V" at his prayer spot to reveal the sublime, deep blue skies. On paper he tried to capture the warm breezes, the caressing sun and symphony of song birds. He began to notice the simple things that were here - and it sparked imagination. All the while, asking this god or whatever it was for help to see clearly, help to live this life. He wondered, *what waits beyond these mountains?* Sweet possibility answered in her soft and soothing voice.

Boundless adventures lay in store

Allowing Life to flow, magnificent visions to behold once beclouded by a thousand screaming thoughts emerged. He had been asking for the power to do this himself, as if how he always thought could just be reorganized or rearranged, and this new sight thus found – up until now. Right now, he just prayed out of pure desperation, beginning anew, surrendering even this notion, and cracking the hard shell which encased it. From here, life-long ways of being and limiting beliefs began to give way through invocation of the greater Truth within.

***

Trains chugged, whistled and whooshed past daily. A picnic table in the open grass provided a peaceful perch. Endless tracks lay between him and the mountains to the East, going everywhere and nowhere. Kevin sat leaning into one hand holding his head up, elbow on the table, counting the cars with a glazed gaze: "One, two, three … forty … eighty-one … hundred and seven. Wow!" *A hundred and seven cars.* What was in them? Who was in them, and where were they going? How long must these tracks be, and how far did they go? Kevin found wonder in nearly everything, especially the possibility of a vastly different, better life. Where was his life going? Maybe he could work on the railroad, see new places and new things, new people and new towns, endless mountains lining vast countryside - he longed to be free the way the train seemed to be! He could work anywhere and do anything.

Then it hit like a ten-ton brick – he would fulfill his life-long dream of becoming an actor! Every hair up and down his spine stood straight up as the chill went through – that was it. He would be famous soon. Now that he was sober, nothing could stop him. He'd always wanted to be an actor. One time he told Dad, "I want to go to L.A. and do it!" Dad replied, simply. "Then go."

But he lacked the courage to go. There was the one television show he'd done for the History Channel some ten years ago, but that was as far as he'd gotten. This is why the business went bankrupt, to clear the way for his new career and an old dream. As the hot sun cooked the thoughts to well done, he wrote about it, and did so almost every day thereafter. Grander worlds danced in the realms of imagination, and he intended to visit them all in the flesh.

The delusion of somehow conquering life was part of what was actually causing the suffering. *Is life not something to be conquered?* Maybe it was a gift and could be cherished. This notion began to emerge, and it felt much better. Still, he mostly fought screaming monkeys, loud as ever. At least now, though, he was becoming aware of them.

More will be revealed …

The universe is always conspiring in your favor

Connecting

In the first step of this new work is the admission of powerlessness over the very mechanism that keeps in place the thoughts, feelings and actions that cause the behavior to continue. And, the admission that life has become unmanageable. This was something that he had always known, yet hid from: He was powerless over the booze and drugs, over life itself. It scared him to even consider letting go of the vices that had been in place so long. Admitting the problem had never done any good. It had happened many times: *Man, I gotta quit. This is gonna kill me. I can't take another hangover like this. What happened last night? Where's my car? Who is this next to me? I need more.*

Admitting this in a group seemed quite perilous. And try as he might to quit the madness and lashing out the way he did - he never could stop. The usual cycle was:

An intense using/abusing spree (which was sometimes just a hard night, but towards the end, several weeks to months long, until it went constant), culminating in destructive events affecting himself and others. Heavy remorse followed, accompanied by begging and pleading for forgiveness (with the intention of control of others and situations), and then a (short) period of "being good." The process was repeated over and over like some Mobius strip. The damage done had varying degrees of severity, and the groveling for forgiveness and promises of it always being "the last time" were only words without substance.

He could write about these things in his journal, even talk about them - yet the brainwashing, wherever it had come from, was firmly in place like worn out old recordings, playing over, and over, and over:

You are unlovable. You're in the way. You can't do it. It's too hard. You'll never make it. You are not good enough. You are fat and ugly.

Being alive for Kevin had always been missing one vital element: A true connection to life and others at the essential level. Better than or less than, for sure – but never a part of, always separate.

A problem cannot be solved at the same level of mind in which it was created

The problem with the problem *is* the problem. There is no problem with the solution.

Much of the time, solutions came through others in the group.

Jake was 31. He always held his right hand over his mouth with only the forefinger extended along his cheek like he was pointing to something left of him, thumb up toward the eyeball – maybe it was also for keeping his mouth shut and not divulging anything. He flipped his disheveled brown hair always to the left, because the part was on the right. Large, nervous brown eyes also showed he was curious about this whole thing.

One day, Jake spoke up: "I've been letting go of needing to know *every move* my girlfriend makes, and just focusing on myself, my part in our fighting all the time. Been prayin' about it too, praying for her … tryin' to forgive myself." This kind of talk was shocking.

The notion struck a chord in Kevin as he tried to fight back tears. Why was this so? He was learning things that seemed unfathomable from the confines of the life he had come from, just weeks ago. An attractive power was in this circle of fellows. The more they opened up, the more these old themes began to lose their power. He started considering possibilities outside of them.

One of the greatest examples of this was when the issue of choosing one's own conception of a Higher Power came up in those first days, and the brief, fateful exchange with Christian. It seemed the god of his understanding, until he had gotten here, had not worked so well - for the insanity was always there. Or, maybe it had worked perfectly. After all, he had tried prayer:

But, praying from *old* perceptions and conceptions, through a fabricated thought system of what this god was, in lieu of direct experience. The same people that had helped shape his world view taught him much of this, but it had been *him* that had accepted these teachings, and only *he* could surrender them - and seek his own god.

"Fake it 'til you make it" was very different from being right. Going *directly to the Source,* admitting he had no idea what a god even was and praying anyway; this lifted veils and revealed doorways that when walked through was like falling into infinite love and safety, where everything was OK. With no idea which way was even up or down and admitting it openly - this is where those tears had begun. Would they ever stop?

Step One. *We* admitted …

Here, too, is where a connection to Life began. It is possible to *choose* a god that works for you. Not better than or less than, but a part of, a belonging.

And it was here he began to own the screaming monkeys, the limiting perceptions, the misguided ways, and expose them willingly in this safe place - a chance to see them for what they were. To realize, *this is not who I am. Surely not who I would be had I any choice.* Did he not have the ability to choose? Wasn't he always choosing? One genuine look inside may offer a clue.

So, he wrote about it and shared it all, taking the same chances he saw others taking, risking exposing these cherished secrets, always before hidden, and especially from himself, ignorantly protected at any cost.

This sense of belonging to a safe place where people supported each other - a community - was resonating with something inside Kevin. *I've never even considered looking at* me, *what alcoholism and addiction is … never felt anything like this. What is happening to me? I feel like just letting go of everything, but can I?* The ever-present emptiness was diminishing, the monkeys' screams less shrill. Staying this course filled a more essential need.

A broader vision was emerging, once too obscured by a smaller mind's prison walls. For once, he belonged – something sought after this whole lifetime.

Out of our greatest despair comes our greatest opportunity

***

The little things can become the most gratifying joys. The experience of being present was unfurling like a tender spring blossom. Kevin began loving the simplicity, like going to the cafeteria with the copious food and being with a group of people that were together for a good and common purpose. Sometimes their families were there, too, and visible was the mix of emotions. So much pain, and yet so much love in this place. Go deep enough into one and you find the other. Providence was moving through this newfound Sanctuary. It was palpable.

He was making friends. One day, in the movie room, there she was (the next potential victim). Long flowing brown locks in big, looping curls begging to be stroked trailed down her shoulders, luscious hazel eyes sparkling across the room caught his, giving his feet wings. He quickly found an excuse and floated over, introducing himself:

"Hi, I'm Kevin," he almost drooled out. "Do you know when the movie starts?"

"Oh, I'm Terra. In just a few minutes," she answered, her massive diamond wedding ring nearly blinding him and removing the wings instantly. He came back to earth with a thud.

Even though she was taken, the two became friends and shared many intimate conversations about life, surely getting closer than either of them should have. It was always a challenge not to get caught. If they did, they would likely be thrown out. Sitting out along the tracks one day, Kevin shared his dream of becoming an actor. "I'm going for it as soon as I get out of here." Terra got quiet for a moment.

"What is it?" Kevin asked.

"I'm related to a well-known actor. I don't like to talk about it much, though." Her reply carried residue of something, guarded and careful.

The hairs shot up his back, an army coming to attention; his whole head tingled this time. This had to be more than coincidence. The pieces were lining up - it all made so much sense. Yes! This is what he was supposed to be doing, exactly where he was supposed to be: Treatment, to get clear, meet Terra, and become the greatest actor in the world. He decided not to push for any more information, for now. Play it cool. And so instead he went on to tell her everything he sought to become, slipping back into the tired old delusion. Terra listened and encouraged.

The pathways around the facility were perfect for walking and for talking. All the good food led to over-indulgence. Kevin began to pack on weight quickly. If he was going to become adored by millions making movies, he better start working on the perfect physique now. He'd always worked out, but in manic spurts, even taking up body building. Always with the main focus being to look good, to be attractive; maybe if the outside looked good enough (an impossible achievement) the inside would come around. So, each morning before lighter breakfasts he committed to at least 25 minutes of push-ups, sit-ups and the like. Plenty of walking and jogging was good for cardio.

Another friend he had made was a man from Group. Shane was hyper. Intelligent, too; one could tell by his deep brown eyes. Shane was cautious, though. He had been here before, at treatment. Relapsed like so many, "trying to figure it out this time, where I went wrong," Shane said with a lost look as they walked and talked of many things. What was discussed did not so much matter, but the honesty and sharing time together did. The warm June sun was glorious today, and didn't hurt his skin so much now. Soaring eagles sent power and strength as they strolled along, and the rolling hills sang of adventure and possibility. They walked all the way to the "In" gateway, which was also the gateway out. Kevin walked to it many times, alone. He would gaze out beyond the threshold, wondering. Gleaning new hope, the light was expanding.

Thoughts create feelings, feelings create experience

You are the author of your life story

The Mirror

So much was changing in such a short period. For the first time in a long time, there was positive movement. In all the blaming of others: Family, girlfriends, jobs, people, places, things, judges, cops, situations - there was *always* one common denominator, one person that was always there: Kevin.

Who you have been is not who you are, it is only who you have been

Yes, he was literally writing the next chapter through surrender, and that chapter *was* surrender. Somehow finding the courage to share with others the good, the bad and the ugly, he would get feedback and, to the best of his ability, accept it. Offered solutions were working when applied, and none of it would he have ever thought of on his own. He began to see the value in *listening.* Apparently not very well by the comments he was getting: "Take the cotton out of your ears and put it in your mouth. You've got a bad case of the 'I know' its."

To everything Sarah spoke of in the first days Kevin would say, "I know. I know! I know it, I know that. I know I know."

Until the day she said, "Kevin. May I remind you – you are at inpatient treatment? Maybe there is something you *don't* know."

Upon this revelation he slowly began to accept that perhaps he did not know it all - in direct contrast to what he had always been: The ignorant know-it-all.

Inherently, outside the confines of dogma and agreement, there is no particular way of being that is right or wrong or good or bad more so than another. It is what it is. Rather, any way is creating certain results – and *we* are always *choosing* our particular ways of being. The thin cracks in the shell allowed just enough light in to see. The writing helped dissipate the darkness, transforming the way he thought about life, shifting actions and creating new direct experiences - which were far more favorable.

Are these the results you would choose for your life?

Peace and serenity, perhaps a better definition for success - not dollars, not status, not being right. Things have a funny way of working themselves out. Each day has its own flow, and allowing the flow was much simpler than trying to manage it.

Controlling the universe was something he was never any good at, so why had he fought and clawed and struggled to try and do so? And so burdensome. This was still reflected in the writing: "Conquer" these things, "Figure it out." But, with the praying and *listening* and practicing simple acceptance, the need to try and control began to diminish. This gave way to peace, and realizing the profound value of just letting go.

***

What was happening was the gradual trickling of attention from the always thinking little mind, to the heart. Here was peace. However, living inside of rote thinking for many decades was not going to be overcome in just a few weeks, try as he might and wanting it all right now.

The heart hears what the head cannot

Attention waned - in the head, always thinking, was the conflict and disharmony. In, from and through the heart was serenity and softness, and time seemed to fade away and take care of itself. The heart helped direct the mind in a peaceful way.

This was a safe place, away from the lonely diversions. Here, Spirit was allowed a chance, which he began to *feel*. Moving toward this glimmer was now his greatest asset. It was not form or matter, not material, not any of the false idols always sought after. And none of these things even came close to providing the comfort It did. And so, this practice of being heart-centered began to take, and like freshly planted seeds, grow toward the light.

Let go and allow

~ Chapter 6 ~

Sink or Swim

With graduation came the distorted notion of having reached some pinnacle, but it was a short-lived fool's paradise. It was a false summit rooted in myriad forms: Ego, self-pride, self-aggrandizement, forced confidence and certainly that old partner in crime, delusion. Kevin had gained a plethora of facts and knowledge about this disease that had all but killed him - but this will not keep one sober. Self-knowledge is useless against the first drink, and it's the first one that gets you drunk. Or the first whatever.

He would now get to see what lay beyond that gateway. But, even in light of the excitement of travelling and the adventure that lay in store – in a huge and complex world - fear infiltrated every thought. It was daunting to imagine a sober life without the guidance and protection they had just left. Where would he go when they got back home? Could one month change a lifetime of habitual living?

Shane and Kevin had managed to arrange travelling back home together. Laughing most of the way and making the best of riding the old Greyhound, they set out on their way to new lives. The bus pulled into Seattle. They promised to keep in touch, but as his last connection to the once-Sanctuary was about to separate, Kevin began to feel a knot form in his gut.

This town he had thought he knew so well, the sights even; the familiarity of it scared the hell out of him. And what about when he got back to Mom's? How was he going to clean up *that* mess? He really did want to do well, but without the safety of The Sanctuary he began to shiver inside a sinking emptiness. He desperately did not want to lose the connection he had experienced, lose sight of the light. Praying about it helped, but still he longed for the spot along the white fence and the bird's soothing melodies, the community. Finally, the huge double-accordion doors of the bus flapped open with an evil *"Whooosh."* It seemed to yell, "Now get out and see if you can make it!"

And, it was standing right there, shell shocked, at the desolate bus stop in the middle of a bustling, intimidating megalopolis, that another simple, three-word prayer was made of pure necessity. It would be of so much help: *Please take it.*

In the silent moment the serenity came he was transported to a safer place, even standing in the chaos. A deep inhale breathed it in, welcomed it. It was like Kevin's fear had weight and mass, and was taken away from him with the exhale. "Please take it," spoken aloud under the clamor of the selfish city. The action brought instant relief, and he clung to it all day long.

At Mom's waited the Explorer he'd run up against the curb. A few pathetic belongings that served as reminders littered the interior along with gross food wrappers and other disarray. And the old rollerblades. He wondered how Sheba was doing with Sis. The bleak bedroom in which he had abused so many things waited, too. Every damn thing reminded him of the torment, the drugs and booze, the mental illness, the wrenching emptiness. His mom had let it go on, probably because she did not know what to do. Well, there he was, 38 years old, nothing to his name, and going home to Mother.

Back at The Sanctuary, several people had strongly suggested living in an Oxford House in Yakima.

Mary was a likable counselor. Her intense, knowing eyes shot right through him the day she had made the offer: "New town, sobriety, different people. Summer in Yakima is great. Ya' might wanna consider it." He recalled the incident as if she were standing in front of him this very instant with her hands on her hips.

"Nah," he had replied, avoiding eye contact. "I might find one back home, but I'm not ready to come live here."

Here was the awkward tug back into the old ways, back to living off Mom. It was like stepping back into the quicksand you'd all but drowned in. How quickly one can forget.

Two connecting busses from the downtown Seattle terminal delivered him to Mom's, some twenty miles away. With the near-empty duffel in hand, he walked into the old 55-and-over living community, up the driveway. A blooming hydrangea stood guard at the familiar brown deck with the white aluminum overhang. Those few alabaster plastic chairs on the brown faux-carpet floor did not welcome him to come have a seat and stay a while.

Lost as ever, the knot was growing with each step. It found the very pit of his stomach now. But, at the same time, it was a sweet summer day. At the bottom of the few stairs that led up to the deck, he paused. Something was different. There was a peaceful and overall calmness - why had he never noticed before how pleasant and serene it was? The warm sun lay like a golden blanket upon the day, well-cared-for flowers swayed in a gentle breeze, fuchsia, yellow, crimson and pink, talking and singing, sharing their easy happiness. Rhododendron buds were poised to pop open any second, and others were already clusters of pink trumpets. Trees and shrubs shone their myriad greens, singing along. Against the living blue sky, the crisp voices of several birds picked up the melody, sweetening it ever so. The birds again ... they sounded like *his* birds! The ones that had brought so much comfort at the prayer spots. Were they? They certainly were familiar; had they flown all this way to be with him? Kevin came alive with hope.

It's going to be OK. I'm OK! Now I'll get my life together, make work what didn't before, clean up things with Mom, with work, with my family. Fantasizing how *he* would do it all, just like that, Kevin was catapulted right back into his head and treacherous old control seeking. That false confidence, that pretense that always had it all figured out, returned in a one-breath instant. Delusion reigned as he climbed the steps, head held high.

The serenity was nice, though soon there would be the marching band, the congratulations cake, and the party with the "Welcome Home!" banners. Probably a whole mess of people heralding his arrival would commend him on his new-found success. He beamed with self-pride. Mom was probably going to fall to tears of joy at the very sight of him.

"Knock, Knock." He never had before knocked on Mom's door, but felt awkward now and thought it the least he could do - besides, he was about to be praised for all his hard work and wanted to seem humble. But the energy, of which he had now gained only a slight ability to sense, did not feel in alignment with any welcoming committee. This was affirmed when she opened the door:

"Hi!" His voice was thick with enthusiastic expectation, manipulation flying about like a hundred fish hooks on invisible line.

"What are you doing here?" Mom's voice was sour, and her face matched.

No cake, no party, only disappointment. His stomach dropped below the surface of the Earth. What about the grand plan he hatched only moments before? Her face said it all. Decades of her enabling came to an abrupt end in this moment, and he knew it for the truth it was.

"You have a lot of nerve coming here after all that has happened," she said, angry and still basted in the residue of all that had transpired. "You've done enough damage." He could tell she wanted to say a lot more, but she held her tongue. This was as much grace as she could show him right now, in light of the nasty messes he had left for her, all he'd thrown away now. It all festered unsaid in the stale air between them.

The need to look good and as if he had it all under control overruled any chance of a breakdown – but only barely. Regardless of the tremendous despair he felt in this moment, he only said, "I know." There it was again. "I know." But he did not know.

"I just came here to get some of my stuff." It was the first arrogant reply he could think of.

She let him get a few clothes and some mail around an uncomfortable silence; it felt weird inside. His old room was spit and polished. *Such a mess* he had left for her to clean up, - and she had, as always - but that had been it, the last time. Mom was done. Such a mess. Oh, the disgusting things he had left in that room.

And, so, he got his keys, fired up the banged up Explorer, and drove off with one odd wheel. It must be hard for Mom not to give in, not to reach out to him in his suffering, comfort him the ways she always had. Surely someone must have talked to her, coached her - but it was the best thing for him, for her, for everyone. The fear and loneliness, the sense of loss, began to set in like nightfall in the forest. The creatures began to stir. Monkeys grew restless. Hunger pangs echoed in the late afternoon air.

Please take it! Please, *take it.*

No sooner had he turned onto the highway than he spotted the car of an old drug dealer. How weird is that? Or, how appropriate. Neon signs of each well-used bar taunted like oasis in the desert. He was panicking while trying to keep calm. He only knew the old ways here. Old "solutions" screamed at him to feed the way he always had. Nowhere to go, nothing to his name anymore – *Please   take   it.*

Kevin drove aimlessly in the direction of the house he'd nearly gotten blown away in just weeks ago. *Another* dope peddler in a dented-up Honda Civic with four different colored doors was stopped at a red light. There was no safe place to go; mental tires automatically began seeking old grooves. He teetered on the line. Despair and old behavior waited impatiently on one side - unknown and uncharted territory on the other, once again. He thought about what they had taught him and what he had learned that once brought some relief and refuge from the raging storm in his head. The self-knowledge was useless. It felt like being on the slick steep slope of a melting glacier. *Please help.* Kevin narrowly avoided turning into the familiar old driveway of the desolate little shack. But he passed by, somehow. *Damn that place!*

I'll go to the nearest restaurant and write. Some relief, maybe. *Got enough money for a coffee.* As it turned out, it was to rent the table - besides, free refills at the 24-hour joint. But he was one lousy phone call, one wrong turn away from oblivion.

On the way to the restaurant, something else came up on the radar: A man who worked back at The Sanctuary. Glenn lived in one of the Oxford houses there in Yakima, and had become a real friend. Kevin had nowhere to go in this old place, no money, no one that was willing to buy the BS he was attempting to sell in the marketplace of denial. And he desperately did not want to go back to the old dwelling.

He knew very little about being in recovery, but he did have a feeling there were many like him in similar situations. He did not even think about meetings, for whatever reason. What he did not realize and fully believe in yet was the guidance and wisdom and sheer power of what he been invoking for the past four weeks. He had been praying in true sincerity and handing over self-will to the very best of his ability, *allowing something* in, something through. But could it really be trusted in real-life? Something had brought him this far.

"I need a phone," he spoke aloud through the dusk, up into the green and red neon lights of Sherrie's Diner.

An old pay-phone hung on the wall off to one side in the foyer. Clutched in sweaty hands was the purple-covered notebook. Showing him to a booth, the pleasant twenty-something waitress with huge brown curls bubbled, "Hi ... this be OK?"

It looked comfortable there, against the window through which he could see the Explorer in the parking lot. "Yes, perfect, thank you. The phone work?"

"Yep, ya' need change?" She was almost too happy.

"Yeah, quarters please, and a coffee." He handed the five over.

"This much? Oh ... must be long distance. Be right back." She turned quickly, her uniform skirt flipping as she pirouetted away, a pancake-toting ballerina.

Nervous hands scrawled anxious words in the notebook that had now become a life-raft, trying to organize enough thoughts for some direction. He glanced at the quarters. Most tables were full as it was rush hour. The aroma of dinners cooking filled the air. Clanking dishes and skipping servers soothed the loneliness, here at the spot next to the swinging kitchen double-doors. Monkeys chattered and pounced, vying for position. There was nowhere to go around these parts, except down. Now, the new faith would be put to the test. He walked toward the doorway and picked up the two-hundred-and-fifty pound phone. Explaining the situation to the operator of the treatment center, he was barely able to get Glenn's number without crying.

"Hello?" Glenn answered.

"Glenn?" Kevin pushed out through a broken, cracked voice, surprising himself. "Thank God you answered. I don't have anywhere to go – I … I'm screwed … I think … I'm gonna use. In fact I know I am. Soon, too. I need help." He was going to use if he stayed in this old place. Lost and alone, he admitted it, which felt like bungee-jumping with no bungee cord.

"You are welcome here; we have a couch you can crash on and we'll get you set up in a room - don't worry, *just come.*" Glenn's voice was reassuring. Kevin was relieved, *so relieved.* It felt like there was actually someone there for him when he really needed it, the *way* he needed it.

"OK. I'm coming. But tomorrow; I'm too tired and stressed out to drive three hours tonight. Thank you, so much."

His stomach was a mess of nervous butterflies. He could not know what lay in store, and realizing he was leaving this old once-home, hope emerged. Maybe an entirely new life was possible, far outside the scope of anything he had ever known. His soul longed for nourishment. From inside the problem, the solution always seemed to be the same-old, but now he was moving away from that self-inflicted torment. At the little table with only a coffee, a pen, and a two-dollar journal, he wrote about it. One thing became apparent, immediately, as he searched recesses of everything he'd ever known or felt to be true:

"I don't know, *I don't know!*" He admitted, raised voice in a pleather booth. It produced a glance from table seven.

Perhaps the action of admitting and accepting, writing it, *feeling* "I don't know," was an access code to a new life. A life of opportunity, beyond what had always been? Beyond current limitations?

"I do not know" opened some doorway. The problem, at its core, was in the knowing. The truth was, he did not have a damn clue. The already knowing everything *was* the prison - a shallow, ignorant, self-imposed confinement. Beyond this "knowing" was far greater potential. It must have been this potential that had allowed the strength to actually reach out to Glenn and ask for help.

The work thus far had engendered change, but he'd gotten hi-jacked by the half-ass plan to try and make it work at Mom's again - in the old ways. The best thing she had ever done to help him was to shut that door, to simply say "no," to stop the enabling. No, he did not know what he was going to do, or what living in a strange town was going to be like, what was to become of him - admitting this, an expansive relief and freedom was found. But being alone right now was dangerous.

So he wrote at the restaurant, all night, excited about what lay in store. Besides, someone had been on his mind …

There is a thing often said in early recovery: Not starting a new love relationship for the first year is a pretty good idea. He sure did not have much to bring to the table aside from toxicity. One undiluted glance at the track record found easy proof. Try keeping a plant alive for a year first, someone suggested.

That seemed ridiculous. Terra was beautiful. He had always had a woman around, always looked to them to validate something in him. In fact, he never could stand to be alone. It terrified him. Terra's welcoming, wounded eyes told him she was available, and that was enough. Even though commingling with the females is a no-no for the male patients and vice-versa, he never was one for following *all* the rules. Besides, he needed what (he thought) he needed, and there was a strong mutual attraction. The two had connected at a crucial point in both their lives. Here was at least one thing to look forward to about going to live in Yakima.

Well into the night the ball-point scribbled frantic ranting. He wrote about everything, including the last thing of any value he *might* still own: The collection of musical equipment and his precious drums. But that was put away, and getting at it would be difficult *and* embarrassing. He could not risk it now. Afraid to go anywhere else, he knew what went on at night around here. Until the hand could write no longer and even a whiff of coffee was nauseating did he stay fast in the booth, with no one across the table. There was nowhere to sleep tonight, except the old Explorer.

The sun woke him early, and Green Lake was calling. Just north of Seattle a three-mile path encircled a lake that was just wide enough you could see the other side from any point, but barely. There were always plenty of people with dogs and lots of ducks and geese so he would not feel alone. This place had been a sort of sanctuary for most of his life, as it is for many locals. Just something about it that soothes and lifts a person; it always had for him. The trees here were like friends, too, and some of them he knew well. Weeping willows were his favorite, and one in particular, in full bloom, even looked like Mr. Snuffleupagus. Deciduous brothers and sisters were mesmerizing to watch change with the seasons. The water always felt alive as it melded its colors and moods with the skies; it was calm and inviting, beautiful to behold. It moved him. Besides, Mom didn't wake up early almost ever and he needed to get at some stuff before leaving.

This warm, sunny morning entailed more writing, some reading, plenty of praying, rollerblading, and people–watching, all with reserved anticipation. Thoughts of Marie kept slipping around, but going anywhere near that was asking for too much trouble. The judge had made it clear enough. The mess of emotions and insecurities along with unsure hope (mixed with still being toxic) was uncomfortable at best. His blood might even be phosphorescent – he felt it chugging thick in his veins. Post-Acute Withdrawal Syndrome: PAWS, they called it. After being on so much crap for so long, it can take up to six months to leave the system – certain drugs, years. What else was locked deep in the cells?

Standing on the cusp of a virgin life wanting to change feels so invigorating. He was going for it.

There was much to clean up here in Seattle, having racked up several charges and making a pretty good mess of things. It was not behind him, not even - this would still have its days of reckoning. Kevin knew it would take an extraordinary leap of faith if he was to break the cycles of his former life.

If nothing ever changes, nothing ever changes

~ Chapter 7 ~

Summer of Serenity

The closer to Yakima and the farther from Seattle, the better Kevin felt. Pretty much anything he had ever owned - gone. How weird is that? From a wheeling, dealing business owner to a single duffle bag - he had done it all to himself and was beginning to realize it. Was there something else being wielded? Was there some subconscious mechanism at work? Perhaps it was all part of some grander interworking.

There had been that malignant piece of commercial property back home. Paid over a half million for it, and ran an auto body shop and peddled cars out of it. "Takes a lot of beer to paint a car," had been one joke. He remembered so many times drinking to incoherence and still painting cars, always loaded on something, mixing drugs and booze relentlessly, waking up not even remembering it and with a nail in the head to boot. He *hated* that place, always felt so trapped - condemned to that life, certainly devoid of gratitude. Anyway, didn't matter - it was long gone, and he had nothing to show for it. What a loser. *One damn bag* - oh well, here he was. *Please take it.*

Glenn showed him to an empty bedroom. "You can stay in this room, but only for a couple days. Someone is coming to interview for it, but there are several of these homes in the area. We'll find you one."

The room was perfectly plain. A small bed with a white cotton blanket next to a desk with a chair sat below an open window. It was clean and fresh with no residue of his old life. "This is awesome. Thank you so much." Kevin couldn't help it and hugged Glenn, who seemed to like it if a smile was any indicator.

He had no money, and an Oxford house room did require rent. The three other tenants at the house had similar issues, and shared possible solutions: What they had done to survive, what they knew of that might help. A husky 20-something guy stood near the sliding glass door. Both his hands were shoved in torn up Levi's pockets and messy, unkempt, thick and tightly-curled brown hair almost covered his eyes. He spoke up with a shy, reserved voice, no eye-contact: "The treatment center has a program called 'after-care' for anyone that graduates. You gotta be living close enough to attend the group sessions. They're once a week, and free."

"No shit? That's right, I remember now. I'll check it out ASAP." Kevin had no clue what to do. This sounded good, and he liked free. The Sanctuary was only 15 minutes away and he already missed it. There was a growing sense of gratitude for being able to come to this safe place.

***

Sunday morning. Waking rested, the coffee tasted much better without a devastating hangover like most other mornings brought over the past several years, and throughout most of his life. *One whole month without drinking or using is a long time ...*

Even one second thinking about managing life caused anxiety and fear kicked in like a bad habit. He looked at what was in front of him, instead: Finding an Oxford House, and the guys invited him along to a number of 12-step meetings. After-care started soon, and there was possibility of financial aid. This was a good enough plan for now.

There was one other thing. He left the house, looking for a church in town, searching like some Pagan for a deeper relationship with whatever this Higher Power could be. *Something* had been guiding him, opening doorways, nudging gently, helping let go of the old ways just enough. The God thing ... this is something many struggled with, not only him. Many at treatment resisted the whole notion and seemed agitated most of the time. He had notions of what it was; Warren had taken the family to a Catholic church those few years, but it didn't ring any bells with an angry young boy. It was so boring – him and Sis would fall asleep and risk getting the belt again. He saw and heard a lot about religion and its teachings and dogmas, none of which ever made sense. There was too much conflict, oppression and saying one thing and doing another.

During the stint in jail when Yang gave the bible, he had attended a couple services brought in by an outside church. It seemed pretty rigid - and at the same time there was something compelling about it. Maybe it was the getting together, the break from the cell, the introspection. Upon getting out one time, he began going to the church. The people were likable, but the pastor kept talking about burning in hell (or something like that) if everyone did not acquiesce to a bunch of laid out rules perfectly. It burst his religious bubble. There was a dissonance he could not quite put his finger on, and since being perfect was way too tall an order all by itself, he soon quit attending. It was too harsh. He longed for direction, just not like that. But he would try again.

He again thought about *willing, honest and open*. These principles opened tightly closed internal vaults. How much simpler was this way. Before was always fighting. Trying to prove he was right and everyone else: Wrong. "Being right" was only a façade of chosen illusions and limiting perceptions, so thinly held together by pure delusion. It was a glass house that had come crashing down - the shards slicing him so badly that admitting complete defeat was a step up.

Right now, the willing part was the willingness to admit defeat and surrender, set down the old ways, even if just for now. One could always pick them up later if desired.

Your misery can be reclaimed at any time

The open piece was simple - accepting ways that were foreign to him, being open to accepting help and guidance. Coming to church was asking for help, as was the praying - in fact, the whole message around moving here to Yakima, his very core intention, was a humble and desperate, *Please help me.*

The honest part right now - not having a clue what lay ahead and the complete not-knowing.

The Explorer found a shade tree in the parking lot of a nice Four Square church. It was only a mile from the Oxford House. The message was light and pleasant, not so downtrodden and dark. In fact, allowing the message in without so much judgment always found a golden nugget. He was a wide-eyed kid, beginning a brand new life, as indeed it was.

This church that found him was much more open, not as serious and in your face. A burgeoning awareness of principles in lieu of dogmas was growing, and in the state of openness, his spirit continued to wake up. After the service, he met several locals. The pleasant younger man who led things was also mayor of the city.

"I'm Pastor Jim," the dapper young preacher said, extending a hand.

"Good to meet you. I'm Kevin, new in town."

"Oh, what kind of work do you do," asked Pastor Jim.

"I'm looking for anything."

"Come see me early next week, maybe I can help," Pastor Jim offered.

Movement already - there sure were lots of nice people here.

~ 65 ~

One leg with a bare foot dangling off the end of it hung all the way out an open window of the perfectly shaded Explorer, into a warm afternoon breeze. Digging through his journal, there was Terra's number right where she'd written it. He studied the girl's handwriting for some time before finding the gumption to call. Quite an audacious thing to do, considering.

"Hey, I'm here." Kevin paused, listening. How would she respond?

"Oh, I'm so glad you came," Terra's voice and intonation confirmed the silent invitation.

He was quite fond of her, and could tell she liked him. The problem was, she was married - and, worked at the treatment center. Two big no-no's. But following directions never was one of his strong suits and that apparently had not changed in just a few weeks. Many people had even gotten kicked out of the treatment center for commingling with the opposite sex - they did not want you diverted in any way, and took it very seriously, making examples out of many unfortunate individuals of both sexes. Still, they were drawn to each other in that unstoppable way. Maybe, it was the blossoming of a summer romance.

***

Being back at Mom's and close to all the wreckage for even less than a whole day had paralyzed him. Leaving there was the best choice. In doing a geographical move, you can go anywhere in the world; the problem is that you take yourself. But here, there was a chance to actually change, to look at the "yourself" you think you are, and choose whether that is who you wish to continue to be. This introspection could set one free. He was willing and inspired to continue this work of which he had only skimmed the surface. It is recommended to change just one thing, some said: Everything.

The support groups were 12-step meetings; they had done a few in treatment. Entailed in the treatment program, the counselors had carefully (and at times painfully) taken them through the first five steps, so he had some familiarity with them, and a chance - a good start. Most of the counselors had been right where he was, and they were now living sober.

The fourth and fifth steps were extremely confronting: *"Made a searching and fearless moral inventory of ourselves. Admitted ... the exact nature of our wrongs."*

He had searched for, found, written and shared more ugliness about himself than ever before, had seen the source of much of his deep resentment. He had been honest and shared with another person his most hidden secrets, as many as he could be find, at a time when all of it seemed too much to bear. And all of it was more beneficial than he even had a clue right now. It was highly recommended to continue with the meetings and the step work in a program of recovery, with guidance. Sarah told him that she believed in him, and that had given him hope.

Glenn and the other guys hovered around the coffee pot, talking in the front room. It felt good to share the morning's events. "Let's do the noon down at the old church," Glenn suggested.

Off went the gang.

In the front of the room sat a man who was like a cartoon character. "Hi, I'm Niko, alcoholic."

Niko was huge. He spoke like he had a mouth full of marbles. Must have been 350 pounds, with a round face and belly to match. A thin, white, well-worn cotton shirt with the sleeves cut off stretched around his huge torso, about to split at any moment. The legs of the miniaturized chair in which this could-be Sumo wrestler sat trembled just below the butt cheeks hanging off either side.

"I've picked a topic from *Daily Reflections.*" It was the same book Kevin had been given at treatment – he loved that book!

"After I read it, I'll call on people … please keep your sharing around three to five minutes. You can pass if you don't feel like talking." Something about the oversized man was comforting.

The topic was: *Trusting a Higher Power, especially in the midst of great change.* "You can share on this or anything that pertains to alcoholism and recovery, please."

Some attending were calm and peaceful, some were not, and all kinds of states in between. They shared, one at a time (usually) about themselves, their lives, their experiences, thoughts and opinions. It was a safe place to hang out where people were actually not loaded (usually), but rather came together to share recovery and help each other. Just like at treatment. He liked the new language, liked most of the sharing, and liked the people, instantly; he *related*. It was packed, and it was blazing out, so the door was open with a fan blowing the hot air around - in more ways than one. He liked this getting together. Several girls wore scanty outfits - he liked that, too.

Pretty cool, he thought, listening to the people. The notions he heard today that hit home: *Take what you want and leave the rest.*

Look for the similarities, not the differences

The meeting was closed with the Serenity prayer. Another shade tree outside the old church was perfect for gathering under, and soon a smaller circle was formed.

"That was good in there, and hot. Feels good out here. I'm Kevin."

"Ah, welcome. Niko, but you already know that. Yeah, it was. Welcome now to the meeting after the meeting. There's usually three … one before, the actual meeting, and one after."

~ 67 ~

It was largely an extension of what went on inside, lots of alcoholism and recovery talk. He identified with these people. "You didn't introduce yourself in there ... want some numbers?"

"Sure, that'd be great. Only know a couple people in town." Kevin liked this nice fat fellow, and watched him, with great interest, lumber on inside and only seconds later emerge with a schedule and a pen.

***

Terra was always on his mind, and she had agreed to meet. Strolling along a park's pathway, just being with her was a dream come true. They made small talk of the hot sun and welcome breezes. It was slower here than in the busy city. Butterflies stirred as they hugged goodbye.

Kevin thought about his mom as he crawled into the old Ford, which he wouldn't even have without her help. She always bailed him out, but those days were over. Here he was. *Please take it all.*

But then, better thoughts came. *Wait ... I'm not alone.* A blast of extreme longing was replaced instantly by a sense of unity. *Those people were so nice and helpful at the meeting, and at the house; I have a place to stay, I have somewhere to go, I have these phone numbers ... and The Sanctuary - it's safe, and soon I'll be signed up to go there again.*

It felt like a good move, so far. Something was looking out for him, it had to be. The trees, as they swayed in a soft wind, seemed to acknowledge him. A lone eagle showered down love and peace as it circled in an open blue, endless sky.

A Way Is Made

Hot July sun beat down on the porch of the white house on the corner. A flaming gay guy's blue eyes flared wide as he flung the door open. Apparently, the sight of Kevin was up for discretion. After a good and awkward once-over from shoes to scalp, Mikel welcomed him into the living room where the others were. There were four of them in the house, and they could not have been more diverse.

"Come in, have a seat. I'm Kip." Six-foot Kip was a lanky fellow with shorter blonde hair and wide, almond shaped cat's eyes. He spoke like an automated machine, a cynical robot almost. "This is Dan, and Arvin. You met Mikel," He said, extending a bony index finger in each direction from a long, thin arm.

"Hi, I'm Kevin. Thanks for having me over," he said as he plunked down on the crème-tweed, fairly stained loveseat.

The living room was humid and stuffy, and the house smelled like four dudes lived in it.

"Cold drink? I have two kinds of soda, or water." Kip yelled from the kitchen.

"No thanks," Kevin answered, scanning the old place. At least it was moderately clean. Furniture was sparse, albeit sufficient. It sat upon well-worn hardwood floors. A large comfy chair almost matched the couch, but the loveseat did not even come close. Kip carried over a 3-ring binder and set it on the chipped up, old-school wood coffee table with an amber glass top. He leaned forward and opened it as the other two took a seat.

Arvin was short, skinny and darker skinned, almost bald, and kept chewing his fingernails as he rocked nervously in an easy chair. Arvin was sort of alienesque. He seemed … diverted.

"OK. Welcome. So, here's the deal – you ever live in an Oxford House?" Kip was feeling him out as he reviewed the paperwork and spoke almost in binary.

"Nope, my first time *ever*. Just got here yesterday. I'm from basically Seattle, a little north of it. I couldn't handle it there, need to be here for a while." Kevin could feel the guys processing data and creating possible scenarios until a loud Dodge truck ripped passed the house and rattled the front windows.

"How long you been sober?" Dan asked quietly by way of a deep voice. He was a large man, at least six feet and three inches tall, with a real soft presence. Small, round chocolate eyes gave a look of authentic interest. He placed his hands sideways on each knee and leaned in, bald sweaty head first, in an attempt to listen better, inquisitively squinting one eye.

"Just about a month. I went to treatment close by, just got out." As Kevin spoke it, Kip shot up and almost squirted orange soda out his nose.

"At the place just over here?" Kip pointed behind him.

"Yeah, great place." Kevin answered with a certain amount of pride for completing the rigorous program. "Why?"

"And you know Glenn?" Kip wanted to know.

"Yes, he saved my ass. Gave me a room for a couple days till I get my own place. I like Glenn."

"We both work at the treatment center. I'm grounds maintenance … hard work. Glenn is in the office."

"Yeah, he helped me a lot when I was there. Hey, you guys do a great job on the place. Small world, eh?" Kevin felt a connection already.

Over the next half-hour, they explained the Oxford house way. The phone rang four times but nobody budged. A muffled message being left reverberated down a hallway. Things were run in a sort of democracy, with a president and a secretary and a treasurer, and you were voted in, *or not*, by group majority. Since he never had much of a problem charming his way, he figured it would be a breeze. Though, as the meeting went on he began to doubt this, doubt himself. This old dichotomy again. Too good, not good enough. *Just let it go,* he thought. Besides, trusting whatever had gotten him this far was doing a way better job than he ever had. These contrasting thoughts flashed through his mind in nanoseconds, more than once.

They asked about his situation, intentions, meeting attendance, and ability to pay rent. The phone rang again, but only twice now. Arvin tossed a look toward it, but that was all.

"Well, since I just got out of treatment I don't have any money yet. I went home, but knew I wouldn't make it, so here I am." It was an honest reply. "Hey, could I get that water?"

"The treatment center has a program called ATR, or something like that … they might help pay rent if you're in after-care," Kip offered on his way back to the kitchen. He was the president or whatever and did most of the talking.

"Yes," Kevin exclaimed, "I heard about that, I'm going to sign up for it tomorrow. What's it stand for? Already Tried Relapsing?" Upon which a bellowing laugh shot out of him, drowning out Dan's chuckle. Arvin paused for a moment of contemplation. Then it hit and he busted up.

Kip replied completely literally, without so much, even, as an eye twitch. "Ha Ha. Access to Recovery." Oh, Kevin could have some fun with this guy around.

Kevin was enthusiastic, maybe too much. "What's next? Thanks." He took a gulp of room temperature water from the hazy mug.

"Well, we'll vote on it after you leave. If it's a 'yes' we may be able to work with you on the rent, and you'll have to give a UA right away. If you pass *and* can pay rent in a reasonable amount of time then you can move in." Kip's eyes flapped shut as an arm raised in the air with one finger pointing up, "Oh. Almost forgot. There's a 10:00 p.m. curfew for the first month, then it changes to 11. And, if any of us *even suspect* anything we will ask for a UA immediately. Is that a problem?"

"No, not at all." Kevin was willing to do just about anything to lock in a room, even if it felt somewhat like an accusation or a criticism. He did not like being criticized.

In the old days, just a couple months ago, this all would have been "a bunch of BS" and he would have slammed down his now empty glass and stormed out - but not today. In fact, he kind of liked it, because he *really was* sober and had made the commitment to this new way of living, and actually liked the accountability of being tested on it. And so, he agreed to all of it.

"Give us some time to discuss this. We'll vote on it and be in touch," Kip said as he stood up and peered out the window, "after I mow the lawn. Good luck with ATR."

"Thanks you guys, talk to you soon. Hope I get in." Kevin flashed a nervous, hooky smile. "Bye."

***

Back at Glenn's place he shared the details of the interview. "I just *gotta* get that room."

"I'm sure you will, as long as you are truly not using and are giving this whole recovery thing an honest shot," Glenn said, peering kindly at Kevin through round, wire rimmed glasses, one hand stroking his beard and the other latched onto a coffee mug.

"I am. I really am. And I *so* appreciate all you have done for me. Thanks again for letting me stay here, and for being there when I needed someone so badly." Kevin felt like crying, and almost did, overcome with emotion. It felt good to let people help, be part of a community, but so awkward.

"That's what we do," Glenn said and then gulped down one last swig.

The phone rang … *the Oxford House.* "We voted. Can you come back?" His heart raced in a mix of emotions; would they let him in? Of course they would. No they wouldn't - this again. Kevin's emotional state was tender on a good day.

Let it go. Please take it.

Mikel answered the door again, this time with a cute little smirk, chin up and half cocky smile as if he held a secret. *I'm in, I can feel it.* But then he saw the other guys and they seemed to have a different vibe; he just didn't know. It didn't matter, he liked the house but there were others. More, he just wanted to get on with life, and this was a major step – a safe place to live. Oh, what was going to happen?

It was like these guys enjoyed the power of having another's fate in their hands. They did a good job at stretching out the small talk and letting the decision linger like a low dull hum in the room … *what was it going to be?*

Finally Kip spoke up. "We voted you in if you can pay the rent and pass the UA."

"Yes!" Kevin raised both fists in the air in victory.

The pee test would be a breeze, and he had faith in the rent coming through. Even if it didn't come from this ATR he knew he could make it happen. After passing the UA, they gave him a couple weeks to come up with rent. He could move in tomorrow.

Thank You.

***

It is astonishing how life can change so conspicuously in a blink, and time can seem to literally stand still when one begins to move in the direction of greater Self-awareness. Something beyond description occurs.

Please help guide my day.

The search for a peaceful place to pray, like the spot at The Sanctuary, became the priority. And, knowing when and where was his next meeting. That little schedule, which was decorated with phone numbers, had plenty of options. Much had changed in only a few days.

It seemed like aimless driving, but the Explorer must have some divine GPS. It brought him right to the spot. The black and gold SUV pulled all by itself into a parking lot overlooking a powerful, winding river. It was so loud it drowned out most other noise. The thought occurred it might be a challenge to throw a stone across and hit land, it was so wide. The river tugged at him. Kevin was amazed taking it in. Would he have found this blessing on his own? What was it that touched him so much here?

A concrete pathway wound down alongside its bank, disappearing into an enchanting grove of trees. From the vantage above, it was a twisting trail down into a rabbit hole. And oh, was it ever. The trees beckoned him in, gently though. *Grateful for these old rollerblades.* Somehow, they represented freedom. On a bench, above the white water rapids of the Yakima River, he strapped them on and hit the trail - but only after several minutes of breathing the scene in, committing each nuance to memory. A dragonfly appeared suddenly, two feet from his two eyes and made itself known.

Wind caressed the wings he sprouted on the way down the hill. The sun poured its life-giving warmth upon the day, beside this glorious waterway. Holding both hands out with arms fully extended, he faced his palms into the wind and spread his fingers wide, opened his mouth full and let out an "Ahhhhh," skates picking up speed, hair whipping in the wind. *Flying feels so good!* Entering into the grove, the path flattened and the river calmed, flowing softer now as it leveled. The entire energy changed. Immediately he knew he was being watched, but in a good way. He felt the friendliness of the surroundings. Stirring creatures of all sorts acknowledged him.

The virgin path - perhaps it led to some verdant new adventure. Snaking along with the water, the birds were talking, chippering. There must be hundreds of them. The sun filtered through the trees, fusing its way in, as a squirrel darted across the trail, tail twitching high, flying to the other side and then skidding in the dirt. It turned around quickly and up on its hind legs in a puff of dust, miniature front paws dangling, all in one swoop. He seemed to say "Hey! Who are you? Watch where yure goin'. And welcome."

A happy couple walked by with their black and white curly-haired dog. The day sang a perfect melody. There were no monkeys here. Ah, the experience of being present. The song birds soothed his soul, and he was able, somehow, to feel part of it all.

There was nowhere to go and nothing to do, except this, right now. It was peace not much known. Some part of him began remembering ... but what? He spent hours on the trail just being, crying, laughing out loud. It was calm and beautiful, this new freedom unfolding right before his eyes. Its only access was surrender. He sat quietly for some time alongside the river bank until a meeting the guys suggested felt necessary.

At the beginning, they asked for any newcomers to introduce themselves. "Hi, I'm Kevin, alcoholic." Then they asked if there were any visitors. He was both. They welcomed him and passed another schedule around, the men writing their number on the back. Something weird, they said - they actually *wanted* you to call, that it helped them, too. What did they mean? He did not know.

Sitting in a circle, they shared one at a time, more politely than at the last meeting and less confusion going on in general. Afterwards, a man gave some of his time.

"Hey, nice to meet you. I'm Fred. New, huh? That's gotta be somethin', moving out here from the big city," said the calm man with the gold watch. A yellow polo shirt had a cell phone sticking out of the single breast pocket and a hairy arm out of each sleeve.

"Oh, yeah ... need to get solid in this recovery thing. It's feeling good to be here. Back home was scary." People were breaking off into small groups of twos or threes, just chatting.

"Want me to show you some of the better meetings around?" Fred offered.

"Yeah, that'd be great."

Fred must have been fifty, not quite six feet tall with a fairly large belly and salt and pepper hair. He was casual in demeanor and his cargo shorts and clashing flip-flops. Kevin could not help sizing him up.

"Here, let's see your schedule ... I know this one on Monday is good, and ... " Fred leaned on the old piano in that room and must have circled twenty meetings in the half hour they spent there. He shared about each one, gave general directions for the location, and a little on his take on them. Fred seemed to enjoy the whole exchange, and for Kevin, it turned out to be a real blessing.

"Thanks Fred, for taking all that time, appreciate it so much." Kevin decided Fred must have been sent as an angel disguised in goofy clothes.

He soon began going to each meeting Fred had taken the time to share about and circle. He sure had no clue where to go; he would flip that schedule open and the circled meeting stuck out like a freshly-hammered thumb. Every time would remind him of Fred's kindness.

At home, he shared with Glenn and the other three guys hanging out all the good that was happening. The gang was all smiles; something happens when life moves in a positive direction, people get that way. Happy, looking forward to life, and sober - this was certainly different.

Lying in bed under the open window, Kevin poured over all that had transpired in the short time he had been here. It was surreal. The next day he would go to The Sanctuary, see what that brought - it was the first place he had ever really felt safe in a long time. What exactly was it that caused this? Not sure just what it was, his eyelids began to close with the intention of finding out.

Planting Seeds

The Explorer passed through the gateway in. This time, the little signs on each lamp post appeared very different.

Today is the first day of the rest of your life

He was beginning to believe that. Some pieces were falling into place.

Each day is a new beginning

Maybe a lasting better life was possible. There was now a warm enveloping feeling about it all, so different from that toxic first day. Now, the beauty of the landscape underneath the huge, open sky was brilliant and inviting. The golden sun disk was no longer as scary as it had always been. Those peaceful soaring eagles were now carrying a more discernable message. And the little birds flitting about, jumping from tree to tree, offered their songs to anyone who cared to listen. Even the insects did. This time, he felt it all noticing him.

The new hope was unfamiliar, intimidating, yet inspired. When he walked toward the office to see what he could do about getting some aid, he recognized the walkway he'd been taken down that first day, just over a month ago. Eons had passed in the handful of weeks gone by. A newcomer was being walked along the same path, his head hung low. Kevin could not help feeling for the guy, wishing the best for him, relating to how he must feel. All this he had not, only a month ago, the capacity for – it seemed. A curious feeling stirred through Kevin. Something within longed to connect to this suffering person.

People were coming and going, doing the deal he had just done. He liked being back here - liked feeling a part-of, and was beginning to feel just that.

Entering at one side of the building, the first door on the right was the ATR room and services office. Several filing cabinets sat underneath clear windows looking out over the lawns and rolling hills. Three women, each with a desk and computer, were working behind a counter on the right. On the other side, three double-seat chairs and a few magazines on a small table waited. The place was neat and organized, even smelled clean, and the ladies were kind and pleasant. One stood when he entered.

"Hi, what can I do for you?" Her pink gum smacked as she spoke.

"Nice day out. It is so beautiful here. How are you today?" Kevin redirected.

The comment and question set in motion a five minute conversation with the women about the weather and potential activities in the area. "What's this I hear about a program for help with rent money?" Kevin was trying to come off parenthetical, when in fact was quite purposeful.

"Oh, Access to Recovery. Great program if you qualify," Fran bubbled, loosened up from the small talk. Her perfectly round glasses and red hair tied-up on her head made her look like a happy librarian.

"They will pay up to four hundred dollars rent if you're in after-care and don't have another way to pay, and have an Oxford House or the like that will take you."

The light went on, three for three ... as good as funded.

"They will even give you a gas voucher each week, along with some money to get clothes for work," she said, handing the forms over the counter.

"Sweet!" He needed gas money and some clothes, too. A little mischievous greed kicked in, but it felt awkward. *Do I have to pull some con on everything?* He really did need the help. Here, there was a chance at another way.

He took his time with the application, enjoying the continuing small talk and the interaction with the ladies, but still trying to coerce and get the benefits of ATR immediately. Always wanting everything *right now.* They said it would take at least a few days to process. An opportunity to practice patience - it felt like a wet sponge.

At any rate, he left the office extending appreciation: "Thanks Mary, Susan, and ... Fran, was it?"

"Yep, got 'em all right. Thanks Kevin. Bye," Fran called after him.

Walking the opposite direction from the parking lot and around the grounds, slowly, he finally came upon the sacred spot. A searching glance found no one near. Willing knees found the old familiar earth. The birds came and greeted him with their beloved melodies. Stillness fell upon the day, a stillness which could speak. It said that all things were in their perfectly-imperfect place. This dawning of a life he could not quite yet fathom … It said not to worry about any of that. The groups inside were meeting, sharing, and watching films. He did not have that safety anymore. Yet, he sensed everything was going to be all right.

He tarried, taking time just being, did some writing at the picnic table near the tracks. Feeling a little lonely now, he decided to go, head toward another meeting. It was another stellar July summer day: Still, calm, and hot. He had only a few commitments and plenty of time, a car, a bed to sleep in, a place to live, and was not using. He did not even want to right now. Life was looking fairly awesome.

One day at a time

Mikel called and gave the green light to move in. After the meeting, he thanked Glenn and gang for all the help, and packed up. The homes were only a mile apart. He could not wait to tell the guys.

His room would be downstairs. Fine, it was much cooler. The room was dark and stuffy, the furniture not arranged in any good way. In fact, it was downright cluttered as well as being stagnant. Everything was drab brown. Someone had set up a divider row of dressers between two beds with various tables and clothes strewn about - no Feng Shui practiced here. They acted as if it was the least of all the rooms, maybe because it was shared. But looking past its present arrangement, like Kevin himself, it just needed some help.

Kip said there was another guy coming to share the room; he had tried to go home after treatment and knew he wasn't going to make it. Just like Kevin. Coincidence?

Tonight he'd sleep in the room as-is. Tomorrow was the Fourth of July. The place to be, everyone said, was the fairgrounds. A huge celebration was planned with several Christian rock bands and lots of fireworks for sure. The pastor cum mayor was also the MC. Terra said she would be there, and the guys from the house also. Everyone, it seemed, was going.

Codependence Day

Rising early, Kevin made his way to the kitchen and a roomie clanking dishes.

"Coffee?" Mikel asked. "The cups are right heeeere … and there's the cream and sugar," he said, pointing, wrist flapping, surely being purposely obnoxious when he spoke.

"Thanks" Kevin mumbled through cobwebs – usual, until a few sips at least.

Mikel was fully awake, drinking java and anxiously peering at him, out the window, back and forth. Obviously, he wanted something. "You going to the meeting - A.M. AA?" he smirked, drawing out the last "A" long enough to be noticeable. He looked 50 but acted 15.

"Ummm… yeah, sure," Kevin retorted, taking a sip from the steaming cup.

"Give me a ride? I don't have a car and I'm *tired* of walking – we leave in a few minutes?"

"Sure… Let me get ready." Kevin contemplated getting dressed around a few more gulps.

On the way Mikel filled him in - from his own perspective - on the house and its tenants. Mikel was somewhat cynical, and was attempting to enroll him in it, but Kevin declined the invitation.

Only a few minutes from the house, the meeting was at the same church he had attended Sunday. The world was shrinking in all this serendipity, and he loved it, for whatever reason - a whole world existed outside of his usual norm.

It was another meeting with intriguing people, sharing, coffee, and way too many doughnuts, pastries and cookies this time. The Fourth of July celebration was the hot topic. There was a tangible buzz in the air. Many of the people attended this meeting before going to their day jobs, and they said coming here offered a great way to start the day. The meetings, usually (and this one did), ended with the serenity prayer, for those that wished, standing in a circle and holding hands. At treatment, Group ended in a circle, arms around each other, saying this same prayer:

God, grant me the serenity to accept the things I cannot change, courage to change the things I can, and wisdom to know the difference

This prayer was changing Kevin. Its meaning, to him personally, would change and transform, sometimes even between meetings. There can be much more to it than just spoken words – if allowed. This holding hands and praying would have been ridiculous to him before. Here it was providing him with great comfort and unfamiliar results - like so much he was being shown.

At the meeting after the meeting everyone was talking about all the to do's going on around town, and most agreed winding up at the fairgrounds after the barbeques - sober - was the favorable plan. Terra would be there, and just seeing her alone was worth going.

After the meeting he returned to the river. Spent the whole morning there this time, loving the peace and tranquility, in an almost constant state of prayer, which was not anything like he thought it might be. It was *being connected* to the spirits of things, people, places ... this was the god he was coming to know. More the subtle flow of life *through* life than some figure above, looking down doling out judgment, fickle and angry and punishing yet all powerful and kind - that god he never could understand at all, let alone trust.

It had been just a few weeks ago at treatment during the struggle with how to even begin this relationship with a Higher Power. A man in his group who was Native American handed him a coin which had a Native American prayer imprinted upon the back of it. As Kevin read, the words spoke a truth he never could. A secret passageway of awareness opened. Like a sweeping autumn gust had it come, precise and right on time:

Great Spirit

Whose Voice I Hear In The Wind

Whose Breath Gives Life To The World

Hear Me

I Come To You As One Of Your Many Children

I Am Small And Weak

I Need Your Strength And Wisdom

May I Walk In Beauty

It spoke of what he was really seeking - a more profound connection with Life itself. The stirring message on this little coin had happened to come his way and offer its essence. Here on this very trail by a beautiful river was revealed the peaceful, soothing flow of the natural world. And so much more.

When you commit yourself to something, Providence moves

He had been reduced to only a few possessions, not even enough money to pay a few hundred dollars for rent, minimal clothes, and a vehicle that he would not even have without Mom's help - and these rollerblades. Funny how the skates were the most valuable material thing he possessed today, he mused. The musical equipment was worth lots of money, but he shoved thoughts of it away.

Kicking along the trail, the sun baked his bare skin. The wind whispered songs of freedom. The water roared and splashed and sounded its grandeur. It made the sweetest music. He practiced giving the river the stuff that caused him pain. He imagined the thoughts that tormented him as matter. While acknowledging the swift, powerful essence of water, he let them go into the center of its flow, and marveled at how easily it took them. Each time he felt the thoughts lose their hold, replaced with simple wonder and the easy beauty of his surroundings. It all infused through, good medicine. He could feel it healing him, working from the inside out. This easy power knew him and the help he needed, fully willing if only he asked - and he did. Tears streamed down his cheeks, tears of happiness, of knowing the tenderness, the miracle of this nurturing.

***

People milled about the fairgrounds. A band was setting up on a huge center stage. Carnival rides, food booths and games lined the outskirts. The atmosphere was alive with celebration. "Small town Fourth-of-July, pretty cool," Kevin whispered out loud but only to himself, taking it all in. A fierce orange sun was low in the sky now, hovering just above the mountains. It was surreal, being here.

A Christian rock band fired up on high, the music was thunder and lightning coursing through a swirling electric sky. Twenty-foot tall speakers on either side of them, thousands of watts of raw power blazing guitars and booming drums - the vibrations rippled through the whole crowd, which amplified the effect even more. The music shot through Kevin as he raised his hands in a "V" and sang the hooky chorus along with the whole crowd, loud and wide open:

"Let the flood gates open ... I feel You in me ... Let the flood gates open"

Roaring applause after the grand finale finished the set. Kevin headed backstage, intending to meet the band. On the way, just coming off the stage was the MC, who was the pastor, and who was the mayor. After only a brief and clumsy chat, Kevin excused himself with "See you at church."

The band not only rocked, they were pleasant guys. "Thanks for a great set. I *loved* it." The whole thing made him think about his own love of playing drums, making music and performing. His imagination flew far beyond where he stood, in a moment of contemplation ... somehow he knew, he would play again.

"Hey. You guys know anyone looking for a drummer?" This was always the best way to land a gig, just asking around. With no solid leads, Kevin departed backstage. "Thanks guys, I'm gonna go check out the festivities." Dusk was slowly shifting the entire vibe.

An electric, radiant quality buzzed through *everything*. Life was alive like never before. Not even fully dark yet, a thunderous boom preceded a shower of red fire in the sky, then silver, green, and blue tracers sizzled towards earth in myriads of colorful torus. Kevin hurried over to the racetrack, east of the stage, where they were being launched from. Dazzling the eyes, explosions mixed with the noise of the rides and the music and the people – everything felt in perfect rhythm, true synergy.

Mom always loves fireworks. The thought bounced in. *I'm going to call her right now.* He longed to share this new found wonder, this easy happiness, the serenity he felt, how much he loved being sober, and to wish her a happy Fourth.

"Hello?" Her voice was reserved and cautious.

"Hi Ma. Wish you could see these fireworks, it's beautiful here tonight." His tone was awkward, as if masking something. Mom did not have much to say.

"How's Sheba doing?" The question caused a pause.

"Your sister had to give her to a new home. Apparently, she attacked someone."

"Oh, crap." He let it go right there – of course she had become aggressive. Asking why would only incur the risk of some kind of accountability.

More silence. Take a lot more than one sober month and a handful of current promises to repair too many damaged relationships. *Please take it.*

"Well, happy Fourth of July and we'll talk soon." His voice was light to hide the sadness.

"Happy Fourth, Kevin," she said wryly.

He found the best diversion as quickly as possible: Terra.

"Hey! The fireworks are going. Did you see them? Totally awesome!" He was so happy to see her. From the many occasions talking at the treatment center, he knew quite a bit about her situation.

"Yeah, very nice. Just getting my three-year-old a bite to eat." She tossed a head nod toward a young boy running figure eights. "Hey Brandon, come 'ere, meet my friend."

The boy stuffed a used up paper plate in an overflowing garbage can and ran over. He was not shy.

"Brandon this is Kevin, shake his hand?" Terra crouched down to eye level with the boy to see if he was interested.

Kevin held his hand out but the scowling boy did not take it. "Hi five?" Kevin rerouted, holding his hand straight out instead. The boy lit up immediately, swung, and laid a perfect one down.

"Nice work," Kevin smiled, raising two fists in victory.

Terra smiled too, enjoying the exchange. Brandon kept running wild as they walked the fairgrounds. They had to reel him in every thirty seconds.

"Great kid, sure has lots of energy." Kevin liked kids, at a distance. "So what's going on with you?"

"Oh … well, it's all so weird at home. I'm tired of the fighting, the not getting along. I sure wish it was different." Her presence was weighted, her head even hung when she talked about it, watching her own fingers play with some wrapper in her hands. "My teenage son, Devon, is tired of it, too. He is my stoic one. Different dad. He watches out for me, that boy does." Just speaking it brought her head up and her spirit, too.

Kevin could tell she wanted out, and fantasized in the moment about being her rescuer.

"Why don't you leave?" It was a leading question.

"Working on it … I worry about Brandon, being so young and all. It didn't used to be like this," she answered, and then got quiet.

"He's an addict too, right?" Kevin asked, even though he was pretty sure of the answer.

"Yeah, and he's in active addiction, I never know what's going to happen, if he'll be home or not. He's gone a lot and comes home trashed, and often angry." Terra's voice was heavy and morose.

"Does he get violent?" Kevin wanted to know.

Terra just looked at him with those big, gorgeous and sad eyes that said it all.

"I gotta get home soon, get this one to bed," Terra said, shifting the conversation.

The fantasy was growing now; he *would* rescue her. That was a joke; he could not even help himself. But, denial runs deep and conning himself was something at which he was *so good*. But did she even like him? He knew she did, and he also knew, beyond the self-deception, that it was too much too soon for either of them. Still, he couldn't get past his need to look for himself in a woman, just as he had always done, and especially one as beautiful as her - no, he was not strong enough for honoring that, and he would play every card he had to win her favors. Besides, they needed each other.

"Well, here's my truck." She motioned toward a small blue Toyota 4x4. The two shared a long hug goodnight. Butterflies danced as fireworks exploded overhead.

"Nine-forty-five, crap - I gotta go! I'm parked way on the other side, talk later." Kevin ran across the street, Terra's "Bye" rang out behind him.

Running through the crowd, he came upon the guys from the house, but their curfew wasn't until eleven. They saw him, too.

"Hey guys, on my way home right now. Having fun?" He was huffing and puffing and hyper.

"Yeah. It's ten till, ya' gonna make it? Don't worry if you're a couple minutes late. We'll be home soon," Kip said.

"K thanks. See ya' at home." Kevin ran free toward the car, weaving the crowd, loving the whole vibe of this night. It felt so good to be sober, even if delusion still lurked like a pack of hungry wolves.

He could not wait to get home and write in his journal - the new way of sorting things out, the kinds of things that can drive a person insane. He got to see in the writing again the confusion and insanity of his thinking. Each time the bringing it out of his head onto paper caused instant relief. Self-awareness is the genesis of real change. Tonight's journal entry allowed a valuable revelation.

The ego likes complexity and confusion. In the writing, he kept referring to *evil*, and beating and conquering this permeating disease that had him. As long as he fought something outside of him, he was a victim. Evil was a *perception*, and he began to see it - it was his own head fighting his own head. As long as *he allowed* it to continue there would always be the conflict. Screaming monkeys.

It was like trying to head-butt himself - no wonder he felt so insane all the time. A realization came: He connected to the river and the trail, the wind through the trees, The Sanctuary and mountains, the eagles, the birds always singing to him, even the trains. What was he exactly handing over? *It was his thinking.* The way he saw life – tired old perceptions, which were not even real. Unless *he made them real.*

This "evil" was actually self-imposed, and, was *transformable.* Here was releasing old ways. There was a choice: Operate from stale old stores of pre-conceived notions, or, allow fresh inspiration to be a wiser guide, unfettered by fear. He was being shown through the step work, the sharing with others. He had always relied on his own power (thinking), which was always too thin to suffice. So what was it that was guiding now, instead? Trusting this invisible, natural flow of life is when he *felt* peace, serenity, and release from conflict. It was simple.

True Power does not come from mortals, It comes through ...

***

Deep, dreamy and full, it was a good night's sleep. Kevin woke rested, did the AM A.A., and returned to his new home. A waterway trickled past the house, on the other side of the street. He sat beside the little stream in the morning sun, feet dangling just above the water, rejoicing in the delightful day. The tree and plant people held his birds. The winged ones sang to him and to all the humans going about their day. Again, silence and stillness became available beyond any noise. He was beginning to enjoy this more than anything.

Several ducks came to say hello. He watched them for some time, their diverse colors, little eyes seeing him, feathers soft upon the water. They were peaceful beings. Making a mental note to share some food next time, he dubbed it a good spot and would come here again tomorrow. This was all meditation, more good medicine. He thought about the day. There was much to do – he decided to let a Higher Power handle all of it and spoke the words aloud to the universe. The commitment brought the inspiration to pay Pastor Jim a visit.

"I know some business owners. I'll put the word out about you looking for work. You try the Work Source Office?" Pastor Jim offered.

"Nope, I'll try it." Kevin shared some about his situation. It was steeped in delusional thinking. But, he had made the choice to practice honesty. It felt much better than lying. Pastor Jim did not flinch.

The guy from treatment was coming to interview back at the house. Whoever it was would be staying in the brown room, too. He silently hoped this guy was going to be OK. Little did he know it was a man already befriended.

"I went home and the very first night drank some beers … it scared me that I couldn't just not drink, so I came right back here to where it was safe." JP wanted to give sobriety a chance. Kevin was happy to see him, and how their stories were similar. They had gotten along well at treatment but were in different groups there. JP had to go through the interview process, which Kevin now got to be a part of, and was voted in easily and right away. Now there were five of them living in this house. What was going to happen? Would it be OK?

One day at a time

They all sat in the living room and talked about Oxford House living, the barbeques and get-togethers around town in the recovery community, and about how it worked in general. They talked about living in the house, and each guy shared some of their story. You could cut the bravado with a knife, each of them still trying to look good and avoid the undeniable reality that their lives had come to this: Not able to make it in the "real world" and now barely able to pay some 400 bucks rent, let alone much else. Yet, they shared a common bond.

The room looked even darker when he showed it to JP. It was full of stuck energy, even a novice could tell; it reeked of broken souls that had dwelled here and not honored the place. One of those basement windows that sit up near the ceiling was plastered with leaves and dirt outside, filthy on the inside, and glued shut. It was the style that had a cut-out in the ground around it on the outside, for a daylight basement. No light came through it though, and the brownish furniture was barely visible. The rest of the room was also a mess; abandoned old clothes decorated the room, draped lifelessly on wire hangers. It felt like a dungeon.

But there was potential and the fresh vigor that JP and Kevin had was about to change all that. They looked around the room, at each other, and said in near-unison, "Let's give this place a makeover!" Before starting, they asked permission and got an apathetic response from the others. "Yeah, do whatever you want."

"Dude. What do you think about this: We'll move the beds on either side of the room and put a dresser next to each, and pitch this one," Kevin said, pointing to a dilapidated old dinosaur chest of drawers.

"That sounds awesome. Like, who *lived* here? This place is almost depressing." JP's tone was even funny. His presence brought a welcome lightness to the place.

Kevin laughed out loud. "Almost? It is! We'll fix it up in no time."

They cleared, cleaned, tossed, arranged and laughed. Laughed and laughed. This was so much fun.

"Whose clothes are these even?" JP raised his upper lip, pretending he were someone else. "No wait …" He said crawling inside an armoire, giggling. He came out with a goofy looking coat and put it on. "I'm a drunk stoner loser, stuck here."

Somehow even this was funny and the two cracked up.

"Pitch it." He said, whipping off the coat. Kevin echoed, "Pitch it!"

And outside the door it went, into a growing pile of other items on their way out.

Rule #62: Don't take yourself too seriously.

JP plugged in a light he picked up off the ground and clicked it on and off a couple times. Nothing. "I'm sure. What a douche bag, whoever lived here," clicking it again as if now it would work.

Kevin grabbed another table lamp and same, no light. In fact, the only light in the room was a lackluster ceiling light in the center that could hold three bulbs, but had only one. It was a miracle, they guessed, that the one even worked.

Trust God ~ Clean House ~ Help Others

Kevin remembered hearing this at a meeting. All the praying he had been doing was the first trust … trusting something he had never known - even calling it god (aside from cussing or last-ditch-effort-triage) was shaky ground. He usually thought about it as Spirit or something to which he had not already attached a stigma wrought with confusion and negativity.

And here they were, literally cleaning house, helping each other - at a time when both of them so needed help. It felt good to have each other's company, and they were happy as could be in this moment.

The room began taking shape. The beds were placed on either side of the room, a dresser next to each. Kevin's bed sat below the window, JP's across from it. The center of the room was now wide open. Bulbs were found upstairs for the table lamps now shining on each dresser. The ceiling light took special ones. Even a small task such as going for specific light bulbs provided a welcome adventure and just enough purpose for the day. It was better than chasing down dope and nursing hangovers.

"We'll get a few of those at the store when we go back out," Kevin said pointing to the coverless fixture. "I found the cover in a drawer. I'll put it back on after we do."

Just like with their own rooms and closets of the past, old memories and ways of being; they had cleaned house. Out with the old - or at least take a good look at it, clean it up, and make it useful - and in with the new.

The armoire was opposite JP's bed, kitty corner from Kevin's. And, with a thorough vacuum job the place was much fresher and way more open, an altogether different room. It was huge now - the only thing left was getting the window open, and that would take tools.

This cleaning, arranging and reconfiguring may seem trivial to some people. But Kevin was beginning to realize the subtle interdependence of a human being and its environment. A new thought, a better feeling, even the simplest action, was all helping create an expansive burst of growth.

It is an inside job

~ Chapter 8 ~

Unfinished Business

Alcohol and other drugs taken in extreme excess will wreak total havoc on a human being. On one such occasion some eight months back, at the old shop and under such duress, after hours of peering outside through a small peephole between tokes of various drugs and with stale booze oozing out of every pore, paranoid delusion convinced Kevin that the shadow of a tree was something much more terrifying. After peeking out one last time just before sunrise (when it is most dark) at the motionless figure, he called the police:

An indurated voice answered. "911 - your emergency?"

"There's someone with a gun. Outside my shop!" He ranted, convinced but not convincingly, for the people he was calling had seen and heard it all, and to them he was just another low-life calling during witching hours. And the area from which he was calling at some 4:20 a.m., around the shop and that skanky highway, was quite seedy. Why had he even chosen it in the first place?

"We'll send someone out," she said, sardonically, taking the address and his *full* name.

In no less than 20 minutes the boys in blue had arrived. The authoritive "Knock Knock!" reverberated off the empty concrete floors, bounced off the lifeless walls and then through his heaving chest.

He scurried down the ladder and swung the front door open. Two large officers greeted him, their faces twisted in sarcastic judgment. One of them announced with a smirk:

"Well, there's no one with any gun, but you do have a warrant for your arrest." They invited him outside for a complimentary pat-down and immediately discovered a small bag of a white, powdery substance, which of course, he had no idea how - he stated emphatically - it had become lodged in his right hand pants pocket.

They smiled politely, their job nearly done. "Watch your head," one cautioned as they loaded him in the back of the cruiser.

Calling the police on himself, as well as having the drugs in his pocket in the particular amount that was there, were all in perfect alignment with a greater story unfolding.

In one view, it could be said this was bad luck. But with a different view, was there something else at work? He was soon to learn much more about such things. From the shotgun and the fly, to this trip to jail and the ensuing charges, a profound purpose was indeed percolating. But:

It will require acceptance and willingness to be revealed and realized

All these months had gone by now and no charges - maybe he had become lucky and the police had given him a break and just tossed out the bag of drugs, or maybe they used it and pretended it never happened. (He surely would have if he were a cop.) But they had not, and, as if on some divine cue, charges were filed. He now faced a felony drug possession rap. Mom told him; the mail had come to her house. He had somehow managed to elude any felony charges up until now. Being convicted of a felony is bad news for many freedoms in the world. Here was one of those "yets" they talked about in treatment: Haven't done that, *yet*. What would the next one be, were he to pick up again?

***

JP and Kevin loaded themselves into the rig and took off toward Mom's house to get his last few possessions, which did include enough hand tools to get to work. Two lost souls. How much fun they had, standing upon the threshold of a brand new life, unsure and with very little, happy and excited just for the pure possibility that lay in front of them.

It was a two-hour and forty-five minute laugh-fest, making fun of the other guys at the house, cackling like two hyenas. At some gas station-pit stop along the way, they found a figurine. It was a three-headed Tiki-doll. They played with it like kids for hours - the three faces on the thing even *looked* like the guys they lived with.

JP danced it on the dashboard. It came to life! "Look at me .... I'm so cool," imitating one of the dudes at the house. "Grrrr. Grrrr! ARGHHHH." JP pounded the doll up and down on the dashboard as if it was throwing a tantrum, just like Arvin had done more than once.

Then he redirected for another tenant. "A.M. A *Aaaaaaaaaaaaaaa.*" It was too much as the Explorer swerved and all but side-swiped a Volvo wagon and barely shot back into the proper lane after a drastic over-correction. They were ripe for a driving-while-dying-laughing charge.

Tears ran down Kevin's cheeks. Everything JP did made him laugh. Tiki provided hours of fun. Taking turns, one in the driver's seat and the other mimicking their housemates, they cruised at 70mph down Interstate 90, abdominals aching and jaws spent from too much boisterous hilarity.

After procuring Kevin's last few tools and some mail, including the envelope with the felony charge, they made one more stop: The old shop. A sinking, grotesque feeling filled Kevin but he tried to act cool, collecting a few items he had left there. It was obvious: *I am not welcome here.* Even the few trees up the driveway spoke it to him, in addition to the scowling glances from the people. They knew him.

"Let's get out of here," Kevin said, a thick black cloud nearly forming right over his head as the gas pedal clanked onto the floor in an attempt to elude it. The truck lurched onto Highway 99 as the thought flashed to drive by Marie's, as he'd done a zillion other times, to check up on her. Rarely a day went by without some thought of her. JP could easily feel his friend's pain, and provided a welcome diversion of silliness as the Explorer found the road back, instead, through bluer skies, to their sanctuary-basement-hideaway.

"Hey, like, I'm putting this thing somewhere … those douche bags will never know," JP said with his signature cocky sneer, suppressing another possible run of giggling, holding Tiki above him for a moment as if to pull power from the universe itself. "It can be, like, our guardian or something." And so it was dubbed, as he set it carefully upon the desk between their beds.

The room was even brighter with its new Tiki-guardian.

***

Waking up with the sun, the early meeting was first on the agenda. Just a few additions and their room would be finished. One of the few possessions Kevin had left to his name was a computer speaker set-up which consisted of a subwoofer, four surround-sound speakers, and a built in amplifier. It could go way loud. The computer was long gone.

After the meeting, Kevin figured out how to hook up the amp to a little portable radio and CD player. They suddenly had adrenaline-instigating, pounding, *loud* rock music. Both of them, being rock drummers, loved it. JP air drummed with his index fingers as drum sticks, making his best rock-star face as Guns-n-Rose's *Paradise City* shot through the sound system, filled the room and sizzled to life. More fuel for this awesome summer day - much to the dismay of the frazzled roommates. The sun blazed at over 100 degrees, the figurine on the dresser danced with the pulsating bass as they both laughed and danced and banged heads without a care in the world right now.

The window cut open easily. Cleaning around it (letting the light in and allowing a view out), they washed it and found it could be propped open, allowing a welcome, fresh cleansing breeze to enter. The opening was just large enough for a human to crawl through - their own private fire escape. With the usual upstairs front door-open-and-fan-blowing-the-hot-air-out set-up, it created a refreshing flow-through. It was a smaller window, but clean and open it turned that room that was, just a couple days ago, a stagnant and stale, stuffy, cramped little dungeon, into a breezy, light and open space with plenty of room. Just right for two separated brothers beginning to find their Way.

When the others came to see about all the noise and commotion, they were shocked to find what used to be the cruddiest room in the house was now the coolest and lightest room, full of vivacity with these two inspired, crazy guys living in it. No one had even known the walls were actually pale, an eggshell white.

"Wow, this place looks great," Dan loudly exclaimed. Kip - deadpan as always: "Pretty cool, guys." Mikel just grimaced at the blaring speakers and whipped his head around flippantly and then stormed off. Arvin only scowled. JP looked at Kevin, at Tiki, and then back with his lip going again. The laughing almost drowned out the ripping guitar solo flying out of five well-placed speakers, and they had to fall onto their beds to avoid collapsing. The other guys could only wonder, "What was so funny?"

The day was beautiful as any in recorded history, the room done. The boys set out on the town to see what was going on.

A Gift?

Kevin was looking forward to the first day of Group. If he had stayed in Seattle, he would almost surely be loaded by now - at least lost in that place which was now worlds away. He cringed every time he thought about the past couple years, of facing the wreckage of it all. A lifetime, really. His stomach dropped - he felt like the biggest loser ever for all that had transpired. He'd made a fool of himself, had done it publicly - but that did not matter anymore. He was here now. Not only would he be lost there, as he was immediately each time he returned, he would not have the nurturing of this after-care program. He needed the support of the group, the safety of Sanctuary, and guidance. He was willing to do the work, and, probably for the first time ever, to really listen to others and follow direction. But only so much.

Take the cotton out of your ears and put it in your mouth

He went into the office, greeted Mary and Fran before inquiring. "I've got Group tonight, and was wondering ... heard anything about the ATR?" He told them again about the Oxford House and the rent situation. "Have a seat, let me check it out," Fran said. He waited nervously.

What if I get turned down? Then what?

And right there, sitting in the double-vinyl chair, the office fell into a blurry background and he toppled headlong into reverie:

I guess I could ... get ... a job.

gulp

A job. That was a joke. The once-big business owner with money flying around everywhere was now here, reduced to this. But owning that business had been the real joke - he hated it. He felt lost and alone, trapped, and no amount of money could fill the hole in his soul that just got bigger and huger and more tremendous with each passing, agonizing day. No diversion ever filled that hole. But they almost always succeeded in hurting others. He flashed back even further into a most unwelcome retrospection, which had knocked on the door of his memory during the trip to The Sanctuary, that first day, in the Caravan:

It was the height of success, at least in his addict's ways of judging success: A few employees, plenty of business, making his own hours and overusing as much as he wanted. He and Marie were going to Montana, sporting his fancy red convertible Camaro Z-28 - and with plenty of money. Marie let him drink to his desire. However, he had to hide the pills he always obtained through a peddler that supplied potent narcotics with unpronounceable names, pills that temporarily killed the emotional pain every thought seemed to bring.

And, less than a year ago he had rekindled his relationship with cocaine. It had been fifteen years since he had touched it. Back then, it had its claws deeply embedded, a rabid demon-monkey on his back. This scared him so bad he (somehow) put it down and swore it off – had let the booze and softer drugs do the work of suppressing whatever it was he always was hiding from - until now. By the time they left for Montana, the pills and other drugs, the booze, even in their powerful combinations, had quit working. Monkeys spilled out of the glove box, poured from the trunk, pounced on the hood, filled the whole Camaro and dominated every breath.

In the little fanny pack strapped to Kevin's waist was the small pharmacy of narcotics and plenty of powder. Marie hated drugs, so he made sure she was clueless. His business, a ship with no captain, was left to be run haphazardly by employees that knew he was not all there. As they drove, he requested Marie stop at every damn gas station along the way so he could "go to the bathroom," where he snorted another line and popped another pill or two or three or five. They stopped at various bars and drank. When she went to the bathroom he would pound her drink after his and when she came back she giggled as if it were "cute." She only ordered more. It was anything but cute. He had five to her one, and off they went. He was becoming grouchy and pissy and his face was clogged from snorting crappy cocaine. "Why are you so plugged up," she asked. It was explained away as a sinus problem, which she only accepted for convenience, always wanting to believe him. Kevin was a ticking time-bomb.

He could not get high to any kind of satisfaction - no matter how much he took or how many drinks or what combinations. The whole day had been like this, the worst ever. They finally arrived at a motel - it was late, and he was exhausted and touchy and empty and desolate. And so loaded. At check in, something set him off and he was extremely rude to the staff. Marie glared at him, miffed. "What is *wrong* with you?"

He miserably grumbled something off and blamed them for being jerks and assholes. More booze, that would do it - they went into the hotel bar. A mirror caught his glance and found bloodshot, enraged eyes against the white wife-beater tank top – god, he looked like hell, staring back at something he *hated*. Hated! He promptly ordered a *glass* (not a shot) of straight vodka and downed it before Marie even had two sips of her mixed drink.

Marie turned to the bartender. "Any live music around?" She loved live bands, and since there was more booze, he'd go.

"Yeah, 'bout a mile down this road right here there's a joint with a band 'til two." It was only one now, still another hour for drinking. Off they went.

A guitar player shredding out monster chords on his Les Paul greeted their entrance just five feet inside the front door. He tossed his long hair up, down, and all around out in front of the cranked-up rock band. Marie began banging heads with him and dancing, and Kevin excused himself into the bathroom for more coke. Still, *Can't get high!* It was *agonizing*, so he popped *more* pills which he did not even know dosages for or names of or even what they were for. He staggered back to the bar and got a Jager and root beer, one of Marie's favorite drinks, in a pounder glass. "Too much root beer," he scoffed, glaring at the bartender with death beams, attempting to slice her in two. The unphased rougher-looking gal apparently enjoyed a challenge and draggled over on task with the bottle, filling the nearly empty glass - and not with any more root beer - which Kevin immediately pounded. And then another. Marie was doing her best to have fun. Kevin was hell bent on oblivion, driven purely by demons. All the while the monkeys screeched, louder, louder, louder. Nothing would drown them out.

~ 92 ~

Closing time.

Marie insisted on driving. Kevin used the full force of the death beams on her now as she kept a steady gaze on the highway. She knew what was next. Maybe if he were cruel enough to her, *his* monkeys would *shut up.*

He berated her about anything and everything, projecting as always, all his worst fears and self-loathing upon her.

"You're fucking worthless and you'll never be anything!" The rough and pain-ridden voice matched his condition.

"This stupid fucking trip in this *damnable* place! I should've never come. Fuck I hate this place! And I hate you. I HAAAATE YOU!"

Marie replied, fearful, *here it comes.* "What? I thought you wanted to come … what is *wrong* with you?"

Angry, raw, red eyes were swimming in a saturated skull, which was now bobbing, blood thick with poison.

"Fuck it all! I just don't care anymore. *I don't care, do you heeeaar me?"* This time he got so close to her face and peered at her with the most satanic look as full of hatred as he could possibly muster.

Marie was reduced to confused sobs. "Oh my god Kevin, you are possessed. Please stop it!"

He only slumped back in the seat now, morose and gross. *"Fuck it. Fuck it all."*

She always took so much abuse from him, the vicious cycle; if there were to be a later he would grovel and tell her how sorry he was and that it would never happen again. She would finally give in and forgive, until it happened again. And it would. It had always gone on like that, round and round.

Angry demons lashed at his every cell, ripping scabs off wounds that never healed. The monkeys had turned violent now, and no place was safe from their gnashing, glistening teeth, from the nameless pain. There was only the tremendous rage. The toxicity, fuel for this raging fire. A tormented mess, in every way, the self-loathing at an all-time high – Kevin, at an all-time low.

He snorted a drizzling mess back in; it sounded nasty. *"I hate my life! I hate everything!"*

"You sound terrible. I'll drop you at the room and go get something for it." Marie was concerned, but did not know how to address the true problem.

Kevin stumbled into the hollow room and fell onto the bed. Time was only some unfortunate blur. Marie acted like nothing had happened, as if some reset had occurred. "Here, brought you some antihistamine for your issue." She was trying every way she knew to help. Kevin promptly ingested it, and of course more than the recommended dosage. Trying to watch TV and go to sleep inside the gross fog, he yanked out a bottle of booze they had brought.

Marie complained. "Oh my god! You're gonna drink *more?*" Ignoring the comment, he took a long, hard, antagonistic pull off the bottle of vodka. That he had taken in as much as he had this day, and was still standing, is a tribute to the magnificence of the human body. He did not know he was doing his best to kill it, for he was only trying to numb some unconscious agony. Having at this point drank surely close to a gallon of hard booze and taken more narcotics than a horse could handle, not to mention the other crap, he remembered the anti-anxiety/sleeping pills he had conned some detached psychiatrist into giving him. Trying to be shifty, he popped two, maybe three of them. *Doesn't matter anyway.*

"Now what are you taking!" Marie was dumbfounded.

"Shut the fuck up! I can't believe you ... who do you think you are? And how could you sleep with some fucking asshole. You probly wanna fuck every other guy, too. Whore!" It was allusion to someone she had dated during one of their many break-ups. Kevin slurred much crueler words also as he raged on.

"I give up with you, I give up." She was defeated and crying.

Then he finally shut up, as he began to pass out and drift off to a toxic wasteland in the fires of hell. Certain death waited there.

The gurgling/snoring/choking whatever it was that ensued was keeping Marie awake. Besides, she was pissed at him. He had been cruel to her; but he always was. She kicked him, trying to shut him up, to no avail. When she got up to go to the bathroom and turned the light on, she was shocked to find him dark grey and purple and not breathing. His body had given out, and long after many bodies might have. The respiratory system shut down, heart too strained, it all just finally *shut down.* And here they were, in the middle of nowhere, a fact he had just hours ago condemned, far away from any medical assistance. She kicked him, shook him, implored him. *"Wake up or I'll call an ambulance!"* No response. He was gone.

Frantic, Marie grabbed the phone from the dresser and dialed 911. "Oh my god, he ... he's not breathing. He's not breathing! Please help me, I think he's dead, or, or dying!"

"Calm down, ma'am, just try and focus. What happened?"

"Calm down? He's dark gray for Christ's sake! I think he was doing drugs, maybe ... ummm, he for sure drank a ton of alcohol. Oh, God. I told him!"

"It's OK, we're going to help you."

They instructed how to perform CPR through her distraught tears. Not sure if it was working, she continued, breathing for him, pulsing his heart for him, receiving directions from some unseen helper, trying to listen, hold the phone and perform the instructions. Thoughts raced through her contorted mind. *What if I fail? Will his family hate me forever? What will I tell people?* Chest compressions, breaths. Tears. "Oh, god, no. No! Come on, breathe, breathe! Don't do this to me, please."

The closest hospital was 45 minutes away and any ambulance, the same. Marie was desperately trying to save the life he was as desperately trying to end. To her it must have dragged on forever. Despite all her work, he was still not breathing when the ambulance arrived. They put a tube down his throat but even that was not working, and things were not looking so good - depending on the perspective.

Marie followed the ambulance in the flame-red convertible, scared, frantic and confused, not knowing if they would be able to revive him. Was he dead right now? She had always reproved him for his excessive drinking and using: "I don't want to wake up to a cold, dead body!"

***

A peaceful, enveloping white glow of blissful encapsulation faded from soft and warm into a moving, shaking and bouncing pale-white blur of horror. Kevin emerged from a fathomless place. Beautiful peace gave way to a thick haze of disconnected terror and bewilderment as he slowly came back into his body - head pounding, every cell wrought with never-before-felt pain and discomfort, barely able to even move crusted eyelids apart to reveal red, tattered, eighty-grit eyeballs.

"Whaaat   ...   where ...   ? "

"You quit breathing," the paramedic answered. Now he vaguely realized that part of the white blur was the ceiling of a moving ambulance. "We're bringing you to the hospital – you had checked out, we couldn't get you going. If it hadn't been for your girlfriend you would be dead right now."

Kevin was confused. Part of him *wanted* to be dead. Part of him was trying to figure out what had happened. Where was he? He could barely move anything. What would happen now? Was he somehow paralyzed? He fell back into a sick slumber.

Waking in a hospital bed with all kinds of IV's in his arms, he felt like the worst kind of shit. The nurses were quite concerned, and Marie - he could see her through the window – was just horrified, and looking a frazzled mess from the trauma of the situation and what she had just been through. The old delusional underlying commander kicked in, and the highest order of business now - not wanting them to find out he was on drugs. Duh! What a joke, like anyone *didn't* know. But, denial is a cold, deep ocean in which he had been swimming for decades. Manipulation, a skill well cultivated.

Never had he felt physically worse in this whole life, but still remained rigid in this steadfastness to not be "found out." They said they wanted to do some blood tests but that would require his consent. "Hell no," he slurred, aggressive and petulant, ripping out the IV's – they were not going to expose his addictions, these would be protected at all costs. After all, he knew how to manage his life, obviously. He staggered to the bathroom, stinging urine drizzling out like barbed-wire, every molecule of his being *hurting*. The room was definitely spinning.

The doctors, nurses, and especially Marie, all looked on dumbfounded at his sheer level of self-obsession and disrespect for life. He half realized the gravity of the situation, but the denial won over even here. He thanked them, all but sarcastically, for their help.

"Really," he said, "I appreciate what you've all done, but I'm *FINE*. We're gonna go now," and he headed toward the exit. But he was not fine. He was tore up bad, and knew it. Blood tests would reveal what he was unsuccessfully hiding at any and all costs. He needed help. *Some* kind of help. Marie was mortified in utter disbelief.

"Get in the car," he ordered. "Let's go."

She had followed behind the ambulance for 45 minutes of sheer agony, not knowing if he was alive or dead, and now he wanted to just leave? Numb, she slowly slid down into the seat behind the steering wheel of the sleek red Camaro and could only stare straight ahead in her own bewilderment.

This, of course, was not the end of the using, although he *truly tried again* to stop, but simply could not. In fact, not even 24 hours passed without ingesting more toxins. He should have died all the way that night.

Something is keeping you alive

***

"You've been approved," Fran announced, snapping him out of the morbid recollection. "You'll have a check for rent soon, and you'll get a voucher each week for 35 dollars' worth of gas. You also get a one-time voucher for seventy-five bucks for a local store so you can get some clothes, if you need that."

"Oh, that's so great." (Most of his clothes had been in the back of a car he was driving several months back, which was not even his - pulled over and taken to jail on yet another warrant, the car had mysteriously disappeared with all his clothes in it.)

The universe was now showering him with gifts. Coming from where he had, dancing around death's embrace, to be here now - this was against all odds. Yet, here he was, overcome with joy and happiness, at a time when many might look upon the situation as nearly hopeless. To him, this moment was the greatest thing he had ever known.

In nothing is everything

~ Chapter 9 ~

A Great Shift

"I must feel my way. That means to listen to the call of my heart." These exact words were written in the journal today. Very different from fighting and conquering. Something, it seemed, *was* happening.

The daily prayer, the writing, the conscious letting go, the work done at treatment, were all working in ways that could not be fully grasped with an analytical mind. It was only through action, practical application and doing the work that the power of this letting go of the old ways and allowing new ways to emerge was realized. There was far less fear, less loneliness and less conflict - than ever.

It was the beginning of a wonderful summer of possibility. Not even a week had passed, and already life was very different. A far cry from that first night back home, when Kevin had been wrought with fear and impending doom. He had listened to his heart, actually made a decision to *listen* to Spirit, and then to act even through the din of screaming monkeys.

Being engaged in activities that nourished this Spirit, a subtle realization was growing: *I do not have to fight anything.* There was nothing to conquer. *Nothing is even there.* When he simply listened to his heart and followed its easy direction, the monkeys were quelled.

Keep It Simple Sweetheart

He was becoming someone else, someone unrecognizable as the old Kevin. As a result of beginning to live these principles, what was emerging naturally was a calmer, gentler, inspired soul that was happy to just be. Never before had he known such peace, and always before had he fought.

But there was still much work.

At least two meetings a day, and sometimes as many as five, became the new spots to hang out. Barbeques, get-togethers, events, potlucks, sober parties, there was all kinds of stuff to do. Kevin just found himself happy, way less encumbered. Each day was an opportunity to practice praying, which, these days, centered in handing it over: Any and all of it. The warm summer mornings, mindfulness, ducks upon the water, gently tearing a piece of bread off, feeling it, calmly tossing it to them, watching them take it, observing their little habits, the passers-by on their way to work, the rising sun, the breath in, and out – it was practicing meditation, and it was happening as a result of slowing down.

Every day has its own flow. Within this flow is a softer, more natural and peaceful way to live. Anyone can align with it through simple surrender. Accessing a higher level of awareness within and actually being guided by it is a *now phenomenon*. He could stop anytime he became confused and again, hand it over, - *let go of it* - whatever it was. Fear was usually what caused upset, and as someone shared, fear was just an acronym:

Forgot Everything's All Right

***

In addition to beginning the day in surrender, he was also spending lots of time at the river, doing much of the same. Toxicity was slowly dissipating and as it did, he felt better and better. Each time he shared at a meeting, he purged stuff that was inside his head; with each journal entry, a similar anomaly occurred. Struggling was actually a choice among many possible choices, and simply letting go was a much better-feeling choice. *Please take it.*

Poof, gone … strange.

Things have a way of working themselves out

He liked living here. Life was transforming into something once deemed unattainable, especially being so far down. Often, he marveled at the grace of whatever it was that had allowed him to live, and was beginning to see this grace in every living thing. In the program, many called it a Higher Power. This was an appropriate way to call it, for whatever got him here was surely a power greater than anything by which he had ever lived. Maybe it was a more integral power. After all, it was inside of him – this is where it was first felt and realized, underneath everything he thought he was, beyond the toxic stuff found and cleared through the process. Recovery … maybe even more accurate: *Discovery.*

He was beginning to love what was found by practicing this art of allowing.

The old life's *perception* of being a victim of circumstances was shifting, and new possibility was emerging. It came through inspired action – by letting go of old, stale and limiting thinking. A fundamental shift from "this won't work for me" to "anything is possible" was happening. It seemed this Higher Power had something it wished for him. The trick was to let go of what was *in the way* and holding the old perceptions in place and impeding direct experience - but experience of what? Life and living was not what he always *thought* it to be.

The thinking, where he had always been invested, was so commanding that he could not eradicate it on his own; *he simply lacked the power.* This one delusion, that somehow the power must come from here, was perhaps the most limiting belief held.

Out of no way and out of nothing, a way will be made

***

She was so soft and tender.

"Hi," Terra said, gentle and full with welcome.

"Hi," he replied, in almost the same sappy tone, long and drawn out.

They hugged for a good minute. "How's your day?" Kevin whispered in her ear, just before releasing.

"Good, worked all day. It's nice to be here with you in this quiet place," she said, gazing out over the park's perfect rolling lawns. A paved pathway wound around, down a grade and disappeared. They couldn't see where it went, but a pond caught their separate eyes at once.

"Let's go down there." Kevin motioned toward it with a head nod. A large maple and a couple elms lined the path. One larger elm near the pond agreed to let them settle under her, a worthy sanctuary from the hot day.

Terra spread out the blanket she brought, half in the sun and half in the shade. "I've been thinking about you all day," Kevin said succinctly. "Thanks for suggesting this awesome place."

"Oh yeah, what you been thinkin'," she inquired.

"Been thinking this," he said, extending his hand. In it was a couple pages folded twice over.

Another love letter. "Did a lot of writing today and couldn't help myself."

"Ohhhhh, thank you." Her captivating eyes shimmered with the water. Her precious face blossomed into a huge smile. What romantic notions would he bestow upon her this time?

"Read it later, when you have more time. I want you all to myself now."

Their eyes locked, the place fell even more silent as they drifted slowly into each other, lips melting together as two flames becoming one. Old Mother Elm sheltering, they tumbled to the blanket, rocking in warm embrace.

There was something both of them needed, and they were more than willing to share it – or seek it, in each other. It was all so nice, yet at the same time an all too familiar dysfunction was present, which was evident in many ways: One, she was married and living with her husband. Two, he was fresh out of treatment and standing on shaky ground, teetering, and still living largely in delusion. Three - it was the treatment center where she currently worked. But, like attracts like, and their respective shortcomings somehow validated each other's. Sure, he was in love, again, and didn't care much about keeping plants alive, anyway. And she was seeking an escape route from her current situation.

Nonetheless, it was mesmerizing, and it felt imperative to be together.

~ Chapter 10 ~

Settling In

New ways of showing up in the world inspire new actions. Choosing prayer and meditation as the foundation and cornerstone allows the ability to take steps into a set of principles that will change life forever. Not only that, it just plain feels good.

Between JP and Kevin was a fairly wide scope of skills, and they had a damn fine time together. Kevin was good with fixing cars, and JP, being a window installer, had similar talents. They began cavorting through the streets of Yakima, searching for broken cars and cracked windows, and just talking with people about their businesses and whatever else presented itself. And laughing at anything and everything – no one was free from innocent scrutiny.

The outings in the small town were more of a people meet and greet, and didn't produce much work. A few odd jobs were procured - good for gas money and some extras, but it proved to be more for just hanging out, having fun, and some companionship during this dubious time in their lives. Certainly, it was a time where neither of them knew what to do, and a time in which the future was one giant unknown.

Potentially dangerous so early in recovery, they also started to check out local live music; such things take place in bars and upon slippery slopes. They were rockers, raised on the stuff, and more - raised on the lifestyle: Partying, angst, and self-indulgence to the max. Being in the clubs, he could feel the proverbial tire slipping back into the same old rut in the road, where losing balance was too easy. Kevin did not much like these places any more. They were too sleazy, and - a reminder of a life he had grown to dislike and was choosing to leave. Honoring the curfew, they always made it home on time. Only then, JP would sneak back out through the little bedroom window, conjuring who knows what trouble. Maybe that was why it had been glued shut, Kevin thought, watching JP scurry out of it while insisting his roomie cover for him if anyone asked. Kevin had a sinking feeling about this, and it was the beginning of their taking divergent paths.

The life Kevin was beginning to know was a direct result of following directions that he did not create, but rather received. Through the suggestions of others, through daily prayer and meditations, the ability to listen with the heart was growing. Crawling out a window to go to a bar against house rules was not any direction that he had received. Besides, he loved waking up early, beginning each day in surrender, being sober just for today, one day at a time. He liked going to bed with a clear conscience, knowing that he had followed inspiration and divine guidance, what they taught at treatment and what he had been learning at the meetings, to the best of his ability.

At those meetings, there were people that were obviously at peace, and they talked about how they practiced the program and lived. He listened as they shared their experiences and found when he practiced what they did, he often got similar results. He also heard from people who were much edgier. When they shared about what they did, it sounded uneasy. He chose to listen to them, but not do what they were doing. Any chosen way creates certain results - he began to see the value in *listening*. People are always teaching.

Are these the results you would choose for your life?

***

The next several weeks were surreal. He continued to practice forgiveness, for himself first, then for others and sometimes simultaneously. Friendships blossomed and most were with sober people, many of whom attended meetings. He looked forward to seeing and hearing from them. Accepting circumstances he had always fought so hard to try and control, they seemed to always work themselves out and dissipate. It was baby steps. Kevin even quit worrying about what Marie was doing.

Serenity comes through surrender

The less he struggled, through acceptance, the lighter he became. The life he had come from was all about domination, scamming, controlling, and winning. But for what prize did he fight so hard?

No matter what material possession or status was ever achieved, there was little serenity, only more wanting more. Here, where he was right now, less really was more. Everything was almost backwards, upside down. Whatever it was, it sure felt good. He liked not always trying to figure out his next move, how to outsmart the next guy, how to beat the game and how to "win." Something was working for him, not him working for it.

Here, every finger he had ever pointed at the world he had somehow found the courage to point back at himself and say, "What is *my* part in this?" Again, this was shown to him by others. Found here was the fact that he had a part in every complaint that he had about the world - the biggest part. If he could not change the world, maybe he could change the way he thought about the world. Seeking to control situations is optional. Through simple surrender and observation, he could see:

Things have a way of working themselves out

Dad used to say that to him all the time.

His parents had fought a lot, and for some obscure set of reasons, he had somehow blocked out any memories of early life. There must have been a lot of abuse and violence though, that much he suspected. Dad had been an alcoholic as well. Through what he always called "a series of miracles," he had become sober around the age of 50.

When Kevin was an early teen they began a fresh relationship after years of no contact. Dad was even welcomed back around the whole family and for most holidays and celebrations, and became Mom's close friend, even though they never got back together. Here, his father taught him as best he could and tried to warn him - but never pushed too hard the issue of where the treacherous path of the partier might take a person. Looking back, his using tendencies and over-indulgences probably horrified Dad, this great teacher of acceptance. Dad let him do what he felt he needed to do, follow his own destiny.

They would talk for hours upon hours. Dad was his best friend. Many times at night, they would stay up into the wee hours on the phone, laughing, just being silly and talking about nothing and everything. He always loved that, and often thought of Dad as timeless and ageless, that there was no age or generation gap. They related so well. They shared more than blood; their souls were eternally intertwined.

When Dad died eight years ago, it was the greatest tragedy in Kevin's 30 years of being alive. He had been a heavy smoker and the cigarettes had slowly killed him, a horrid way to go and very painful for those around to watch. Over the years his breath and body was taken, slowly and insidiously. With so much resentment about Dad passing, he now had a grand excuse to wallow in self-pity. He recalled that night he received the word after too many long nights in ICU. Dad had passed.

Kevin stood on his own front porch ready to burst. A storm raged in the cold, dark cruel sky, wind howling through eternity and relentlessly whipping trees in a bitter now. Pain-ridden gusts biting skin, long hair thrashing his face, Kevin raised a clenched fist to the sky cursing life. "I'll show you, damn it! I'll show you ALLLLL!"

If he could have only seen with different eyes, he might have realized the storm raging was only his father waving to him, the wind, nothing but Dad's love being shared again, playfully. The gusts were him caressing his boy, telling him everything is all right. But this night, Kevin could not see or feel this.

Instead, there was only *rage*. Death scared him assiduously, beyond measure, but the fear masqueraded as anger. *Always as anger.* Perhaps underneath it all was his own obsession with mortality.

***

At least every weekend there was an outdoor barbecue or two, along with any number of other events throughout the week. All sober. He spent lots of time at the trail, skating along the river. Terra came sometimes and they would lay out a blanket along the river's edge. The relationship was heating up. Often, she would come to the house for a walk and talk. Naps, both with and without Terra, in the middle of hot days in the cool room were blissful. Between meetings and Group was the best time. Gentle breezes flowed through that precious little window. A book was always near. Never had been much of a reader, but now he looked forward to turning the pages and following the story, or learning something from the recovery literature. JP was doing his own thing, but they still hung out often. An occasional car repair was done together, but since there was no garage, it was often difficult.

One warm, still day, relaxing at the waterway outside the house feeding the floating fowl, a thought crept in: *There is nothing left of the old life.* Everything he had ever known was gone, and he was happy. That old life had actually been in the way. Was it ever real?

Though he loved the Oxford House, it still had its challenges - five recovering addicts in a confined space can be volatile. But this transition, this stepping stone, was a huge blessing. He'd already outgrown it, and it was only the end of the first month.

Terra came for a walk around the neighborhood. Rounding the very first corner, there sat a most captivating house. A lovely garden of myriad rose bushes and lively shrubs inside a white picket fence surrounded the yellow home. Something about it was extraordinarily inviting. And, it had a garage … a small one-car, but he had worked out of one that small before. In the window of the house a sign beckoned:

FOR RENT

Both the front and back yards were shaded with plenty of trees. The white trim of the house accented the fence just so. One large apple tree dangled over a hot tub next to the garage. *What is it about all these trees now?*

Here, at this house, on the trail, at The Sanctuary - there was just something about them. They had become friends. *Talkative friends.*

Pointing, Kevin blurted, "Look. That house! It's awesome, gotta be at least two stories. She looks ... alive. She looks like a Sadie." The house did have quite the personality, and he couldn't help giving her a moniker. Evidently Terra liked it too, judging by her smile.

"Your enthusiasm is cute," she said with a "dream on" undertone, as they passed by the place.

At the bottom of the sign was a phone number, and that was all. With a nudge to call it, Kevin began dialing on his cell phone. "What are you *doing*?" Terra insisted. "You don't have any money, how will you rent *that* house?" He didn't know either, but that was of no concern. Somehow, spending all this time in the heart had offered a strange ability to consider possibility. "I'll just talk to them," he said. "You never know ..."

The pleasant voice of a young woman answered. "Hello?"
An inviting greeting.

"Hello, calling about the house," he said, moving the phone away from his mouth and blowing a kiss at Terra.

They walked on, even as he listened on the phone. "The rent is $1200 a month," Debbie continued, "and there's a damage deposit of $400. If you'd like to see it, we just live across the street and two houses down. Why don't you come by about four?"

"I'll stop by," Kevin answered. "See you then."

Now what had he gotten into?

He tried to convince Terra how awesome it would be to live in that house. She wanted out of the toxic environment with her soon-to-be-ex. He'd like to move on from the cramped Oxford House, as much a blessing as it had been. And the garage, fixing cars - he was tired of being broke.

"I swear, Sadie's alive ... I can just feel it," Kevin said.

They talked about the yard, the gardens of blooming red and pink rosebushes, the bursting rhodies and eating fruit from the trees. They agreed; they both loved the house. Still, Kevin felt something obfuscating Terra's ability to fathom the whole prospect.

After she left, Kevin went back and walked around Sadie more thoroughly. She was a fine home. He pondered the meeting with the homeowners over and over, vacillating between concocting some grandiose story and telling the truth. Honoring the commitments of willingness, honesty and openness, he opted for the truth.

The owners literally were right across the street; he was nervous knocking on their door. An affable young married couple opened the door.

"Hi," they spoke in unison, big smiles on their faces.

"Hello," he answered, "I'm Kevin." The awkward before-business-handshakes took place.

Small talk out of the way, he got right to it: "I went to the treatment center just outside of town, then tried to go home. I knew I wouldn't make it, so I came back here and got into an Oxford House." He pointed out the white house just past their rental. "Just happens to be right next door to your place.

"I've lived there for a few weeks now, and would like to move on. I'm also in after-care at the treatment center, and there is a program where they pay up to $400 of my rent per month. I'm on state assistance so that's how I get food and some spending money. Not quite $400 a month. I've been in the trade of fixing cars most of my life ... I'm good at it, and could easily make some money out of the garage."

Debbie and Mike didn't flinch. Many may have sent him kicking rocks. Instead, they knew about Oxford homes, and of the treatment center. "We know some people that have gone through there and have great lives now." More affirmation.

He also told them about Terra, that she worked and would share expenses. "Terra's Dad, he, well ... let's just say I *know* we can make the rent."

He was sure of it.

No money, fresh out of treatment, had lost everything and was starting over. He told them the absolute truth - truthful where he would have lied before, willing to show this uncomfortable vulnerability. It was a nice conversation, and he truly did not care if he got the house or not; he was just excited for the adventure anyway, practicing the art of letting it flow. Sharing stories, they chatted for the better part of an hour.

"We'll discuss it and be in touch. Thanks for coming."

Hands clasped behind his back, Kevin walked slowly along the sidewalk, each step in freedom, no urgency for anything. Where was he headed? He had no idea what was to become of any or all of it. None of it mattered ... he was here now.

Get a Job

Business was much slower here than in the big city. Rows upon rows of rolling metal boxes lining freeways back home provided the opportunity for plenty of auto body work. It certainly had its downside, though - frustrating rush hour traffic, crawling along, so many bereaved people. Doldrums and monotony, the quiet agony – countless souls grinding out the commute, performing upon the treadmill of day in and day out work, and for what? It seemed to project from their faces, palpable discomfort in work which to him was always horrifying … but why? He always *hated* that traffic, that whole life, and certainly could never hold down some nine-to-five job. Even the thought made him sick to his stomach.

Here, life moved much slower and that was good, but fewer opportunities for work. Not being one that gave up easily, he shifted the focus a little, and it was to pay off big time.

Pastor Jim had mentioned Work Source, basically an unemployment office. He'd go there. One could apply for jobs on the spot. *If I could do anything,* he thought. Imagination took over. He liked people, was learning much by watching and listening to others. Plus, he had been cooped up for most of the last year in the dreary attic at the body shop doing drugs and guzzling booze.

A master dishwasher (if there even is such a thing) in his early 20's at a hopping restaurant, he loved the fast pace and the people, and fit right in slip-sliding on wet tile and tossing porcelain around. Being around people right now seemed a good start. Pretty much any job was going to be OK, this much he decided on the way inside.

"Thank you," he said spryly to a nice man who'd shown him in three minutes how to use the entire system. Within minutes, as if by divine synchronicity – there it was. Listed on the computer screen was every possible job. *Wanted: Waiters and bartenders, cooks and dishwashers.* The eatery was to open soon, right in town. *This is it!* Feeling as good as hired, he called the phone number and got the manager. Sherry sounded like a nice woman, pleasant and sweet. "Most positions are still open. Can you come in Friday?" Two days away. Yes he could.

An interview. How cool is that.

New Job, New House?

It was a fine summer day. The plan: Chat by pen with the mysterious listener of Dear Journal, and hit the trail. Fondness for writing in various coffee shops, grocery store seating areas, park benches and the like was growing. He settled upon just such a perch. Being around people felt necessary; oftentimes just sitting and observing passers-by was comforting. He wrote of their activities, no matter how trivial, in addition to intimacies, hopes, dreams, and aspirations. Many times, by seeming pure coincidence, random conversations would provide some jewel of wisdom. Perhaps this chance connection would lead to some other opportunity, and often did. It was a roadmap, a flow, which became accessible by just letting life be life. Submerging into this odd bliss of simplicity was fascinating.

Who would have thought plain old sitting in peace would lead to a random conversation that led to a car repair job that further led to a friendship? He began to *experience* these small miracles, presenting in the midst of the stillness - they were *everywhere.*

Settling into a perfectly cream-and-sugared coffee, he composed another Terra love letter – could not wait to see her.

He thought about Marie, again. Talking to her was a bad idea with the no-contact-order and all the damage done. *Just leave her alone* won out over *but I wanna,* and for once he actually did. But there was so much there, still, unforgiven. Nonetheless, the judge had emphatically stated one more violation would be an automatic felony. He was free of those, for now anyway.

Suddenly, a monolithic boulder fell from the sky and crushed every other thought. The very day of arrival at The Sanctuary was also Marie's birthday, the third of June. *How appropriate.* Putting the two together had been buried under all the self-obsessed turmoil. Feelings of pride rose, but inadequacy caused him to leave abruptly. Monkeys clambered upon the giant stone, pouncing and shrieking. *You failed with her! Just like with Selena. Just like every relationship you've ever had. You don't deserve your clean date to be on her birthday. Loser! You'll never make it. You will always be alone.*

The Explorer loved taking Kevin to the river, especially in such tender condition. It was an easy 99 degrees even with the windows open and flying down the express-way. Tears came again from the bench at the top of the trail, overlooking the water where it was most rapid and roaring. Praying kept doing this to him. Or was it this place? They were no longer only tears of despair, but something else now, somehow comforting, cleansing.

His heart was emanating, radiating, far beyond his chest. It felt like omnidirectional radar sending and receiving unlimited information in all ways, to and from everything. He read and sat, watched and listened, imbibing the whole of it. Slipping into the skates, he kicked along the river once more, growing fonder of each day. Especially here, within this encapsulating, warm peace. He would go to the noon meeting and then see what the day had to bring. Marie would love this river trail, too. How long must it go on for? Where did it lead?

In spite of the melting heat, nearly every seat held a body for the duration of a fine meeting. A few of them hung around after. Life and upcoming events were good fodder for convo, and soon interrupted by his cell's ringtone. *The new house.* They wanted to meet, discuss some particulars - they had questions. *Wow.* How had it gotten this far after being so honest with them about his situation, especially having next to no money?

True prosperity has nothing to do with money

~ 110 ~

They agreed to meet that evening at Sadie, the fine yellow home. Everyone hoped Terra could come as well. For Kevin, it was semi-critical, or so it seemed. He called her.

"Oh my god, can you believe it? What if we actually *get* that house?"

"That would be something," she said, sounding mostly unenthused. Considering her situation, he could understand the melancholy. After all, her family was in shambles.

The stellar summer day was good for another walk and talk. Heat rolled off the pavement, waves radiated and then disappeared into the ether, distorting the view down the long, hot street upon which they strolled.

"I don't know … it feels like a lot." Terra was on the fence. "I've got a big load. Umm … how would it work?"

Brandon would live with them along with Devon, who was 16. Kevin didn't mind; it was a large, ample home, and Terra could even have her own room, which she insisted upon, anyway. The more they talked about it, the better an idea it became. Yes, she would come to the meeting tonight, at the house for rent, with their potential landlords.

The shade in the driveway offered a respite even from the penetrating late afternoon sun. The white Oxford house on the corner next door sat in a way where the same sun just cooked it. It was always way too hot inside. Even that old fan in the front door and all the doors and windows open barely made it bearable – it was quite miserable in certain rooms. But that cherished room downstairs … it sure was nice in there. Best room in the whole place, now. He thought twice about giving it up. The yellow house was an altogether different direction; Sadie was shaded, cool, and much more inviting. One glance at gorgeous Terra and the choice was a no-brainer. If Mike and Debbie would let them rent it, it would be their home. But was he listening to the deeper guidance?

Inside felt good. The kitchen was the whole corner just right of the side door they entered; its windows graced the front rose gardens and cool grass inside the white picket fence. Terra stepped into sunlight that poured in the living room's giant picture glass. Through it, the landscape was a surreal portrait. Two bedrooms and a bath completed the main floor. More windows revealed the backyard; the hot tub awaited. It needed repair, but Kevin was already soaking in it. Pink and yellow rose bushes surrounded the tub along with a variety of blooming perennials. A grandmother, cragged-limbed apple tree had an old swing hanging from one of her largest branches, made of two pieces of fuzzy old rope and a mossy two-by-six. Perfect for children. It creaked back and forth eerily. *Is someone already there?*

Downstairs: One large, open room, another bath, and a laundry. Nice space, but it had an unusual, odd feeling – an unfamiliar energy ... couldn't quite recognize it. *Leave it alone, for now.*

The cracked and crooked driveway went past the concrete stairway that found the kitchen door and onto the glorious one-car garage. He'd check it out later; for now, it was all about Terra liking the place.

The whole property was protected and watched over by some arborvitae and smaller cedars. Poplars were sentinels down the entire length of the drive. This place offered a golden opportunity to give life here a chance. Standing in the shade of the same poplars, the two couples encircled the front of Terra's little Toyota pickup. Kevin shared about the potential job and the restaurant. Terra listened, quietly.

"Yeah, by the hotels; that place has been closed for must be five years now," Mike said.

His wife chimed in. "I read an article about it in the paper. We've been wondering what was going to happen with that place for some time. Being right there on the walking trail is a great location. It will be a total success."

Kevin wondered about the trail. "I know I'll be working there, I can feel it. When I was talking to Sherry, their manager, I just knew."

They were responding to the enthusiasm and confidence. The four discussed treatment, financial aid, and the rent. There was the car business, which he could work from the garage.

Then it happened, after a brief silence in the serenity of the warm summer evening.

"If you can come up with first month's rent and the damage deposit, you can move in. We believe in you and want to help you get going on your new life, in your new directions."

Kevin could not believe it. Terra, could not believe it. A mix of emotions swirled between them. The whole thing was fantastic.

Giddy with excitement, Kevin stood on the threshold of uncharted territory, even again. "Woohoo! Thank you." The familiar old fear tried to assail, not good enough and couldn't possibly deserve this. *Please take it.* In only seconds was it gone.

They could tell the landlords were truly happy to help. He and Terra could make it. Terra thanked them, also, though he sensed that she was unsure of this whole thing. He tried to compensate her doubt with more enthusiasm, even though they were equally lost.

The sun continued to dive toward the mountains as their leisurely footsteps again rounded the neighborhoods. "This is going to be great. Don't worry about anything, we'll be fine," he reassured her.

Mustering all the charm and ability to convince her he could, soon she was feeling better about it – for she really did want out of her situation. Neither had any idea what they were doing, and both knew it. Kevin remained steadfast and sure, maybe for her sake.

It was one day at a time; the way of living he had chosen to accept and try on like new clothes. See how things fit. At first, they may feel weird, unfamiliar, but after a short time they start to feel better. Pretty soon you're wearing them all the time, loving them. Was it possible to not have to worry about tomorrow or yesterday, and be here now? Not really caring whether or not they got the place, what could a phone call to a number on a "For Rent" sign hurt?

Detachment is a powerful way of trust and faith

***

Friday. Day of the interview at the restaurant, and Terra's dad was going to send some money to help. ATR would assist with rent so long as it was a clean and sober environment. Sadie was just that. Kevin was light, not a care in the world, almost - except those pesky criminal charges, including felony drug possession, an impending bankruptcy and a plethora of other gut-wrenching scenarios, scenarios he never thought he would face. Still, he chose to believe it would work out. This simple faith followed by inspired action was vastly more powerful than what *might* lay in store.

Please take it – Gone.

How strange. This little prayer, which was only one possible choice among millions, and required only a nanosecond to utter, sent the worry or frustration or fear from right between the ears through heart-center, bifurcating and reconfiguring it. And most times, within seconds. In that flash of feeling negative emotion, the choice of forgiveness was now an option. Where had it gone? Had it ever really been there in the first place? *He* did not "do" anything with it, and yet taken away it was. The whole process seemed to transcend linear time and affect the past, present and future, as if they existed all at once: Or, never even existed to begin with.

Go Ahead, Interview Me

It was obvious the old restaurant had been closed for years. Tables and chairs were stacked dusty along walls and amidst milling workers. Beyond the mess Kevin could see the perfect answer to his employment issues.

A bakery complete with pizza ovens begging to be used sat to the left of the main entrance. Straight ahead was an open kitchen where the cooks and servers would be seen preparing food. Opposite the bakery and up two steps was the ominous lounge. The main seating area was staggered up and down, plenty of nooks and crannies with booths and tables. The west side's whole wall and half the ceiling, angled at 45 degrees, was a giant solarium of windows facing the river and open sky, filling the room with natural light. A paved pathway between the majestic river and the patio was quite familiar. This pathway was called the Greenway, hence the name of the establishment: Frederick's on the Green.

The place had to be 5,000 square feet at a shy guess. It flowed nicely, a fine restaurant arrangement. Yes, he would work here.

"Hello," he said to the tall woman. She was kind, focused, strong and on task.

"I'm Kevin, here for the job interview."

"Ah, I'm Sherry. We spoke on the phone." She was congenial and offered a firm handshake, her silver-blonde hair bouncing from the vigor of the exchange. She was surely old Viking soul.

"Nice to meet you. Awesome place." he said.

"Oh I just love it, too." She adjusted her large glasses by a forefinger and thumb on each swooping temple. "Here, have a seat."

In a corner booth she divulged plans for the place and its projected opening date – one month away. It looked more like six months to him with all the dust and disarray, but he just smiled and said, "Great."

All that isolation over the last year – it felt so good to interact again. A saw buzzed in the background and gave way to a nail being hammered into place.

"When can you start were we to hire you?" She had to yell just a little.

"I'm wide open," he shouted back. He did not mention the curfew, but that would not apply anyway because he *knew* they were getting that house.

"You're hired. And with a personality like that - you're my bar manager." Her giant smile was bigger than her hairdo.

Wait – bar manager? How is that going to work? They said to stay out of slippery places and slinging booze in a lounge was just that. But, he was not in charge. Something had brought him here. The ego stroke sure felt good, too. All in all, it was a nice place and the energy felt right. Sherry must have heard him thinking and offered some auspicious information.

"Since we're starting fresh, we won't get our liquor license for several weeks after opening, could be longer. Have to apply for it." He waited for the other shoe to drop.

"So, you can be a server while we're waiting for the license; that way you can be working right away."

It was perfect. Way better than he could have dictated, and all he'd done was show up, again. What was happening? A house, a job, a whole new life … *and* sober?

Kevin did not even recognize himself. Not too many times had he been able to do anything without worry and delusions of control, and yet here he was, flourishing within a state of as-complete-as-could-be surrender. It certainly was not giving up that got him here – it was a greater, more subtle undoing. He hovered above that table, remote-viewing the odd scene in the messy old building, realizing such once-impossibilities.

Life gives unto life itself, and you are but a witness

"So, I for sure have a job, then?"

"Yes, you are hired. You're welcome to come check out the progress, lots to do, *lots to do ...*" Sherry sang the second one, observing the worker's bouncing hard-hats. Two cute girls and one nervous young fellow waited on a bench, next in line. Sherry chuckled as she put a fist on each hip.

"Thank you," he said, and as she went to shake hands he hugged her instead. She giggled, obviously enjoying it.

"This is going to be *awesome*," Kevin said, and practically skipped out of the place. It was simple joy that found the greatest happiness. No matter how trivial a thing may seem to one, to another it can be a golden treasure.

Now, about this trail. Where must the pathway lead? It sure did feel familiar. On this glorious, hot and sunny afternoon was he freshly hired and had a real job. It had been a long time. He always felt like more of a prisoner than a business owner – trapped and alone. But it was always well-hidden. The restaurant would surely be bustling with all shapes and sizes of people. It surprised him how much he actually looked forward to that – it was more than just a job, much more.

Perfect time for kicking along the trail. He'd leave from this very parking lot. Again, the lush greens of trees and plants of all sorts and colors along the river's banks danced with the wind. Raptors overhead peered down. What did it all see? What did they want him to see? Sweet air tasted clean and felt good, even the sun did now. The skies were bluer than ever. Why was it all speaking to him? How? The river flowed along, easy, just as this new life materializing before his very eyes. In this moment, the realization came: All that had disappeared, an entire lifetime's collection, perceived and clutched onto as if it *were* who and what he was – he never even needed any of it. In fact, it had been inhibiting any real growth. The kind of growth for which his Spirit longed.

The next curve became familiar, the spot he usually turned around on "the other trail." But it was the same trail. Until now, he had not ventured past this point, or known to where it led. The trail whereby such peace and serenity had been found was the guide. This place of equanimity led right to the new workplace. *Right to it ...*

Just Like That

Waking up was magical now – the morning ritual with the waterway, the ducks, the wonderful coffee that tasted better every day, the rising sun, and the freshness of each morning.

Each day is a new beginning

At the morning meeting, Kevin shared of all the opportunities popping up like daisies, the countless blessings, and about his growing gratitude. Journal writing helped him to articulate. It was a good meeting, full of powerful sharing. Today's message, a cello's crooning. Summer buzz filled the room, that way it gets early in the morning when people know the sun is going to bring the heat big-time and the beach or a boat upon the water becomes the prime directive. It was another thing he had hated about oozing toxicity from every pore – that sun and heat on sticky skin felt so uncomfortable, only a short time ago. Today was a different story.

The meeting paused and a short break. Time for announcements – there was a lot going on with the great weather. A barbecue being announced caused him to blurt out loud. "That's me!" Everyone giggled. He wanted JP to come, but hadn't seen him in at least two days, maybe more. If he saw JP, he'd invite him.

So much going on. Kevin was giddy like a little kid. At The Sanctuary, they said that you stop maturing when you start using, and that when you stop using you are emotionally mature only to about that age - or less.

14? I'm 14? It did feel like it. Likely, he was much less mature than that, sober now only a shy three months. So awkward to be in the body of an adult with the emotional state of a wounded child.

Nonetheless, he was full of a cleaner energy now and charged with anticipation of a bourgeoning life. More was coming, too, he pondered with child-wide eyes. Nine cups of coffee and six cookies did not calm him down any.

Terra was working, so off to the trail again. This time skating the three miles to the restaurant and putting the pieces together from yesterday was the plan. The plethora of birds chirped their melodies, perhaps signaling his arrival to the other wildlife, announcing his passing by; maybe it was a greeting. He chirped back, over and over. Generous winds rustled his tree families; in some places the river was calm, and in others the white water crashed down amidst huge boulders. Certain stretches of trail found more people, other parts, no one. People's homes, some nicer than others, shared the way. The path occasionally intersected with streets, danger spots where there was too much gravel and a possible wipe out. Kevin cruised along on the blades, allowing himself to be a part of it all.

Finally, the restaurant came into view, nearly underneath one of the nicer hotels. Its sign facing the highway overpass - *must be a quarter mile high.* A main thoroughfare went right past; along it were several other hotels, restaurants and retail stores.

"This place is gonna be busy; I'm fortunate to have this job," he whispered out loud, stopping for a moment to sit on the lawn next to the outside patio. The river wasn't 30 feet away. One man under a yellow hardhat carried a board on his shoulder to a radial arm saw on the patio, buzzed it to size and took it back inside. It was a mini-beehive of workers.

On the return trip, Imagination painted pictures of what it would be like, working. He smiled the whole way home.

***

Off to another meeting at the old stone-and-brick church downtown; more listening to the shares, people watching, and of course, partaking in the coffee everyone knocked but drank nonetheless. After the serenity prayer ended the hour long session, there were more connections to be made. Those already befriended were a pleasure to see again.

In back of the room a large, sliding partitioning wall separated the meeting space from an unseen room. Kevin peeled open the accordion-style wall just enough to slip through. It was incredible inside. Sunshine poured through huge stained-glass windows, painting the room in breathtaking rainbows of soft, warm primary colors. Larger-than-life statues of Jesus and Mary were magnificent to behold. Renaissance art in elaborate golden frames decorated the old stone walls above rows of finely crafted wooden pews. He took a long, full breath in through clear nostrils, and could taste it at once, all of it. He let it in. The peace in this sanctuary nourished his soul. It felt different here, now, having let go of his stigma attached to such places. Just months ago, those preconceived notions would have overshadowed this direct experience - *this feeling of belonging.*

Every heartbeat was a drum, each breath coursed through altered, more pure cells. The room, a thousand faceless eyes, breathed with him. Every color filled him. *There is nothing needed not available in this moment.* He was moved to pray for a minute, which turned into a few, and then a few

~ 117 ~

more. Outside, the buzz of dozens of people in their busy-ness and getting on with their day slowly dissipated. *Life,* he thought. *Just life going on.*

"It feels good to be a part of it, *thank you."* The whisper-prayer ended the session, but there would be many more.

Terra called. "I'm ready to go. So nervous - and excited!" The landlords did say they could move in if they had the agreed amount, and it looked like they did. With the several hundred Kevin had and the aid coming on the first, he would have close to half. She would contribute the rest.

He pushed aside the nagging feeling this whole situation was way rushed and entirely selfish. He still had not the capacity to consider the gravity of his actions and how it might affect Terra and her family. This perturbance could easily lead to future tripping. Worrying about the future had always fostered stagnation and procrastination, kept him stuck in situations he did not want to be in, frozen in fear. He opted for the new choice instead.

The Grand Experiment: The choice to simply trust. But trust *what?* Trust the principles that had been a lighthouse on the foggiest nights. Prayer and meditation were the foundation, and then taking inspired action. Guidance always comes through listening.

Look at all that had transpired thus far, in only a short time.

From the Nothing a way is made

August

The guys at the Oxford House could not believe Kevin and Terra commandeered the sweet place next door with next to zero dollars. JP finally showed up. Kevin invited him to come live with them, an idea Terra was less than thrilled about.

"Uhhmmm, I'm, uhhh, like ... I moved in with Bethany. We're getting ... *married,"* JP said in a sardonic tone.

"Whaaaaat?" Kevin belched in response. "Wow. Here I thought *I* was moving fast." It made him feel like he was moving too slowly.

That they would be living right next door to the guys in the white house on the corner was somehow comforting. Maybe, if home got weird, he could hide out there. The lease was signed with just enough money to satisfy the agreement. Terra had tons of stuff for the place, and that was good because he surely did not, except the loud stereo and few tools.

The heat was always the main topic of conversation, and usually followed any greeting. "Hey, how you doing today? *Hot out,* shee-whiz."

Terra's son, Devon, was a strong boy with a good back. He, Kevin and Terra managed to load up and move all her stuff, which included plenty

~ 118 ~

of heavy furniture. It was enough for a whole house, and fit perfectly in Sadie. Even though it was blistering out, their trees provided shade and relief. The subtle nurturing from the plant and tree people, from nature, was providing so much comfort. And the feeling of belonging.

An anomaly caused Kevin to pause in arranging the downstairs bedroom. No one else was near. The light went off. Then, it went on, all by itself. Two more flashes. He messed with the switch, - that did it, for a minute - then again it flickered, on and back off … strange. It did not feel like an electrical issue.

The switch sat in the wall at the bottom of the stairs. He handled it, again. No, that wasn't it. *But it has to be.* He flipped it up, harder, then down, then flicked it up and down about ten times. The light had some mind of its own.

He forced it firmly in the "on" position, as if more effort would surely fix the issue. The light went very purposely *off,* and as it did the hairs on the back of his neck stood straight up. Skin turned to goose flesh. The temperature dropped an easy twenty degrees - all this in a quantum flash. The undeniable presence of *something* permeated the space. For a moment that was an eternity, he froze. He *was not* alone.

The angry light came on, went off again - an obvious warning. The confrontational energy, palpable now, shocked him - his gut turned, mind raced. Kevin sensed immediately it was an apparition - a young boy. How could he know any of this? But, in his mind's eye, he saw an angry young face and it wanted them *out.* Kevin swallowed hard, moistened colorless lips.

Intuition, that silent voice, intervened.

Stay calm and speak your truth

Obeying, he sat down on the bed, closed his eyes and took a slow, recalibrating breath, acting now as if accessing some other form of communication was possible. It happened automatically. He felt the spirit all over him, the room, the house. Then he opened his eyes and acknowledged it:

"Hello …" Kevin spoke aloud, feeling quite silly, not knowing what was going to come out of his mouth next.

"Uhmmm … we are here peacefully, and … we would like to stay. We are, uhh, beginning a new life and need a place to stay that is safe – we need help right now. We mean you no harm, and would like it if you would let us stay here with you. Maybe we can even help each other."

The apparition faded away as the light came back and the space warmed. The room was assembled without further interruption and that light, as long as they lived in the house, never flickered this way again.

***

The house went together nicely. The restaurant was set to open in two weeks. A "Grand Opening Night" was planned - the whole staff was scheduled, the whole town invited. The event was in the paper and everything.

Another trip to Mom's; Snohomish County had sent a court date for the charge of felony drug possession for the cocaine found on him the time he had called the police on himself. He was hoping they had done him a favor and conveniently forgot about that little ordeal – maybe they had considered his situation and felt sorry for him. As he would find though, Providence was doing the favor *by* pressing charges.

The Saga Continues

Qualifying for a public defender was easy, being all but flat broke. Thumbing through the paperwork for the charges found a phone number. He made the call from Yakima to the lawyer in Snohomish County as two monkeys slapped him upside the head back and forth.

"Mr. Lowdermilk?"

"Yes," his lawyer answered in voice reserved for the riffraff of the universe.

Kevin gave him the case number. He could hear the lawyer shuffling papers. "Well, you've been charged with felony drug possession."

Tell me something I don't know, Kevin thought to say, but, *better not.* "What are my options?" He tried to hide his nervousness from the cocky voice at the other end of the phone.

The man continued: "You can take the felony and do just ten days in jail, since it is your first one." Lowdermilk spoke with an obvious residue that said, "You'll just be back in a few months." Kevin knew a felony was bad news, but he could do ten days standing on his head.

"Or what," Kevin responded.

"Well, in some cases, if it is a small enough amount you were caught with, they will let you do drug court."

Drug court? What the hell is that? Whatever it was, it did not sound good and it sounded long. It had been a fairly small amount. He was always diligent about not getting caught with the stuff and yet here it was - his first felony offense.

The lawyer was mostly curt, but at least made an attempt at being pleasant. He probably had too many cases to deal with. Lowdermilk said he would do some research on Kevin's case and history and see if he qualified for drug court, talk to the prosecutor. Now they had him by the balls. How was this going to affect the new life he was enjoying so much? What about sweet serenity, now that it was compromised? What if he had to go back and deal with this, leave Terra and their home? He writhed in that sick feeling that had only taken a short leave of absence. The past was catching up fast, and more was probably coming. *Please take it.*

Life had been a certain way: The business, the status, women, partying, possessions, rock bands, manipulation, *control.* It had all been in place. Then some rogue fire comes and rages, clearing everything in its path. It is violent and harsh and devastating, leveling what had been. But as neo-seeds break through after the forest fire, so too does growth follow that may not have been allowed under the shadows of what was now destroyed. Before long, there is a new forest, young and full of life, the ashes of what once-was nourishing and helping it grow in the sunlight.

So it is with a life being blasted to bits. If you share with certain people about having a tragedy or massive conflict, they may congratulate you for your opportunity.

Well, he had criminal charges, a foreclosure, bankruptcy, treatment costs, speeding and no insurance tickets, and was living with a married woman. Hospital bills, on welfare, still toxic and no one from the old life even wanted to talk to him. Opportunity was really knocking!

One day at a time, one moment *at a time*

***

Sadie was working out well; they were getting settled. Kevin loved making breakfast at sunrise, in the coolness of an early morning kitchen. Sometimes, Terra's friends would come over and join them. They liked showing off their new home – they were actually *living* in it. Amazing … simply responding to the inspiration of a moment and telling the truth - the rest really does work itself out. He was trying to practice this same principle with the felony charge, but vacillated between acceptance and fear.

Terra was afraid, too, and he could certainly relate. Neither of them had a clue what they were doing. They both knew, although left it in the unspoken, that living together was flash-flood behavior at best. But it worked *today*, and this is how he had agreed to live, as suggested, one day at a time, in the moment. Of course, this was still tweaking suggestions to appearances he liked and rationalizing damaging behavior. He hid behind what had been shared more than once – or, what he'd heard, at least: "Progress, not perfection." Worrying about possible outcomes was one choice among many, a fear-based way inside of which he had nearly always lived. Every thought and undertaking was always rooted in extreme selfishness.

Only he had made life what it was by his own one-way stinking thinking and subsequent actions.

Until now.

Trusting this Higher Power, more and more, he was being shown that there is possibility beyond a selfish and fear-based life.

***

The grand opening was on schedule. The restaurant was being prepared, frantically. Sherry said it was opening no matter what, just days away now. The voucher ATR provided for a local clothing store had purchased decent waiter attire, and the gas voucher would get him there. Something was meeting every need.

Group was going well, and several meetings a day embettered a recommendation made during inpatient: 90 in 90 they advised, a meeting a day. One counselor, Jesse, who had inspired him very much had said, "Heck, why not do 180 in 90? If you really want to impress me, do 270 in 90." Jesse had aimed high himself.

Kevin liked a challenge and was on par for the more ambitious number, maybe even better. The meetings provided a safe place and something to do, sober. The program offered a "design for living" – in addition to instant community.

Also during inpatient, the counselors at The Sanctuary had taken turns in the movie room sharing their story - most were addicts, too, as their stories revealed. He learned a lot from those stories. They were real; they had lived it and had changed their lives. They found a better way of living. Kevin looked up to them in this way, and for guidance - he *let* them be his teachers. One counselor, Roy, was so funny that his lectures were like going to a comedy show. The whole place was in an uproar from beginning to end. At the same time, there was an authenticity in the content that landed, hitting the mark perfectly.

In the depths of comedy, great sadness is often found, and vice-versa.

Jesse, during one of his lectures, shared of a book, *The Seven Habits of Highly Effective People* by Stephen R. Covey, and about how this book was impacting his life. It was *how* he talked about it. Jesse's inspiration shot through Kevin and became his own, reaching him in the depths of their interminable unity. It was one more signpost pointing the way, moving Kevin to approach him after the lecture and ask more about it. Jesse offered, "I have it in my office; stop by and I'll loan it to you." Something about Jesse made Kevin want to take action.

Wow, Kevin thought. *How cool is that?* In the book he learned more about principles and found that reading, especially stuff in the area of self-improvement, was quite nourishing. *Practicing* the principles and suggestions was even more empowering. He had never tried it. When you already know it all, what is there to improve? This deluded perception was being transformed

~ 122 ~

now, slowly and easily. He truly had been an ignorant know-it-all. What a small world in which to live.

The book had suggested creating a *Personal Mission Statement.* He chose to do this - writing when and what was suggested. He wrote this mission statement in the little purple spiral journal, spending a lot of time and attention on it. Refining it throughout the days, he made sure it was in alignment with the new path, with *his inmost truth.* He had to look inside, *really* look, and contemplate: *What* is *my personal mission? My* true *desires? What goals do I really want to bring into being? If I could become anything ... what might that be? What is it that I most wish to accomplish?*

Beyond conscious goals are inhibiting subconscious memes which can be absolved

The things that came and what impeded realizing them were intimately intertwined with his own once-fixed conceptions of Life, of Love, of God. These concepts can be transformed at any time. Why had he never been aware of any of this? It was like putting a different movie in the projector. The personal mission statement proved to be a most valuable undertaking. In addition, the suggestion to write five goals and five affirmations a day was offered. So, on a blank three-by-five card, Kevin did just that. Goals like:

> *I will be honest all day, both with myself and with others*
> *I will look for the similarities instead of the differences*
> *I will look for the best in others*
> *I will accept and practice any suggestions offered to me*
> *I will exercise today*

Affirmations such as:
> *I am content today*
> *I am learning how to live a better life*
> *I am listening*
> *I trust my Higher Power*
> *I am willing to let go*
Which soon turned into, *I am letting go*

Each day, he spent whatever time it took to finish these, and put them on the mirror in plain sight.

Combining all this with the daily rituals of prayer and listening, journaling and the step work, was cultivating this mysterious growing awareness that he was more than his thoughts. He was finding a part of himself that he had always wished to let flourish, but could not. This part was always buried under all the muck in which he felt so stuck. It was the genesis of a completely fresh way of showing up in the world - through surrender. Now, the Lotus Flower could emerge from and through the muck.

Many thoughtful hours went into Kevin's Personal Mission Statement. He scribbled notes; prayed on it; thought about it; he wrote of new life intentions in countless journal entries. *What would I like to become?* He listened for answers, wrote and rewrote rough drafts. Then, a few days before graduation, he put it all together and wrote it carefully on one page.

A photocopy of the original writing of this Personal Mission Statement is on page 259.

Welcome to our Grand Opening

The big night was a disaster. Arriving early was good because he found out they required black shoes, which he did not have - must have missed that piece, somehow. *Damn it! What an idiot.* Maybe Terra would help.

"Hi babe. Can you go get me some black shoes, size 12? I screwed up, again."

A long pause. "Yeah. I guess. Just plain black?"

"Yep. This place is buzzing, it's going to be awesome tonight. See ya' soon - oh, and, thanks."

"Yeah. Bye." She was totally unenthused, maybe even slightly miffed.

He wondered what was wrong. She just seemed so depressed.

No time to worry about that, though; the place was bustling in anticipation of a full house for dinner. Sherry was frantic and so were the cooks, as the kitchen had not been battle-tested yet. The whole thing was a feat of magic and sheer will, considering how it looked just weeks ago. Opening night had finally come and Kevin was in great spirits, body and mind becoming clearer each day. The busy-ness of the place and the people was just as imagined. Some waiters were frantic, and the cooks were as soldiers before engagement. Spatulas raised; aprons on; charge!

The doors opened, and, sure enough, Frederick's on the Green was packed from opening to closing. This part was good, but staff was a scattered mess, an automaton in its infancy, and someone forgot to oil the machine. Some guests waited more than an hour for their dinner, and some left; others were calm, a few threw a disgusted scowl before they stormed out. The staff had fun, anyway, and did the best they could with the situation. Sherry did too, but also took it personally, of course; she was the manager and it was her responsibility.

Overall it went well, regardless of the glaring flaws. More guests were happy than unhappy. It had been a social evening and a raging success. The food, when the paying guests finally got it, was well-received.

The restaurant had no computer system, so the waiters had to use a calculator or straight math to figure tax and add customer's bills. To Kevin, a minor set-back. His brain was pretty well atrophied and squishy. Doing the math, he could literally feel the synapses fire in his head, sizzling, as the neurons shot through once-used pathways, recently abused and all but shut down. One eye would flicker open and then shut a couple times. A wisp of smoke might come out an ear. "Got it," whispered to the Unseen. "Thank you."

Whatever it was, it was fun and he liked it, driving home happily exhausted after an honest days' work, with tip money in pocket and a full schedule of shifts for the next two weeks. He'd made it through half the after-care group sessions now. He looked forward to them. The self-loathing diminished with each passing day, with each share, with each step and every letting go. These meetings happened in a circle.

Jerry led the group. He was a small guy with thick, round glasses, peaceful, carefree and lighthearted, probably in his 60's and soft spoken. Kevin liked him, could tell he was all about people doing well in recovery and their new lives. He would see Jerry tomorrow. It was always charming at the end of each session. Upon the chair's arms Jerry rested his own. He moved only his hands in circles. Back and forth those hands circled, accentuating these words: "Do somethin' nice for somebody and don't tell anybody 'bout it," ending with palms forward and only both index fingers raised and wiggling.

It was always funny. But, what did he mean? If Kevin did something nice for someone, of course he'd want to bathe in recognition. Jerry would just smile, and end Group with the serenity prayer. When Kevin let life be serene it was, and when he resisted, the monkeys ruled.

Back home, still wound up, he told Terra about the evening. She was distracted by a deluge of emotions flooding a heavy heart. He did his best to cheer her up, take her mind off whatever it was for the evening as best he could with stories of opening night. They usually talked before sleeping, of spiritual principles, new ways of living, and helped each other see into one another's blind spots.

But tonight was different. Terra insisted nothing was wrong, but her mood and attitude said otherwise. He asked again, "You sure nothin's wrong?"

"Yeah, I'm OK … just tired tonight." She flipped over. Kevin wrapped his arms around her in the spooning position, trying to close the million-miles-gap between them. The cooler evening breeze gently blew through an open window. He was happy with anticipation of what might come - but what about Terra? They lay there, each in their own world, and slowly drifted off.

***

The newness of the good life in the once-perfect house wore off after only a couple weeks. Challenges abounded, mostly welcome. Even though it was summer, the hot tub was something they wanted fixed and working, and Kevin could pretty much fix anything. He messed with it and found the heating element fried. The part was under a hundred bucks. The landlords said they would take some money off the rent for fixing it, an added bonus. He got it going and actually made a profit on the deal.

Being a waiter was fun, talking with all the people, getting to know the staff, the daily goings-on. Not to mention always plenty of good stuff to eat. Giant cheeseburgers were his favorite. Housemate Arvin was scarfing up the great food, too. Kevin had helped him get a job in the kitchen.

Terra was doing OK, and had her own life dramas going on. The treatment center found out about the two of them, and fraternization was against policy. Someone must have spilled the beans on them shacking up together. It was devastating. She called Kevin right away. "They brought me into the office, all the people in charge, and told me they really didn't want to … but then they fired me!"

Kevin was silent, except for an "Oh man. I am so sorry."

"They said because we are living together they have to." She sobbed. "What do I tell people?"

"You'll find another job, sweetheart," he tried to reassure her, but she only cried more.

Several of the treatment center's employees often came into Freddy's, on the Greenway. In the old days, Kevin would have been at least passive aggressive with them if not directly confrontational. He considered it for a minute. How would he act next time he saw them?

Resentment and blame was the old way now, though still it was the first tendency. But these were the same people that had taught him principles and about how it was possible to choose to live in a different way, through acceptance and love and tolerance.

He recalled again that morning meeting in Anthony's office when he hovered on the brink of being expelled - maybe they were simply seeing what would happen in Group that morning. Would he tell the truth? Was it a fork in the road, some divine test of choices? Maintaining the lies and unwillingness to be open and honest would have been choosing to live still in the old ways.

But the truth had come that day, somehow. Sarah had witnessed it in Group, and must have shared it with Jesse and Anthony - or maybe something more mystical was at work. It didn't matter, anyway. He had made the choice, and they had let him stay.

Yes, it would be hard to be resentful toward them for firing Terra.

A few nights later, six workers from the center came into the restaurant, two of whom were Jesse and Anthony. Upon seeing them, all the happenings at The Sanctuary flashed through his mind in a moment of grateful awareness.

He went up to their table right away. "Hello, welcome. It's so nice to see you." His huge smile matched the sentiment.

"Hey, congratulations on your new job," Jesse said, also smiling. "Nice place."

These people were such an important part of his life, and always would be.

The others looked on, most of them he had talked with before. Still it was uncomfortable, with Terra being fired and all. They avoided much but small talk, and he was relieved they were in another waiter's section.

Looking into each of their eyes, he said, "Thanks again." He wanted to tell them he loved them. They had become his new family, and they were everywhere, as he was soon to find.

***

At the restaurant, with each order: Put it together, serve, converse, add up the bill, clear and set the table. His mind got sharper and clearer with each task performed. Working out at the gym and skating the trail almost every day helped improve the physical. He often wore shirts that purposefully showed off pumped up arms, old vanity returning to challenge. It began to feel silly, like growing out of something.

Never having been sober this long, he was blown away by how good it felt. A typical day involved praying, meditating, writing, meetings, the trail, the gym, working, walks, and praying some more. It was all quite different from chasing dragons.

JP was resentful about the offer to live with them at the new house, saying it should have been "me and you" that had the place, muttering something about "women, ugh!" even though he was as good as married. JP just plain fell off the radar over a week ago now. Kevin giggled out loud recalling that ridiculous Tiki doll. He shared a prayer aloud, "Please watch over JP."

Terra and Kevin drifted further apart, sometimes not talking for days except the awkward "hello" or, "goodbye, see you later." It was all right; he was busy with life and had plenty to do. She was searching for another job and taking care of the kids. Something had to give, and soon.

He decided not to take the felony charge and opted for drug court - even welcomed it, figuring it might actually be a wise move. The charges could be transferred to Yakima County. Life here was good. He went to the courthouse, and those in charge of the program welcomed him in and shared the protocol. He would have to ask Yakima County to charge him. Then, the county of origin would drop the charges. He was doing everything required already and with a positive attitude. There is great value in listening and following directions.

The liquor license was about to come in, and Kevin had trepidation about being the bar manager and peddling booze. But, he would give it a go - more money. Circling vultures wanted that job with the place now becoming a hot spot. He realized how fortunate it was to come at the exact right time, getting the prime positions, and not even having to ask for them. Nope, they had fallen right in his lap, as if it were scripted.

The day came. It was fun at first, but he had no idea what he was doing. *I've never been a bar manager, not even a restaurant manager – I've only ever been a dishwasher.* Sherry had hired him purely on personality. So, after only two days, without even having to say anything, they gave the position to a catty woman, bossy and fairly rude. A way better fit. He didn't want that job, anyway, and genuinely congratulated her. They got along just fine this way. Still, they gave him the prime bartending shifts, and he was happy with that - but not sure if being around the bar and touching and pouring and smelling the stuff was going to fare well with sobriety. *No one will even know, just one shot.* Twenty more monkeys tossed bottles and rattled glasses while he wiped down a disgusting table.

Closing down the bar with each shift, he was grateful that it was more in alignment with restaurant hours than night club hours. Even still, he wouldn't get home till after midnight. It was good money; he could easily pay his share of the bills at the house. Terra was more distant than ever, and he accepted that, giving her the space, sensing a disconnect that could become permanent. Sometimes they talked, sharing their surface feelings, but kept their secrets. He could tell she was unhappy.

There was not much he could do for her, except to learn to show up for himself, first. Without the vices of yesterday, the controlling of others and living in various co-dependent relationships, he was lost. He did not know how to live any other way. The focus would need to shift to learning to live by a whole new set of principles from an entirely different paradigm.

But those old ruts …

~ Chapter 11 ~

New Pathways, Old Patterns

Heavy eyes gave way to the induction, a trance, neither sleeping nor awake, flashing mirrors and fleeting images, whatever reality was or wasn't, stone-cold sober and under a much sweeter spell. Tonight, Kevin soul-traveled to the great solace of the various church sanctuaries, and well beyond. Even though it seemed as if the peace came from the quietude there, the vast space, the magnificent art and statues, the long since passed prayers of the many that had been there before and yet still suffused the room and its contents, this was not the essence. The essence was *within*, a place beyond the individuated "I." He had never looked there, before now. It felt so much better here than living in the head, inside a small, limiting set of perceptions and chaotic, deluded notions about life and the world.

Equanimity really is possible. It was the peace found at the trail, the treatment center along the tree line, with the birds, his little choir of compadres. The same peace found even in jail, between runs; the same peace found in a true hug; the same peace found with every letting go of control. It was the peace that had always been there: In, through and around everything. It was in all things, but first it was in no thing, for it was the stillness itself.

Always had he chosen to fight. This peace could not be who he was. *Don't you know who 'I' am?* It just could not be this simple, surely it had to be complex and difficult – life was fighting, chaos and conflict. These old ways somehow validated who and what he thought he was. But if this were true, why had he always felt so out of alignment with … with what?

The reverie also brought him back to the last thing the inpatients did at The Sanctuary. The fourth and fifth step of twelve: Taking a searching and fearless moral inventory of one's self and then divulging it to another human being – and, some greater power, which many called "God." And a new God was he coming to know his own way. Another first.

Contempt can be so suffocating, and letting go of it so liberating.

Here was revealed exactly *what* he had been fighting – a true looking at and owning his modus operandi; the way in which one shows up in the world. Here could be seen, with help, just what were the screaming monkeys. Upon doing so, they became little, devious, pip-squeaking lies. Lies under whose rule he had lived as if they ordained life and death - surely if anyone ever found out the depth of these lies, he would perish. And, if Kevin ever faced the lies, the dishonesty and self-deception, *something* would indeed perish … and so it was.

With the help of others who had taken these steps, they looked upon these lies for what they were: Just some old used up dwelling place, once lived inside. Admitting these false notions and then finding forgiveness for them allowed a great sense of freedom. Among the groups, the counselors, and himself, peace in the process had been found. This was done together. Little did he know, barely a scratch had been made upon the surface of Self-Realization.

It was amazing; of all the writing, this was by far the toughest, perhaps because it was required to share with someone. He had been admitting these glaring defects to himself, and to the God of his understanding, but this was different. Admitting such things to another human being could actually incur *looking bad*, and this was always avoided at all costs.

Willing, honest and open has its *seeming* drawbacks, and this was certainly one of them. But, the commitment had been made, and with those that were there to help. So, he did as they asked, wrote down as accurately as he could what was suggested, and brought it to Sarah. He was sure it was the most thorough fourth step ever done in the whole world. But it was not even close to that. She sat down with him and shared more of her story and about the process so he could see how to reach even further into the place of hidden secrets and mountains of gooey blame.

"There is more, Kevin; this is a good start - it's just not thorough or complete," Sarah said both stern and guiding. "I ran over *anyone* in my way to get what I wanted. I used people, especially people that loved me. I didn't give a rip about anyone's feeling at all, so long as I got what I needed," she said, channeling the old Sarah long enough so Kevin could see devil horns poke out of her forehead. "And then I blamed everyone *but me* for my problems and self-imposed inadequacies. I just never knew it until I did the work with sincere honesty."

She sure was brutally honest about herself and her shortcomings - maybe this is why she could see right through his bullshit when even *he* could not. She had done the work, and the benefits of living a sober life practicing spiritual principles were all evident. She was living proof of transformation.

So, out to the Altar he had gone, there along the fence, to ask whatever this God was for help to uncover the source of decades of self-deception. Tears of guilt and shame trailed down his cheeks and fell to thirsty soil. Maybe God was these gentle birds; their songs, some kind of solution to soften his grip, holding him up just enough to "see" both lies and Truth. The ability to reach even further into that diseased abyss did come that day. He went back to his room and wrote it all, as Sarah had instructed. More came over the next days, as he listened to the lectures closely and to the others from Group sharing how they were doing it. *And he prayed almost constantly for help, from the inside out.*

One lecture especially made great sense, given by, of all people, the Chaplain at the treatment center. He had talked about the moral inventory. The repugnant things discovered there were like stones we carried around in a backpack. We just kept adding more stones, making that pack heavier and heavier. How exhausting it was to drag it around everywhere, day in and day out.

The Chaplain said, "Drag that backpack one more time, to my office, or to whoever's you choose to share that inventory. Take each stone out. As you do, tell me about it, honestly, until you have placed them all upon my desk. We'll talk about all of it. And when we are done, leave them. Do not pick them up again."

This made so much sense! Kevin had sprouted a full foot in his chair and come alive with possibility. How much of a load it was packing these heavy burdens around for a lifetime! Only, it was carried because he *did not know* there was a choice, thinking he was condemned as this hideous creature he had become. It could all be let go, even *forgiven?*

So, he wrote to the best of his ability, with the tender loving help of this precious Higher Power. It had become the wind through the trees, the same wind that gave breath, and life. It was the Sun and the birds and their melodies, It was Sarah and her uncomfortable honesty, It was the chaplain's message. It was not what he had ever known "God" to be - not by a longshot. It was every single thing that was anywhere, all in a harmony of its own. Becoming a part of this harmony, *allowing It*, gave Kevin the strength to continue and actually follow through with this purification process. And the whole of it was just beyond the thoughts he had always given credence to hold him in place - until now. For now, he was allowing this omnipotent guidance to lead, and It was.

Thank You

The fifth step was next. Sarah had given her blessing on the inventory. Now it was time to choose someone to share it with. They said to pick anyone. He thought about Sarah, about Jesse, even the Chaplain. He prayed about it. There was a period of wafting, of not feeling able to go through with it. But then, after an afternoon walk, he came inside from the same pathway taken that first day. A lone door in the hallway was ajar; a man sat inside the room, alone. Inscribed upon a small brass plate next to the ominous door was the counselor's name. Kevin had seen him many times.

"Hello, Luke?" Kevin's voice was mousy, unsure.

"Yes, how can I help?" Certainly an appropriate question.

"Well, I … ummm. Do you, can you… uhhh, I need to do my fifth step, are you too busy?" God, it felt so clumsy to ask.

"Sure, I would love to. Thank you for asking." Luke looked at his calendar. "When would you like to do it?"

Kevin was relieved. It felt right to ask Luke.

"Gosh, soon. I mean soon. Really wanna do this. It's just so, uh, so *much*, ya' know?" His throat clenched. One cantankerous monkey bellowed, *How about never!*

"Yes, I do know." Luke paused, for a good while. He let his answer echo in a moment of quiet, making sure it was heard. "I do … but it is so worth it, you'll soon see. How about tomorrow after lunch, say 2:00 p.m.?" Luke was not put-out in the slightest, and was even smiling.

"Yes. Yes! 2:00 p.m. tomorrow, I will be here."

He thought about it for the rest of the day and went to sleep restless, got up, and prayed about it. The *Daily Reflection* talked about acceptance and change. *Ugh.*

Right on time, Kevin showed up with a backpack full of stones, notebook of once-secrets, and shared it. The two men talked about *all* of it, just like the chaplain had suggested. Turns out, Luke was a mirror in many ways. There was crying and laughter, and it just plain was not so bad. In fact, it was a giant release and a great purging.

"Thank you so much." Kevin's relief was obvious, and, tinged with awkwardness at having gone to this level with another person. What lay in store? What could possibly be next? Maybe he would turn into a butterfly and flitter off …

"Nice work, Kevin, you've got a wonderful start - and more work to come. Doing a great job."

At the doorway Kevin paused, turned around to face Luke. "Does it really get better?"

Luke pondered for a long moment …

"I wouldn't have believed it could get this good, looking back, if you'd have told me so when I was where you are. And it just keeps getting better." Luke looked a little bewildered at how this could be true. But it was. Kevin could tell it was as genuine a statement as the man had ever made. "There is much more work, though."

Sarah had told him afterwards that Luke reckoned either he was serious about this new walk or he was completely full of crap. Knowing that he had been authentic to the best of his ability, Kevin only smiled and said, "We'll see, I guess." Maybe, he was entirely both. Time would tell.

Next had been the group's most symbolic ceremony, the power of which would be revealed over and over again. It would be reflected in other sacred ceremonies, in every relationship, in each amend, and in every gaze into any mirror.

Just beyond the walking path, the whole group of men, without Sarah now, stood in a circle surrounding a fire pit. These souls that had shared so many buried secrets during these few revealing weeks, who had come to know each other in this awkward and open way, all stood in this circle, arms around one another. While life went on around them - people playing soccer and softball, walking the pathways, summer heat sizzling through breezes and gusts, eagles soaring overhead, a train rattling off somewhere in the distance - the whispers of a transformed life beckoned from a nearer horizon. The serenity prayer was spoken in unison as Kevin's fourth step and who he once was burned and turned to ash in the flames.

The ritual was repeated for each man who had completed the fourth and fifth step. Kevin realized, just as the chaplain had suggested, it was up to him to not pick the stones up again, and so right there did he choose to be free of them. He watched the smoke and ashes drift away, and *let it go*. That was no longer who or what he was.

The suggestion to continue with the step work with the guidance of a sponsor in a program was made more than once. A few weeks would not change a lifetime of habitual scorn, except in a deluded mind. A short and powerful section in a big blue book they were given was dedicated to steps six and seven. In his room, alone, Kevin reviewed what he had just done. Even though he did not understand much of these next two steps, he pretended like he did. Then he went to his sacred prayer spot and sincerely asked the God of his understanding to take these things he had uncovered, shared, and burned.

The old backpack was now much less of a burden, the monkeys only a murmur fading from another focus, the once unbearable load diminished. He was, from this day, never the same.

Thank You. Thank you for taking it

A Moment of Clarity

With the growing awareness, it became increasingly evident that mindfulness is a far cry from thinking. Since this was the case, a choice was made. Thinking would be used for one thing first, before anything else. It took every last modicum of self-will just to achieve this one radical feat. He would use thinking to bring everything through Heart-Center, where the new God was found. The beating human heart and living brain were part of this, yet it was so much greater than any things or parts or being. It was all of all, a Unified Field of Existence. Here was belonging - something never realized in all those years of self-seeking.

The Heart is vastly wiser than the thinking mind

And, the choice was made again and again, as often as it took, every moment sometimes. With no real understanding of how this worked, he instead considered the results:

In this Heart-Center, fear dissipated. It was peaceful and serene and safe. Thinking first, trying to rationally "figure it out," caused suffering. He, alone, *lacked any real power*. Step One.

Notice what you notice

Here was a connection with Something. It was feeling some invisible matrix of absolute flow. Everything was in synchronicity, a divine dance of interconnected systems and pathways. He had never before felt it, except on fleeting occasions, and yet something inside always yearned to know it more. *It must have always been there!* Perhaps it was only obscured by his hard unwillingness to cease trying to go it alone, control and figure out life long enough to simply align with and allow a more integral way. This would require humility.

Listen

The Heart is an undistorted receptor, allowing direct perception in place of "logic" and linear thinking. The Heart receives and emanates pure, essential information and trickles to the thinking mind what it was meant to calculate, instead of the other way around. It happens effortlessly and simultaneously. The overall experience is absolutely expansive and inclusive. This way of communication moves in swirls and spirals instead of only straight lines, expanding everywhere, in all directions, all at once. It is not bound by time or space. Any information along these infinite pathways is available always and instantly. Here was found a better part of him, a better part of others and the whole world. In this Greater Mind is realized the essence of all relations.

True Insight

It had worked so well early on, he began to realize all the prayer was for this purpose: To forego thinking, to which he always felt condemned. His logical mind was always comparing everything to what had long since grown stale - which was where the cause of the suffering originated. It was putting yesterday into tomorrow and living right into it, completely missing the present.

In the Heart is found the Treasure of Life

The journey may indeed be long, but, here, fear and selfishness cannot and do not exist. Seeking to usurp everything falls away. Freedom is a natural result of forgiveness.

Everything was changing – allowing this way of being rang more eternal bells. At any costs, he would stay the course, only ever wanting to be truly helpful, to contribute and fit in somehow, some real way. Of course he was still largely selfish. But the direction of the selfishness, now, was toward allowing this new way and learning to let It lead.

You seek to share what you believe you are, and cannot give what you have not

***

Terra grew even more distant as she drifted away into her own journey. Their separation grew increasingly obvious. The time had come for a conversation devoid of pretense. And, with only a few aftercare sessions left at The Sanctuary, the primates ramped up their cage rattling. What was next? What about all that damage back home? Could he just leave it all behind and hope it disappeared?

Having honored the commitment of making each group session so far, he planned on finishing the same way. But then what? The benefits would end upon completion – but this was OK because of the steady work and decent income now. Still, there was a part of him that was afraid of leaving the place that had provided such safety and powerful transformation.

Just breathe

"What's goin' on, honestly?" Kevin inquired, knowing this may be the night she divulged whatever it was that brought the Grand Canyon between them. She set down the remote after shutting off the television and sat up on the sofa.

"Well, I just feel like … ummm, like this was too much. You and I have our own work to do. Brandon's dad and I, we never had any real closure. It was way too rushed … how we up and left like that." She was looking away as she often did, with only occasional eye contact.

~ 135 ~

"I hear you. It's been my M.O. for a long time, maybe forever: Instant gratification. I want it all right now, and it was no different with how I treated you." It felt good to speak the truth. He had been practicing in the various circles, in the journaling, asking for help with it in prayer.

"Aren't you mad?" She wanted to know. He kicked off his work shoes. That felt good, too.

"No, I'm not angry, weird as it is." Always, before, this would have surely been the case. "I only wish the best for you and your boys. Your husband, too." The sincere assertion made, he settled back onto the couch next to Terra. "Ahh, yes ... it is so nice to relax."

Terra lit up some, making eye contact now. "We can stay friends. You and I share a special connection, and who knows what can happen."

"Yeah ... I think we both need our space right now, learn to live for ourselves. Trust our Higher Power to show us the way." As Kevin spoke it, he recalled someone talking about making a love relationship your Higher Power; he always had, and it always ended badly. No human power ever filled what Kevin always felt so tremendously: A hole in the soul.

"Yeah, I do agree. I'll find a different place," Terra said. It made Kevin swallow hard. Hearing it made it real. But then he thought about it and sprang upright.

"That would be silly. It took us days to move all your stuff, and this house is perfect for your family. I sure don't need a place this big. You stay. I'll find something smaller." He was looking at the wall across from them which had a bookshelf with at least a hundred and fifty DVD's on it, no less than twelve strewn about the floor, and not one was his.

"Are you sure? That would be great!"

Maybe her estranged husband would even move in, but it did not matter the way it always would have before. "Yes, I'm sure. You just focus on what you need to do." His heart was opening more every minute, and hers was responding. Surrendering it all was relieving, and it was the first non-superficial connecting they had done in weeks. Their embrace lasted a full minute, soothing and forgiving. They finished her movie in quietude.

Things ended as well as they could, even in spite of the massive dysfunction. It felt good to authentically care about someone else. Maybe it was because Kevin had begun to care about himself, and in some way the two are connected.

***

Old habits and ways do die hard. Alisa was a sultry, mysterious woman. Many glances had been exchanged during her family visits at The Sanctuary. She was the mother of another patient, Lance. The treatment center has a segment where the family members come and stay for a couple days and actually come to the group sessions, as well as special sessions for only the patient and family.

Kevin's family had not come, not any of them. He had caused too much damage and ran too much bullshit for too long, the boy that cried wolf too many times. So the families came and went, and though it hurt that his had not come, he partly understood their reasons and let it go, replacing projecting blame at them with prayer and working on himself.

Still, every time another's family member came to sit in on Group was a reminder of his own *failure and inadequacy*. It reinforced some childhood wound that was surely there but obscured from awareness. Would this work in recovery, this process, be able to help complete whatever could be this open-ended wound? Was living a life free of having to use and hurt others even possible? Surely it was all connected to what happened with Marie, with Selena, and now with Terra. How many countless others had been affected? Was this why he felt the need to get right back into a relationship before the last was even finished? Would he *ever* really consider anyone but himself? All Kevin's relationships had very similar attributes. They all went through predictable stages, and most ended badly. Was it possible to know lasting liberation from what had always been? From what was happening again, now?

Kevin, Lance and JP had often hung together during treatment. They got along well and always plenty of jokes and laughing. Kevin liked Lance. Throwing a hot mom in the mix can be awkward. One evening, playing cards in the break-room, sparks were flying. The day she left – and he knew she was leaving - he just happened to cross her path as she was heading out, and just happened to have his contact information written upon a piece of paper. Imagine that!

"It was nice meeting you. If you would like, keep in touch." He handed her the paper. "Bye." She slipped the note in her pocket with a devious smile, and off she went. She did contact him, but it was during-Terra, and honoring their relationship (to the best of his ability at the time, yet only true to the levels of his own limitations), he let Alisa know this.

They remained friends, though, and exchanged emails and even pictures. Like a drone being remote-controlled, when it went sideways with Terra, he turned to Alisa. This was just what he had always done ... so hard to be alone, so hard to not turn to someone. Time alone had always been agonizing.

Now, he had to find a place to live. This would be easy, he decided, after how nicely Sadie had come about. On a local bulletin-board, there it was. Custom built on a ginormous property, way more than he could afford, larger by far than necessary, plush and massive: 2000 sq. ft. of living area upstairs, jetted tub in the master bedroom, custom kitchen, overdone like the rest of the house. It was only a long mile away from the last two homes. The central air conditioning on these hottest days of summer would certainly be nice. Even better was that it sat on top of a garage the same size as the house. Complete with electric doors on two sides so you could drive right on through - this would be much more than enough to fix cars. The whole thing was enormous, excessive, way more than needed *and* way out of his price range. He called and left a message.

***

It was a particularly hot day on the trail, even skating half-naked; one hundred and five degrees Fahrenheit. The cell phone buzzed in the pocket of his grey cargo shorts. As if life over these last few months had not thrown enough curve balls. There was another on the other end of the phone.

"Hey dude. How *are* you?" It was a longtime friend. They'd been in bands together for the last 13 years, shared an infectious chemistry, and had teetered on the edge of stardom on more than one occasion, never quite making it. But they had not given up, always working on the music, writing great songs and putting together rock bands that would rise quickly, have their heyday, and then fizzle, only to do it over again. This had been the pattern, and perhaps it was even this that was the fun part, the real adventure: New band, fresh tunes, doing the deal. The music, the scene and pounding the drums was always a stellar diversion from the screaming monkeys. And it was awesome. Until he was overtaken.

The memory caused an instantaneous drift …

He loved the partying. How had it all become so messed up? Somewhere along the way he had gotten into the drugs too deep. Pretty soon, couldn't even come to practice without plenty of whatever the drug of the week was, mixed with plenty of booze - always desperately trying to maintain the facade of having it all together. Over the last few years those demons had gained dominance. Same with work; always had to have the properly distorted state of mind and plenty of painkillers to even do the simplest work, which, this way, became very difficult and often sent him into rage. It got to the breaking point: Too much was never enough.

Frantic insanity increased day by day, every diversion leading to the same place: Despair. And much of it was silent desperation, manifesting in enraged outbursts and inappropriate behavior, followed by groveling and thick, hollow apologies, begging forgiveness, swearing never to do it again.

Could it be that he had been looking for his true source of purpose, belonging and happiness everywhere but where it truly existed? Could it be this simple?

... Snapping back into the body,

"Hello?"

"Dude, it's *me*. How are ya'?" Shackey was calling.

"Oh man, doing so great, just loving this life." Much hovered in the unspoken.

The two chatted about some of the changes, until Shackey revealed the real purpose of the call: "We got a bitchin' band together, a bad-ass one. We got a show booked, *Battle of the Bands*, and the winner opens for a national act."

That's a big deal for an up and coming rock band. The only problem, Shack said, "We need a good drummer - no, a *great* drummer, and that's you. You are the best rock drummer out there, and with you we can do this thing, win it!" Ego stroked ... hook tossed ... target locked.

Everything changed in the moment it took to skate around the next bend, phone tight against his left ear.

Heart racing, pulse pounding, he skated along trying to figure what this could mean, inside and around this diverged life he had been living for only a short while now. He thought about all the variables in about seven seconds. What would be the answer? Shackey didn't like lollygagging.

Had he not gone home and almost fallen on his face? Had it not been just too much? And going back to a rock band, in the bars; was this any good idea? He had a good life here, a good job. But, his relationship had fallen to pieces, yet again. The treatment commitment was over now ... had completed that, at least, which was something, and more than he ever thought he could do. He was between homes though, unsure, and now with the proverbial angel on one shoulder and a hundred and three smelly monkeys on the other.

Shackey was a first-class bull-shitter, as good as they come. He kept on him: "We got a bad-ass bass player, and me and Jimmy've been writing *killer* songs, plus we're doing some of the songs you already know. Record labels are all over us. There's gonna be scouts at the show just to check *us* out *and* hundreds of people ..."

It was all the right stuff.

Now, Shack peddled similar promises about pretty much every show, and every time it happened nowhere near the way proffered. Maybe this show would be different. Kevin *wanted* to buy it, and with stars in his eyes, he thought about it all ... they *could* do it, him and Shack had been playing together long enough. It was way too easy. And *so* much fun.

Target - compromised.

"… and with your beats there is no *way* we can lose - whaddya' say?"

"Yeah! Let's do it!" Kevin caved in a single breath.

Mission accomplished.

"That sounds great. I miss playing, so much." Kevin spoke with a shaky confidence. A foreboding aftertaste lingered in his mouth.

Shack had seen him at his lowest in their last project, Magnificent Cell. In that band, Shack wrote a song which eerily embodied the Montana incident, a tale of Marie breathing life back into his body and of another chance at life. It was a haunting, powerful song laden with ancient tribal rhythms dredged from a time long past. Maybe they would even do it in the new band.

The date of the show, two months and three weeks away, enough time to get solid on the songs and get settled back home - or whatever, at least find a place to stay. They talked for a while about all that had transpired - keeping any real feelings in protected mode, of course, access denied. It kept going back to how cool playing together again was going to be.

Much had happened between them, good and not so good. One honest look and Kevin may have been able to see the same pattern, at its honeymoon stage now, that cycled each time they had gotten together, risen, fallen, and split - as reliable as the seasons themselves.

~ Chapter 12 ~

Leaving a Sanctuary

A dazzling story just begging to be told burned in place of any other thought. Anything could be added in imagination - and spewed aloud, for that matter. This night, Kevin was the star of his own movie, and shared the script with whoever would listen. There were always plenty of willing ears, being the bartender now. Work had become somewhat of a routine anyway. Ah, the ups and downs of a restaurant worker. There needed some boiling hot lava seething through the place.

"My band called, they need me," Kevin said, proudly. "We got a *huge* show coming up; the winner gets to go on a national tour." It was what Shack had said, or something like that - it was what Kevin had heard, anyway, and it sounded good, real good. His eyes enhanced each word as it was spoken, arms waving, sharing about the old days and high adventure now upon the horizon, enrolling a couple guys he worked with in the conversation. "Man, we've done so many awesome shows. Played in front of 1500 with DIO. I even got to meet Ronnie James himself. Love that guy. All the years of rocking is going to pay off big-time with this gig. I love shredding!" Rock-star-face, engage. Air drums, full-on. "Gonna rip it up!" He looked silly banging his head but did not care one bit. Monkeys shook the leaves from their trees in shrill screams.

"So when you outta here," one guy asked, his eyes huge with Kevin's excitement.

"I don't know. Soon, though … prolly just a few weeks." Others came to the bar and asked about his departure - they were *very* interested. The word spread like wildfire.

They are blown away by me, the big rock star. See, I am somebody.
That fragile ego at work again, slowly creeping back. Kevin listened to it,
seeking power from the wrong place.

Perhaps they were more interested in his job than his story. Their
questions, if he had been paying attention, were toward that end. But, a self-
obsessed egomaniac may not be so diligent. None of it mattered anyway. In
his mind he was already out of here, and anyone that likes can have the job -
he was moving on.

15 minutes, the drive home. A middle finger rapped the well-worn
power button on a dark radio. Pulsating hard rock pushed the Explorer's
speakers to their limit. *Perfect.* All windows down, the wind taunted and
tossed howling gremlins through the warm summer evening. Adventure and
angst was the subtext of every word Kevin screamed. Horns began to
puncture the once-halo as they poked through his scalp. He did not realize that
it was all about to travel backwards. A lone monkey with bad breath popped
up and shrieked as Kevin shoved him way back down. No idea what lay in
store, yes, but he was certainly right about one thing: An adventure like never
before awaited …

***

Terra had become a stranger and her amicable behavior gave way to
annoyance. She wanted him gone. He'd need to find a place just long enough
for the remaining commitments at treatment and give notice at work. *I'll
finish everything up here, leave with some integrity. I cannot wait to be out of
here now, get on with my life – sober.* Morning sun's telegraph promised
another hot day as he stepped off the porch and down the street a ways, not
wanting to be overheard on the phone.

"Hello?" Alisa's sultry voice gave herself to him in just one word.

"Hi," he mumbled as his brain flashed an erotic daydream.

Feeling each other out, they talked about hooking up as soon as
possible.

"I can't wait to get out of here. It's so dead, all he cares about is
money!" Alisa insisted.

"I hear ya'. Yeah, pretty bad here, too. Uncomfortable in the house,
we don't even talk. I hadta get outta there. But it's so nice to hear *your* voice,"
Kevin responded, on cue.

They would rescue each other, fix each other.

She seemed enamored with the whole thing, the excitement of it all.
She loved the rock scene, and just had to hear his band as soon as possible.
Kevin's other line beeped in.

"Call you back," he said, and clicked over. It was the people that owned the massive house over on Chestnut Street. Kevin told them, change of plans - going to be in town only weeks, moving back to Seattle, only need temporary housing. Once again, serendipity sang.

"Well, we'd be willing to let you stay there for a few weeks. Nobody's been able to come up with any rent yet and it's been empty a while now," the man said. "We built it for our kids, but they ended up leaving, something about living their own lives. The neighbors next door rent that house from us, too. It's all one property we own. They have a key, we live in Arizona now. I'll call and ask them to let you in and see the place. If you like it, we can come up with an amount that's fair for the few weeks."

"Yes, thank you." Kevin was nearly in disbelief, but so many miracles had transpired over these past few magical months. Something had to be at work. Deciding to let the flow have its way, he accepted the good that was coming from all directions.

Fumbling with the cell phone's buttons, he found Alisa again.

"Oh my God. I think I found a place." He told her all about it.

"I'll come visit!" she offered.

"This is going to be awesome," Kevin said, tears of happiness welling up, pure awe at the gifts that were unfolding. "I'm going to go check it out, call you later." Exactly eleven minutes later he pulled up in the old black and gold Ford Explorer.

"Hi, I'm Kevin. The one the landlord called about?" He reached out a hand.

"Yeah, hello. Jim. I'll grab a key and be right out," answered the pudgy man. He offered a limp handshake. *Maybe he don't like long-hairs and won't want me renting the place,* Kevin thought, as the man made his way through two children and into his house, struggling into shoes on the way out.

The place certainly was huge, and empty. The garage was so big, footsteps echoed - he could easily run a business out of it, but no need for that now. There was no furniture. The only thing he had was that obnoxious stereo that had tormented the guys at the Oxford house, and Terra. He loved that thing. Couldn't sleep on it though, and nothing to cook with. What would he sleep on? The floor?

"We have an air mattress you can use if you like," Jim offered, reading his mind. "I know you won't be here long."

"Thanks. I'll see what the landlord is willing to rent the place for. If it works I'll take you up on it." It was good enough. He called the landlord back.

"I like the place, it's huge. More than I need by far, but … how much?"

The two thousand they were asking for a month was more than he could afford by far.

"How about six hundred bucks," the man more stated than asked. It was a no-brainer.

Kevin responded immediately. "Sounds great," but he didn't have even that – yet, anyway.

"I have a job at the new restaurant in town, and I fix cars on the side. The garage is perfect for that. I *know* I can pay the money – but I don't have it right now. Promise I will. Six hundred - no problem." He was in deal-making mode, and besides that, sincere as could be. Kevin often exercised the coarse attribute of using way too many words.

Silence.

And then, oddly (for he'd no idea who this stranger was), the man said, "OK, we'll trust you to pay, but *please* do. We're retired and need the money; you need to pay us."

Kevin agreed with pure enthusiasm. "I will."

The landlord gave the go-ahead. He could move in straight away without so much as a dime.

When one door closes, another opens

Protected, guided, cared for and watched over – this serendipity was working everywhere. The abundance of kindness he was experiencing, and the ability to actually honor his word - all new. In a way, it felt like trying to balance on a log floating down the river. Could he pay this man his money? Would there be any good direction back home? Providence was moving in ways difficult to fathom, except - *he was living it*. But did he deserve it? It was as if there were guardian spirits all around – flitting and dancing, watching and playing, just ahead of every step, opening doors and illuminating pathways. Right now, the soft brush of angel's wings guided each move.

At the sanctuary of the river Kevin offered a thousand thank You's. The gratitude just plain felt wonderful. There were not enough ways to honor all the good. Why hadn't he died that night in Montana? Or completed any other attempt to end it all?

Terra was a mix of happy and sad with news of the Chestnut place. Not sure what she was thinking, but sure that it was time to move on, he got packing his meager belongings. Since they split in as a good a way as they each could at the time, they decided to remain friends. That felt good for both of them. She helped him pack up, smiling when they loaded the stereo …

She offered a couple blankets and a pillow. That and the borrowed air mattress would make the temporary home complete enough for some good sleep – and whatever else might happen.

"If there is anything you need, I'm just a mile away." He hugged her goodbye.

The stereo sat perfectly upon the mantle. He ran naked up and down the commodious hallway screaming out lyrics of his favorite songs as they blared from his own speakers.

The lush carpet, blissful under bare feet - they had spared no expense on this place. He was so alive and blessed with abundance, if only for this moment. But is this moment not all there ever is, when it comes right down to it?

You are free right now

The jetted tub in the master bedroom belched huge bubbles upon pushing the glowing red button. Settling into the steaming water was medicine to his bones. "Ahhhh." A good book in hand and two candles going he'd found in a cupboard made for a perfect solo evening. After a long soak, he fell into the makeshift bed which let out a strained squeak. He giggled out loud and dialed Alisa. Now he could go for it since he had ended the relationship with Terra - after all, a few hours is long enough between women, right? Simply needing what he thought he needed.

She shared with him how she felt trapped with her controlling boyfriend, and had been looking for the courage to leave for a long time. "We have this business doing construction. It makes tons of money, but that's all he cares about. I feel like a trophy girlfriend or something. I swear I'm *dying* inside! I need some spice in my life. I'm so alone and lost here." Kevin could relate.

With his new-found wisdom, he *knew* he could save her. "I understand, and I'm here for you." Yep, she was the one. But hadn't Terra been the one? And Marie? And all the others? The old cavernous rut in which he was slithering felt mostly uncomfortable. He had to double efforts to push on through an internal gnawing, a rumbling in the cellar. *Ignore it.* Still, he felt somewhat squeamish. He would not let himself look upon something that had been cracked open during the work in treatment. Was he attempting to take back (the delusion of) power and control, which never worked for much but using people and living in the harrowing emptiness?

This time will be different, he told himself, and buried it down even further using a worn-out shovel.

Immediately they began plotting her escape, her coming so they could be together. She laughed at his every joke, it seemed just perfect. They had only time, and a great place to stay - a palace, even. Only two after-care sessions and a handful of shifts at Freddy's remained, a dozen or so good-byes. He would surely end Yakima with a farewell visit to the trail. What awaited him on the other side of the mountains was calling. Alisa would have left right then, except she needed to be less conspicuous than that. After hours of talking and laughing like teenagers, they shared a sappy "Goodnight."

Crashing on the most comfortable air mattress in the world, Kevin slipped off to dreamtime as a king in his castle. But not before a good …

Flashback

Living this way was a reminder of a time:

Arizona. Automotive school, a whim, and only 19 years old.

Josh was a good friend, had gone to the school, and came back on vacation spouting how much fun he was having and all he was learning. The two had been hot rod buddies, with their fast cars and working on them all the time between bong hits and parties. Kevin's pre-rock band days. Lost and without direction, "I'm goin'" was easy.

Sharing with high school sweetheart Katie what he must do, off they went. She would drive down with him and then fly back home. They decided to drive his beloved beast, a forest green 1968 Oldsmobile 442, his very first car he'd talked Mommy into buying. This prized hot rod he had wrecked once and burned almost to the ground another time, both times swearing he would bring her back to life, and had:

The first wreck was horrific.

He was stoned as usual that day. The car had been running poorly, so off to the backyard mechanic it went. Dick adjusted the carb, "That should do it, take 'er fer a test run."

And, down the nearest residential back road he went: 30, 40, 50 mph. The giant bush obscuring vision at the four-way intersection approached quickly. It was looking all right until a Dodge Dart suddenly launched out from behind that very hedge, going as fast down the crossroad and dead-on for a gnarly collision with the massive green machine. The pavement rumbled as the beast roared onward.

If I speed up I can just get in front of him! And the foot went to the floor, even at 55.

The Olds turned into a giant battering ram, perfectly T-boning the drivers' side of the Dart, shoving it sideways across the street and into the nearest fire-hydrant.

The crash was so loud it surely woke the dead. And the man he hit looked dead, head dangling side to side, bleeding profusely. *So much blood.* Kevin could not approach that car, and instead ran in circles right there in the intersection, hands on his head, howling. Had he killed the man?

Later he learned the man had to have his spleen removed and several other surgeries.

After, he promised his mom, who had bought him the car not realizing what a powerful machine it was, that he would fix it. Only seventeen at the time, having no idea what he was doing, and with *her* charge card in hand, he fulfilled the expensive promise. It took many months, but the Olds saw the road again, and in doing this massive repair did he learn much about cars. But the whole thing was devoid of consequences, and full with manipulation. Nonetheless, that Oldsmobile became a part of him.

Shortly after, he had "rebuilt the carburetor" (having no idea how to properly do such a thing). It worked OK for a while until something rattled loose, leaking gas all over the engine. One otherwise normal morning when Katie started the beast in the garage, there was a tremendous explosion:

BOOOOM

The garage walls shuddered. He swore they bowed into the living room. Kevin ran in to see the precious hot rod spewing flames out from under the hood. The wheel wells! Kate's face was sheet-white and scared senseless.

"Get out! Get out of it!" Kevin screamed, arms flailing.

Kate climbed out, lucky to be alive, and off to the sidelines to watch the blazing fiasco.

Frantic, he grabbed the garden hose, but could not get water to the fire, under the hood of his '68 Olds. In those days, the hood latches were on the outside of the car. In spite of the easy access, there was a vacuum-seal. The inferno was raging red-hot and sucking so much air that the giant hood was locked firmly in place. Panic.

Think. Think!

In a single moment, as if in the eye of a storm, he realized that the entire house could burn down ... everything went into slow-motion:

Moving calm and with channeled purpose, he got into the car, putting it into neutral, and - flames raging everywhere - pushed it out. Fortunately, the driveway went downhill only a short distance and then back up, creating a natural bowl into which he pushed his burning baby, in full view of the neighbors. The thought flashed that they must be experiencing some satisfaction from this, after the daily smoke shows and the all-day-through-late-night revving of the beast they so often endured.

By now, someone had called the fire department. As he fought the flames, they pulled up, got out, and leaned against their big red fire truck watching him go as if it were a spectator sport. Why didn't they help? To this day it remains a mystery, but eventually the flames did die down enough to get that hood open and dowse the embers to a smoking, charcoaled mess.

Kevin decided right there never to be a firefighter. "Too much work," he said to himself while surveying the damage. The crowd dispersed. The carburetor had literally melted into two molten piles onto the intake manifold, and anything not heavy steel had burned to a crisp.

Fixable, he thought. Most people would have had it hauled off to the bone yard.

So, both times it had been repaired, with varying degrees of success.

This car - it had earned him a reputation for sure: One time, the throttle cable snapped during an attempted show-off session. The car was a massive beast, with a 403 cubic-inch big block engine (to which he had added even *more* high performance parts), way too much horsepower, and a Posi-Traction rear-end, which meant that both back tires turn, almost no matter what. The as-wide-as-possible-and-still-be-street-legal rear tire's sole purpose (besides traction) was smoke shows, burnouts and doughnuts. And, it was great for pitching sideways around any corner, a feat engaged at every opportunity. These were his "thing," his at the time claims-to-fame.

So, when the throttle cable broke in the shopping center parking lot and the small crowd pointed fingers and laughed, he would have the last laugh; he'd put that whole car together (which may have had something to do with why the cable broke in the first place). Either way, there was no gas pedal, a necessary component for any proper smoke show - not to mention getting home.

His eyes narrowed, mind turning like gears of a giant clock. He took his shoes off, removed both shoe laces, and tied them together. The crowd went from mocking to pondering. "What's he doing?" He popped the hood, tied one end to the throttle on the carb, ran the other end up under the back of the hood and in through the wing-window. Got in, and with a cocky sneer and definite gaze cranked the string back and performed the most righteous smoke show of his career, back tires spinning and relentlessly burning rubber in thick white clouds of stinky smoke. Without a glance back, he autographed the pavement, drizzles on a scone.

At another event, senior sleep-out, where the graduating class slept on the football field inside the running track that surrounded it, he pulled another stunt. Everyone was partying and in and out of tents and the like, when suddenly a (not-so) bright, thickly buzzed idea overtook him. Staggering down to the parking lot and into the Olds, he drove it *up* the grassy hill upon which the field sat, and proceeded to hot-rod around the track, getting her sideways, egged on by cheering, clapping, intoxicated screaming fans.

These antics had earned him quite a reputation, and when those days were over, he was just looking for somewhere else to belong and fit in. Maybe this school in Arizona was the next big show, and having convinced himself of it, decided to make the journey. So, with his girl and a few belongings loaded in the cherished coach, they began the 2800-mile road trip.

On one particular stretch of California highway, a Porsche was a willing participant for a speed competition. 80, 90, over 100mph. A sudden nasty noise clattered through the sweet purring of the big-block. Something was coming apart, forcing them to accept defeat and pull over. She was dead in the water. But, a full toolbox sat in the over-sized trunk. Disassembling the engine just as soon as it cooled, Kevin found that a push rod had failed, which in turn had bent a valve. This meant machine work.

He took the heavy, clumsy cylinder head which contained the bent valve onto the bus, riding with the smelly thing on his lap, much to the chagrin of the other passengers, toward the nearest machine shop.

Butch wore a stained tee-shirt that may have been white at some point, but not today. "Bent valve, hmmph." There might have been half a doughnut in his goatee.

"Can you get to it right away? We're just passin' through." Kevin put on his best "Aww, c'mon."

"Take me a few hours, gotta find a valve. One 'round here somewhere, gotta be," Butch said, scratching his hairy belly with filthy fingers.

"Need a push rod, too, that's what did it. If you could locate one I'd appreciate it."

The engine went back together easily while Katie slept in the back seat. They made the rest of the trip without racing anyone. He loved that car.

Kate flew back to Seattle, and Kevin found a small apartment in Phoenix - no furniture then, either. *Just like here at the palace on Chestnut,* he thought, turning over on the air mattress and squeezing his pillow a little tighter.

Ah, yes, that old apartment – small and claustrophobic. Having been a drummer for only a little while back then and missing the old kit, he put together a "drum set" of five or six different sized phone books. Hitting them with a pair of drum sticks he had procured made different tones, and thus a makeshift practice set. Practice kept the chops up, just in case. Besides, it kept the mind busy and offered a little artistic expression. A water bed in the local paper cost only fifty bucks. Mommy sent down a television, and removing it from the cardboard box in which it came and folding the flaps back over made a do-able TV stand. That was home back in those days, for a short time.

He also found the nearest bar and began to hang out there almost every night, exciting and engaging the drama inherent in such places. Drinking and loose women always topped the list. It was all very cool for about two weeks, and then it began to get way too routine and bland. The landscape was flat and hot and brown, desolate compared to Seattle, and the school quickly became boring and dull. The Pacific Northwest was lush and green, cool and rainy, with hills and valleys, snow-capped mountains, standing tall evergreens and cedars, and a completely different energy altogether – not that he understood much about energy at the time. He only knew he began to hate it there in desert country. Something was drastically misaligned. After only a short time Kevin was out of there, and back home to whatever might be the next saga. He did not know that what was out of alignment did not have much to do with the landscape, the school, the people, or anything else *outside*.

Stepping Forward Moving Backward

And so, now, here he was, headed home very soon to once again get behind those real drums, another shot at stardom. The next big show.

But for today, it was off to the thrift store for a few things to complement the air mattress and jetted bathtub, make the empty palace more livable. A few dishes, some towels, two forks (in the case of a visitor) and a mini-coffee maker did the trick. Morning coffee always provided such comfort.

Alisa would be here soon; they talked every day and each night. The routine continued: Work, trail, gym, hanging around with other sobers, oftentimes three or four meetings a day.

There was one snag: Drug court, but it had worked out almost perfectly. The process for the possession charge to be transferred was taking its time and had not been officially completed. Back to the courthouse, and with some direction and a couple phone calls, arrangements were made to do the program back home in Snohomish County.

Daily plotting of the band's comeback in all-too familiar terms caused Kevin near-anxiety to get home quickly. *How much fun this is going to be, rocking again - and sober.* He and Shackey had an extensive history. They were like brothers and really did love each other in spite of glaring defects in the relationship. Their coming together, from the beginning, was some karmic dance of its own. Kevin shared of his happiness in sobriety, trying to explain new insights of which he had little understanding. Shackey peddled larger than life promises about the band, and Kevin easily bought them, wanting so badly to believe in them again and again.

"How's the gear doing? Safe?" Kevin asked. The question felt stupid and uncomfortable.

"Oh, yeah ... don't worry about it, dude. It's all good," Shackey replied, as per usual.

Kevin was worried. Heeding intuition or scrolling through the history of interactions through the years of their relationship might have avoided further disappointment. But, those old ways ... he decided to believe, once again, that everything *was* OK. That room full of finely-crafted instruments and expensive electronics was awaiting the comeback, all taken care of, snug and sound. Working instead were unconscious patterns hidden in blind spots. Repeating the same behavior and expecting different results.

Years as a musician had amassed a pretty good collection of equipment. The most prized possession was a gorgeous set of nine-ply Scandinavian Birch-shelled drums, some of the finest available, custom ordered from Germany. A deep, full and rich sound came through them. Five grand just for the shells. In addition, a very nice set-up of fine cymbals and accessories surrounded them. It was a beautiful drum kit, countless hours in the making. There was also a beefy sound system of high-quality audio equipment, all kinds of amplifiers and guitar rigs and the like. A room literally full of gear. All of it had been in a storage facility where bands could practice. The place was a party spot for many bands, of which he had done plenty while creating some great music with Shack and the other players.

Many times over the past year Kevin had been in jail, and due to the company he was keeping, each release found more stuff gone upon returning to the shop. The gear had always been safe, however, because it was stowed away at the storage.

On one particular occasion, having been locked up for a good spell, shaky foundations were coming apart more than ever before. Not even the thick veils of delusion could hold together any longer structures that were falling to pieces. Every relationship was strained to its limits.

Mom had let him know (in addition to all the other wreckage occurring), that the rent on the space was not getting paid. The owner was going to seize the contents and auction it off for compensation. Not knowing what to do, the family asked Shackey for help, to go get the gear and look after it so it would not get commandeered. Shack swore he would. When Kevin was released from jail, Shack told him: "Just take care of yourself, don't worry about it. The gear's safe at my uncle's storage unit."

Kevin wanted to – had to – believe. Even though he knew Shack lied constantly, he lived in delusion that this time would be different – time and time again. Kevin lied constantly, too. Looking in the mirror can be so uncomfortable. But, the drums stood for something - this *was* who he was, right? Rock band guy. "Drummer from beyond," the label one loyal fanatic had bestowed upon him. How he loved those fans loving him.

An Inside Job

Everything was falling into place nicely for the move back home. Alisa was going to be here in just a couple days. They were getting closer by talking so much on the phone, making each other laugh when they wanted to cry, and sharing secrets about their lives. Something was being sought from her that there was no way she could provide. Through pure habit and old ways of being, Kevin was looking for his salvation in her, from her - just as he had always done. Perhaps she sought the same from him. There is no way she or anyone else could provide or be the True Power it would take to solve his core problem. It was more delusion, even if around progress in other ways. How difficult it is to see one's own delusion.

There was something Kevin did not fully realize about his newfound Higher Power. Over these last few staggering months he had been *experiencing* it. This power had always been there, *inside of him*. He continued to vacillate between handing everything over to this omnipotent wisdom, and continuing in a learned, limited, programmed, fixed delusional system of thought. Hidden layers of disdain covering a beautiful core; was their removal possible? It was much more than recovery. Perhaps *Uncovery* was a more apt way of naming the expansive process.

***

Alisa arrived, looking hotter than *ever*. Behaving like teenage lovers that hadn't done it yet, they felt like high rollers in this penthouse apartment of sorts, even though all his stuff added together was worth next to nothing. If freedom really is just nothing left to lose then he was close to being free.

At least there's still that room full of band gear.

But, the air mattress and thrift store apparatus did not matter to Alisa - she had been living in an agonizing material abundance in a stale relationship, the topic of many of their late night conversations. No, she did not mind; she was looking for something else. How she loved that he was a rock star. What a story. They both loved the whole adventure. Just two more weeks and he would be finished here, then it was home to the city lights and glamour – or drama, however you look at it.

They drove around the surrounding areas, checking out some sights and mostly, checking out each other. They had a great time, talking and laughing and playing, and of course sleeping together way too soon. It felt almost like a business deal, with fringe benefits, each of them seeking salvation in the other; an order too tall, perhaps, to be filled with any lasting success. But this did not matter from the viewpoint of rationalization. Old operating procedure was all he knew, all he had ever known. At the honeymoon stage it was all perfect, once again.

She would stay only a few days on this trip and then return home, which was some 15 miles south of Seattle. He would wrap it up in Yakima. They were enamored with each other, and so, devised a plan. They would live together west of the mountains, and began looking for a place right away. On her laptop, they looked at houses to buy; she said she had plenty of money. They looked in different areas between where each of them called home, about a 60 mile radius. They talked about how they would start some business, of all the possibilities that lay in store.

As they brainstormed, a conflict began brewing underneath the excitement, a familiar one. Only this time, Kevin had a tool for dealing with conflict: Handing it over, just as he had done out of pure desperation those first tender days at The Sanctuary. Until now, handing it over was done by going to the trail and just being, mindfulness of the river and the trees and the birds and the summer air, meditating upon it all - simple prayers, in addition to the meetings and the daily readings. But right now, it did not seem he could just leave her and go there. A feeling of suffocation began to loom, which he did his best to pretend was not there - instead of *listening*.

The crème leather seat in Alisa's pearl-white SUV was a joy to sink into on the trip back to Seattle. Viewing possible places to live topped the agenda. She hated the areas close to his home, some 15 miles north of Seattle, and loved the ones close to hers, way south. For him, the exact opposite. It was quite a drive from the area she wanted to live to where the commitments to the courts and the band were, back in Snohomish County. And, traffic in a major city can be daunting. But, wanting her happy, he made the sacrifice. They would move where she wanted. Besides, he had no money and was leaving the restaurant job, so she would be the money for now; she would pay the way. Moving where Alisa wanted was the least he could do.

On the day she left they felt they could not live without each other, which was good - because now they weren't going to. They were in love. Something felt strange and weird and rickety nonetheless.

"I'll see you soon, can't wait to be together." Kevin's puppy dog eyes matched the sappy tone.

"Ohhh, me too," Alisa responded, throwing her arms around him in a giant hug.

Waving as she drove away down Chestnut, he looked to the last of the commitments here in town and towards the new life. Future tripping commenced. How was this ever going to work? Scared, he decided to do what they taught at The Sanctuary and at meetings:

Do what is in front of you, and leave the rest to God

Over the next couple weeks, after-care was completed and with perfect attendance. The last days at work were finished (with proper notice, even), and the appropriate goodbyes made. He talked to Alisa every night, and as the day of departure neared they became more and more giddy.

With the last paycheck, there was just enough money to pay palace rent as agreed, six hundred dollars. But then he'd be nearly broke.

I could just leave and not pay it, what can they do? Conflicting thoughts careened around like monkeys playing croquet in clown suits. They had been asking; they needed the money. He needed the money, and struggled with whether to pay it or leave them high and dry. Back and forth it went. Six hundred was a good chunk of change … he decided to keep it.

But, at the river, something beyond what would have always taken the money and ran was present. It was the same voice that had been gently guiding:

There is always plenty ~ Honor your word ~ You are safe

And so, he sent the money, acting as if the intention of stiffing them never even occurred - barely finding the courage to honor the agreement. It took great discipline to obtain a cashier's check, locate an envelope, affix a stamp to it, and actually send it off. The whole situation was another gift, helping transform one more old way of thinking and being. Listening to this guidance would reverberate in ways as yet unfathomable, far more valuable than hoarding any money or possession.

True abundance and prosperity is omnipresent ~ realizing it is but a choice

***

Alisa's sweet ride rolled down old Chestnut and down into the driveway. They stuffed everything into their two vehicles and hit the road. She had broken it off with the boyfriend. Now they were free, albeit without a place to stay. Good thing Mom and Dad were on vacation for a few weeks. They could stay there and look for their new, perfect home.

Here it was again: New woman, new place, new location, almost no possessions. He could not (or would not) fully realize this was moving backwards, repeating time-worn patterns and still again, old ways of being that only served some programmed purpose. Yet, something changed in these past invaluable months. It was the longest he had been sober and actually *experienced* happiness, peace, and serenity.

So they left the place, river trail and all. The once-sanctuary drifted away in the rearview mirror.

~ 154 ~

~ Chapter 13 ~

Short Stay

The honeymoon phase is always intoxicating. What a perfect diversion for the record player needle to get stuck in the same old groove. Living with Alisa and Lance at Mom and Dad's (or Grandma and Grandpa's, depending) wasn't so bad, watching movies and making meals, just driving around. Alisa knew JP from treatment as well, and making fun of him was always good for killing time. JP had hit on her, too, especially when he found out about her and Kevin.

They looked at some nice properties, but since Alisa's break-up was much like a divorce, any ability she had to buy a place right away was on hold. Something about entanglement issues with ownership of the business. Kevin certainly had no money. There wasn't much time to find a place.

Alisa had many acquaintances in Auburn. One of them was another ex-boyfriend. Shaun had rental properties, one that was affordable and available - a mobile home on a large piece of cleared, flat land near a busy street. Shaun also had several commercial pieces, one of them being a good sized shop; a huge step down from the last one, but options were limited, to say the least, and she was willing to pay - just like Mom always had. Alisa got enough money from the bank for both the house and the shop, and gave it to Kevin. He went and met cynical Shaun. *Awkward.* After a short and somewhat strained conversation, he handed over the three grand cash and got the keys for both places.

The loud, industrial park was depressing. He stood inside the vacuous shop. *I have no desire to work here.* The emptiness came like falling into a bottomless tomb. The massive void laughed out loud, echoed through the hole in his soul, threatened to steal him again into the great darkness. He wished he could just go to the river trail. Instead, he brought his tools into the lonely shop, sick, and left right away.

Alisa had retrieved all her furniture and knick-knacks from her old place. She had nice furniture and drapes and trinkets, and it helped turn the trailer into a cozy little home. They worked together to make the place livable, which helped with the creeping feelings of depression. It was decent and comfortable, for a couple weeks. Just like with Terra. But then, something began to change, once again: The all-too-familiar slipping of the once-great manic idea. Honeymoon's kiss was wearing off. Contrivances about each other that had been "overlooked" were beginning to glare. Or maybe it was something else. Either way, the inevitable disconnect began to occur, just as it had every other time.

Kevin could not get motivated to work. He hated this reality of everything feeling not worthwhile. It was a reminder of every other desperate time, in yet another bleak place - again! It came on like a giant mudslide. How he hated this. Gut sinking and trapped again, that feeling that had been there every day of his life, especially in that cavernous shop back home. But was it anything to do with the shop? He remembered too well how that culminated - locked in the attic with as much drugs and booze as possible, trying to stop the hurting, fill the void, and just be OK. It never was OK, and here it was *again*. His mind raced.

Have to get out of here! I'll never make it. Who did I think I was fooling? I have no way to make this work. She wants things from me I am not able to give, be, provide. Damn it! Part of me just wants to die. There must be some other way. But I cannot do this alone ...

What had worked so well until now was gone – or seemed to be. No more treatment center, no more river and trail, could not seem to find any meetings here, did not know the streets or places. It was too soon for this. He had been looking to Alisa and this move to be his savior, falling back into old, co-dependent ways. He wanted to pray, but there was always someone home, and he did not want to look stupid. And the shop – well, he just hated everything about that.

Can't breathe! He wanted to go back to the solutions he had always known, to kill the pain the way he always had, and his mind volleyed thinking of who he could call to get some drugs; maybe he could go get a drink or ten. No, then she would probably throw him out, and there was no place left to go.

What can I do? Have to *do* something. He was in agony, but couldn't tell her about it. Had to look good, had to have it all together – but it was not together, not at all.

Kevin wanted to talk to someone, but felt there was no one. His family probably would not listen; he had used them up with empty promises.

What had been suggested at treatment and at meetings did not even come up on the radar. The nasty little monkeys prodded:

Still *a fraud. Loser. Told you, told you, told you. You will never make it.*

Band practice was a long drive, longer depending on traffic, and several times a week. Sometimes the trip could be done in 40 minutes but it was easily double that at times. Closer to home did feel better. How he longed for the peaceful places: The trails with trees and rivers, a lake, ducks and birds. So many plants of all shapes and sizes seemed to talk to him there. Something about nature brought great peace, if only for the moment. Being around people at the local coffee shops and writing always helped. He did not realize writing was nearly the only way he was praying now, and he was barely writing. Such places must be everywhere, but he couldn't seem to *find* them here. Stinking thinking is an insidious infiltrator. It creeps in and takes over, fast-growing ivy slithering up his brick walls.

And without using daily the spiritual tools that had worked so well, those ubiquitous weathered walls were shutting off the air supply. Sporadic surrender was proving not to be enough. Devious and encapsulating old patterns began to move in for the kill.

Lost and alone, every day and night trying to be OK for Alisa, though both of them knew that this racket was falling to pieces - and fast, slipping, fast.

As added unrest, Alisa was beginning to communicate with her ex again. Steve wanted her back, and was mad as a hornet about the whole thing. He and Alisa had that business together, a home, and a history. The truth was, Kevin felt bad about the entire mess. Everyone was just trying to belong, fit in – figure "it" out. He thought about how Steve must feel; surely there had been unfinished business between him and Alisa. Everyone seemed lost. Tension was building like a giant Tesla experiment.

"You don't even touch me anymore," Alisa screeched. It was true, he didn't. "You just play that damn video game all the time!" He did, sometimes to the point of drooling, if it went too long.

"I thought we were going to get to work? Grow a business!" He had not seen this side of her, she was fuming.

"Yeah, I … Look, Alisa. I'm sorry, this … this was a mistake, I think."

"Ya' *think?*

"What about all we talked about doing? I'm so disappointed!" Both her fists were on her hips and her hair might have been on fire. It had been days since he'd even kissed her.

"I don't know what to say. Something is wrong with me, I can't … I just cannot do this. I'm an alcoholic. A drug addict. I need to get back to what was working, somehow … if I even can now. Please forgive me."

"Oh, yeah, I forgive you. So you just gonna leave? Fine. See ya'." And with that she stormed out of the mobile, slamming the thin metal, cardboard-core door, which in turn reverberated through the feeble shell of the house-on-wheels altogether. At least it didn't tip over. He set the remote down and began gathering his meager belongings.

Almost done packing up the Explorer *again*, the scene turned ugly when Steve showed up. He was angry, and wanted to wreck this home wrecker. The over-sized truck skidded to a halt. Out hopped six-feet-five inches and 312 pounds of palpable anger. Alisa must have told him what was up. Kevin's face flushed and he swallowed hard.

Scared to the core, he prepared to fight for his life. He was trained; Dad had been a life-long teacher of martial arts and taught him some stuff. He knew how to fight. Only, he never used this knowledge, for he always avoided conflict, and never wanted to cause anyone any harm – but this guy was huge! And *very* pissed off – no, he was going to have to fight, if he wanted to stay living. Alisa pulled up with a small entourage in her SUV. *Great.*

"I'm a lover, not a fighter," Kevin often said, but today it looked like being a lover would make him a fighter. Steve approached and verbally assaulted him, both their blood and adrenalin coursing, fight or flight in high gear, either an option about to be exercised at any moment. Super-sized Steve, on the verge of attack, screamed at his rival all the damage he had caused along with the confusion and chaos, and then shared his own credentials with regard to being a certified A-1 ass-kicking machine.

Kevin tried to remain calm. "I'm sorry, really. I'm leaving. We don't have to do this. I made a mistake."

The man did not back down. "Fuck you, you piece of shit! I will wreck you! Hitting on someone's *mom* at treatment? Who *does* that? Loser drug addict!" Steve continued to demean Kevin every way he could, spittle flying, on the verge of attack, barrel-chested and fists clenched.

Spitting nails and chipping teeth, the ginormous man continued: "Get your stuff and get the *hell* out of town, and if you ever *breathe* so much as a word toward Alisa again I will hunt you down like an animal and skin you alive, you worthless piece of trash!" This sounded more than fair, considering the alternative.

"I'm so sorry. I will go. I am sorry if I caused you trouble and for getting involved where I shouldn't have. I didn't mean to mess up your relationship … I'm just so screwed up right now." Kevin groveled and shot a look into Steve's enraged eyes. He meant it, from the heart. "I *am* sorry."

Somehow, through the giant's angry words, Kevin heard something else, beyond the rage. Suddenly, the listening shifted, and his desire for an outcome did, too. In an instant, going from wanting only to save his own ass to actually hearing *something* … underneath or in-between the words being hurled, through what was being spoken. This man was in great pain; he had been hurt too, and Kevin could sense it, *feel* it. And it caused him to do something of which he did not know he was capable:

He truly apologized. He told Steve what he believed to be his own part in it, what he had done and how the brief relationship with Alisa had occurred. He shared with this man some of his own pain (quickly, being aware this guy wanted to kill him and was in attack mode) and how he had desperately reached out for something in his own despair, and that he was now aware that it was wrong. Immediately, the tension lessened, though it did not dissipate. Kevin confessed how he was lost and had not a clue what to do with his life, and did it in front of the crowd that had now formed, giving up looking-good, owning his *true* feelings. He went from trying only to save his ass to being real, and it changed the situation.

Steve responded to the honesty only by not following through with mauling him. There could have been quite a different outcome. Another communication had occurred in some other place, beyond the words and anger and bodies and seeming separateness.

Steve finally left after slamming the door of his pick-up in disgust, in spite of the moment of connection, and then spinning wheels and tossing gravel all the way out the driveway. The crowd dispersed, including Alisa. Kevin finished loading up the Explorer, solo. He took anything electronic, even if it had been Alisa's (living in a lack mentality, you need what you think you need) and left that place, tail between his legs and adding at least one more stone to the old backpack.

One last stop at the shop for his tools, and there was Alisa's once-ex-now-boyfriend-again. Only now, there were no witnesses, just the two of them, one on one. Not knowing if there was going to be a brawl or not, nerves already shot and just wanting it to *stop*, Kevin realized yet another problem: No money for gas, and it was a long way home. The Sasquatch confronted him again inside the shop, this time a little less intimidating but still very angry. Kevin apologized, again. The short time in the group sessions over the last few months had taught him how to interact with others, and he practiced it here. For just a moment, a kind of peace was present, and then it was gone.

"I don't have any gas money, not anything." Kevin said, sheepishly. The giant man was shocked at the audacity. *"You screw my girlfriend and now you want 20 bucks for gas?* No! Get the *fuck* out of here."

On the road again, onto another fairly unwelcome adventure, and this time it was not looking so good. No job, no money, no place to go this time, and no woman. Looking down at the dash, the gas gauge dangled on "E." It was a long drive ahead. He pulled over after a safe distance away from Conan the Barbarian, dug around on the floor, between the seats, in every nook and cranny in the vehicle and scraped up any change that was there: Four dollars and eighty-eight cents. Not much, but it would have to do. He put it in the tank, and hit the highway.

~ Chapter 14 ~

Back Home Again

The only place to go was the band house. Shack and Jimmy lived there along with a couple other guys. The house was just five miles north of the old shop, and a damnable three miles northeast was that dilapidated old drug house. Kevin ignored the calculation. Practice was here anyway, which meant less driving. They'd be rich and famous soon, and it would all be better. A yawning monkey between naps dropped a lone turd in response. *You'll never make it.*

He practiced on Jimmy's old drums, but longed for the birch beauties. Shack kept telling him that the gear was all safe at the mysterious uncle's storage unit in some obscure location, far away:

"Where I moved it while you were in jail," Shack explained, shifting the blame around, mixing it up a bit. "I had to do something to keep it safe, but my uncle is gone right now. We can't get to it."

Funny, he never mentioned any Uncle before the gear incident – *oh, well.* It felt devious, like most of what Shack said, but Kevin accepted the story regardless, maintaining faith (or perhaps delusion) that somehow he would see that stuff again. Settling as best he could on the old couch just a few feet from the drum set and guitar amps … ah yes, the rock band days, alive again. It smelled like stale beer, cigarette smoke wafted in through the windows, booze permeated the carpet and couch, and there were people coming and going at all hours.

The next morning, he found a little java joint just down the street and immediately began writing, voraciously, getting all the madness that was bouncing around down on paper. It relieved the pressure, somehow, adjusting the thinking just enough to stay tenuously sane. But it was not enough. There was an essential quality missing, what had been found during treatment and the time spent living sober in Yakima. Perhaps it was what he was seeking now, reuniting with the path that he'd strayed from. What had been learned, practiced and experienced during those precious months, the closeness to others through fellowship, the daily rituals. These things began to call, or maybe he began to listen, to *remember* – but still, the monkeys were gaining ground, coming from all angles.

Next stop was the courthouse. He found the prosecuting attorney who had given permission a few months ago for the possession charges to be transferred.

"Well, some things … uhhhm, changed," Kevin explained. "I'd like to do the program here."

"You'll have to explain to the Judge why you're changing it up again and see if he'll let you in." They issued a court date, just a few days away.

A gorgeous fall Wednesday. The courtroom full with people sat before a pleasant but stern Judge Masterson. Kevin was called up and explained the situation, again. The man in the black robe conferred with two others seated in front of him for a few moments.

"You do qualify for the program here. You'll need to choose a treatment center and set up an intake interview," Judge said. Not knowing how to even begin to pick one, Kevin chose the one with the best sounding name and headed straight there.

"Have a seat," the lady with brown feathered-hair sitting at the front counter said. She could not have weighed more than 108 pounds, soaking wet. "You can do the intake right now."

This time, he'd tell the absolute truth. It was much easier than the last time where the tears almost ran dry. He was getting better at this honesty thing. It was far less painful the second time, and with some few months "sober" now.

An intriguing man with wire-rimmed rectangular glasses that made his brown eyes huge sat at a keyboard in a back-room cubicle to input the intake information. His fingers were interlaced and rested perfectly on top of his round belly while he looked on, inquisitively, as Kevin took a seat next to him.

"My name is Peter, welcome." He was kind and carefree, almost aloof.

"Please … have a seat. This process shall be a breeze," Peter said with a distinguishably deep, penetrating voice. Maybe he was Greek, with his bronze skin and dark hair. An old soul for sure, and … familiar. Peter's presence was comforting. An inviting and contented quality emanated from him. Kevin pegged him for about 48. Peter was quite affable, and took the information without bias, in a kind, easy way. Next was an appointment with the UA (Urinalysis) department, which Kevin would get to know all too well over the next year. And, just like that, he was in intensive outpatient treatment.

***

This program entailed a rigorous protocol, but graduating meant the felony would be dropped. There would be three phases: Intensive outpatient (IOP), Relapse Awareness, and MRT (Moral Reconation Therapy). What even was the last one?

A signed slip with at least three meetings per week and calling the "color line" every day (if his color came up, a UA by noon) was mandatory throughout all phases. So was being at court every Friday.

Consequences like jail time and community service were awarded for slip-ups: Having a dirty (using) or diluted (guzzling massive water) UA, breaking *any* laws, missing classes, loitering in the program, forging slips, and various other potential stumbling blocks that fell out of alignment with the protocol. It meant walking a thin line for at least one year of his life.

Before graduating it was required to possess one's driver's license, GED, and a job or in school. For addicts and the like, this can be quite an order. Most were in precarious situations and many faced some pretty heavy charges. The deal was, if it was a drug/alcohol related charge - theft to get drugs or money for drugs, forgeries for the same purpose, possession, driving impaired, under the influence and the like - they would dismiss the charges upon successful completion of the program. They had a high success rate for helping people get their lives straightened out and keeping it up after graduation. Usually, drug dealers were not offered the program. If one was caught with more than that considered for personal use - aka dealing - you were considered a dealer. The night of the arrest, Kevin possessed just the perfect amount for being allowed to enter the program. Not too much, not too little … as if it were meant to be.

On the first Friday in court, each participant was called up. Judge Masterson pulled their file and enquired. An over-all sort of rooting for each other was present. There was a common bond. For many it was probably the earliest learning of community skills. It was for Kevin.

It was sure to be quite a ride – take the felony and do ten days would be way easier. It would require diligence in order to go the distance. Kevin was nearly grateful to be back in treatment again, back where it was safe, where they were speaking this new language he had received a taste of on the other side of the mountains.

Kevin had to re-apply for state assistance, and was assigned a case worker.

"Tell me about your issues," the woman asked. Apparently, issues got you benefits. He needed them, and bad: Three hundred and thirty nine bucks a month, state health insurance, and food allowance.

"Well, I'm an alcoholic *and* drug addict. Double winner, right?" She didn't even flinch, except for a nod in agreement.

"Unfortunately, that's not enough." It had worked in Yakima, but now, something was different.

"Oh. Well what about my ADD, depression and anxiety?" It felt spongy to speak it, even though he had suffered from the symptoms of each of them throughout his life. But now it was changing, these conditions had been less severe during the months in Yakima. Moving to that damned place in Auburn though, the feelings of depression came over him like fog so thick you could open your mouth and chew on it. He felt he could not make it without some financial support. Surely, Mom had cut the cord by now. Even if she hadn't, Kevin longed to stand on his own two feet and feel Earth for himself.

There was also that rage; he had always suffered from anger in the extreme, like some giant pressure-relief valve purging too often.

But it was so severe and embarrassing that he did not tell the case worker about it, only saying "sometimes I get frustrated" which had the same smell as "sometimes it rains here" when talking about Seattle in the wetter seasons. It can be sunny, warm and clear, and within seconds - cold, dark and pouring. It can rain grey for weeks at certain times. The anger always came out of nowhere, dumped on everyone around, and after the storm of enraged outbursts, a change again - back to a (manically) happy person, the sun coming out. Always it came again, like some rogue wave.

Usually the anger was superficially directed at someone, and Marie had gotten the brunt of it. Many drunken nights would turn into severe arguments and screaming fighting, telling her how worthless she was, how she would never be anything, how fat and ugly she was, on and on, hurling handfuls of verbal daggers. But it was only projection, berating her with everything *he thought of himself.*

Sometimes, it got violent. There were even times throughout their relationship they had been in straight-up fist fights. Whether it was verbal, physical, or emotional, however the sickness manifested, it was always about "winning" control. The booze and other drugs were accelerant poured on this fire of rage. When it all burned off and the smoke cleared, when they came-to, shards of all sorts dominating the space around them, he would repent through a disgusting hangover, groveling, sometimes for days, agonizing throughout the hours, trying to figure out how to win this forgiveness.

She always gave him more chances but he only lived inside a tormented hell, dragging her along, constantly trying to figure out how to tweak and manipulate external circumstances to appease the screaming monkeys.

Each instance only pointed to a more ancient truth that he refused to accept:

True control comes from no control at all

This was all culminating in dangerous habits, such as procuring high-potency prescription drugs on the black market. Life went downhill fast. The year before the death-trip to Montana, he had found liquid painkillers. They come in that form for people who are so ill that they cannot swallow a pill. Three to four hundred bucks for just one container. Before long, the empty little brownish-bottles with the eye-dropper lids began to collect, here and there. Marie's dad had been on his deathbed on similar stuff, which Kevin stole at every opportunity; there was so much of it around. When Marie finally found out, it broke her heart - but Kevin could not care. All these desperate attempts of control made him feel like such a coward. How much pain could he possibly be in, given the natural gift of a healthy body and an intelligent mind?

What was the true origin of this pain?

At any rate, he would take the powerful drugs and then guzzle massive quantities of vodka or *any* other booze available. Such cocktails were extremely potent, the first several minutes of the buzz producing a blissful euphoria – but then it became elusive, and fleeting. He would then take more and more to try and capture that first buzz. "Three drops" from the eyedropper turned into five squirts, five drinks into fifteen. This mixing resulted in blackout outbursts, often enraged, which began to occur in public, berating Marie before shocked crowds. When he would finally pass out she was relieved, and when he came to, the hangovers were unbelievably grotesque and physically excruciating. The emotional emptiness was a bottomless pit of despair. The only cure that ever worked - *more*. And more never was enough.

Kevin pushed the recollections away. *Go away.* He needed the assistance, help, support. "I have trouble staying focused. My moods are way up or way down. Sometimes I'm happy, but often sad and empty." He realized he was trying to sound convincing, for his bare feet had walked upon the soil of the pathway of liberation.

"Well, if that's the case – you may qualify, but you'll need to undergo an evaluation with a psychiatrist," she told him.

He went to the appointment with the lady-professional and shared the watered down truth, which apparently sufficed. He was grateful for the benefits.

Just like that. A place to stay, spending money, funds for food, and in the safety of a treatment program. The band was rocking. Life was looking pretty good.

~ Chapter 15 ~

The New Walk

"The weather sucks around here this time of year!" The skinny girl in the next chair was attempting to fire up a conversation. They both waited to give a UA at the treatment facility, EMI. Kevin was light today, sober, and in a safe place. It was a relief to be out of that miserable situation with Alisa, free of the confusion with Terra, and single for once. But, what was the common denominator in these short-lived affairs? The thoughts lingered, only for a flash.

"I like the rain and fog. Halloween is coming, my favorite time of year ... I just have the feeling something awesome is going to happen," he answered.

"And it's only going to get worse ... umm, like what," she asked, half hearing what he said only not addressing it until she finished her thought and spoke it.

Kevin did like the Pacific Northwest, the changing seasons, right smack in the convergence zone. Various contrasting conditions came from all sides and commingled, creating weather that could be positively schizophrenic: Ripping winds, rainbows and hailstorms, bright sunshine of blue skies and dark clouds pouring rain, all at once. He was similar, like dark battling the light. Perhaps the weather and his moods were intrinsically connected.

There was the feeling something quite auspicious was going to happen, and it danced tangibly in the air as if one could reach out and grab it. Some of the very first layers of the proverbial onion had been peeled away; there was a lighter load, and a better way of life was emerging.

"Not sure. Like a feeling of impending good coming," as opposed to impending doom, he thought, but did not say so.

"You mean not impending *doom*?" she said for him. They both laughed, and then were distracted by the motley crew around them. Apparently, this is where the crazies came. And he was among them.

A plump woman with a young face and cute curls shuffled a couple papers around from behind the counter as she called Kevin's name. She had taken three phone calls in three minutes and it was ringing again – she answered the call as her chubby, overworked hand pointed him towards a small room with three EMI staff packed in there like sardines in a tin can. Inside, one woman asked him to sign in, and then blow into a machine behind him. A desk just inside the door and two on the other side of the room made it cluttered, but the people were kind and pleasant.

"Hi. I'm Kevin," he smiled, picking up a straw out of a box to send breath into the contraption.

"Hello. I'm Suzy and this is Darleen," the woman replied, looking on through round, silver glasses, pointing to a red-haired woman with a congenial smile.

In this moment was a choice available about what he would make this whole thing mean: Were they out to get him, to make him perform functions he did not *want* to do, to be in *his* way? And not just the ones in the UA department, but the whole place - the ones that worked the phones and directed traffic, the drug court team and the counselors, the judges. Even the other patients, the other crazies; would he let them help, or would he resist and fight it all? A thought came, another flash: *Maybe I'm in their way.*

It was much different from that first day of the rest of his life just months ago. He was not nearly as toxic and not so desperately lost as he had been. Much had happened for sure. There had been peace and serenity, the longest he could recall – *ever*. Then it hit:

Every day is the first day of the rest of our lives.

Instantly, Kevin remembered another teaching:

Who you are is not who you have been, it is who you choose to be right now

The two notions were nearly interchangeable. In this moment, he decided to cooperate, chose to *be* happy and just do what was suggested. He was going to *allow* the process, again – whatever was asked. It felt like skydiving.

They were all very pleasant - when he was. After a successful breathalyzer, he met the last of the three. Rick would be supervising his "donation process" and grabbed a cup and a bag. Off into the bathroom they went. Mirrors at all angles were placed so the endeavor would fall under perfect scrutiny. The man placed himself in position so that there was little chance of Kevin giving anything but an authentic, fresh, 100% original on-the-spot product. He had to go, anyway, and provided a stellar sample. In the obviously unnatural and sterile environment the two shared at this moment, small talk would have been clumsy. He resisted the sudden urge to pass gas and grinned instead. As the session concluded and the awkwardness subsided outside the bathroom, he thanked the man and had a moment of compassion for him and the job he did, all day long.

On the way out and into the rain, he tossed a "see you later" to the girl who had not moved from her seat.

"Bye," was all she replied.

Nice girl … he had enjoyed the exchange with her. He could feel abundant good coming, the same way fall feels coming into late summer. There was another nuance, too. Having this feeling was so much better than trying to connive and get loaded and avoid or manipulate UA's, or to control some situation or someone else, to worry about what Marie was doing, or Alisa, or Terra. There were so many others, too. So many failed relationships, women he had blindly used for his own selfish satisfactions and greedy plastic needs. Yes, there was work to do, lots of it. The willingness came more easily. For now, he found himself happy, and it just plain felt good.

It had been weeks since any meetings. Missing them, he flipped open an A.A. schedule and found one at noon, got in the car and drove straight there. It was in a large room, busy and chaotic, with probably 75 chairs around multi-shaped tables. A four burner coffee maker sat off to one side with two steaming full carafes next to a tray of pastries. *Score.* He found a seat and plunked down. As the meeting began, the attention in the room shifted, almost everyone coming together, focusing. He listened intently to each word of the readings, and there were several. Same when the sharing began. Evident was that many people were dealing with issues similar to his. The meeting was much like the ones east of the mountains. After, he stuck around and chatted, just as before. Liking it quite a bit, he decided to come back again the following day. There was a noon meeting here each day, with a Sunday breakfast meeting at 10:00 a.m.

Aha. I can get back on the right track now. This place is my new hang out.

***

Two weeks away was a party at the band house. Cold River was to play, unleash the songs they had been polishing. Kevin was both thrilled to play again in front of people and nervous about all the partying that would

~ 169 ~

inevitably be happening. He had tools, though; would he use them? New ways of living, visible even now on the horizon, had been brought into the realm of possibility. The part he had not figured out was how to live it here, back in this situation and around the old ways. But, it had been lived those few priceless months. He was determined to pick up the tools again and use them for this event.

So he went to the noon meetings and talked about this fear, listened when others shared, and always seemed to hear just what was needed, which many times came with a suggested action. Often the one sharing did not even realize they were divulging possible solutions for someone else, but something *in Kevin* imbibed it, something beyond conscious thought.

My spirit sees your spirit

Choice: Allow the suggestions to become new actions, or do what he had always done and listen to old, stale thinking.

There is a word for what Kevin needed: Humility.

He was willing, but it did not come easily. After all, the work done thus far had shown what always being right had produced, how deceptive it had been, especially to the one peddling it, and how it had affected him and so many around him; how it *caused* that life of hell. He had been locked in a self-made prison of screaming judgments, perceptions, deceptions and limitations – but now there was a key for the icy-cold door, and it was within reach.

But what about looking good and being cool? That was all an act, anyway - a self-deceptive, thin, lonely act. Being so fake this way caused self-loathing, and it made him thirsty. This precious ego had two sharp edges to it. On one hand it told him just how cool he was, how superior, how much "better than" he was. And then, when it seemed to be needed most, the self-assured cockiness and all that went with it, that very same ego screamed at him: *You're no good, you never were - you can't do it. You're a worthless piece of crap. You are unlovable and not wanted, ugly, gross, and stupid.*

Kevin stood once more at a fork in the road. One way taunted. It was familiar and time tested, albeit a treacherous and dark jungle of screaming monkeys. The other was gentle, but unknown and unfamiliar - with the exception of those few sweet months where he understood what they meant when they talked about "walking in the Sunlight of the Spirit," for he had *lived* it. No one could choose for him. What would it be? Even though it seems like an easy choice, there are many reasons a person goes back to a life that is no good. Perfectly logical reasons are manufactured for not continuing to move forward with awkward undertakings such as prayer and meditation, asking for help and accepting it, trusting, continuing with step work, completing suggested processes, and practicing forgiveness.

If he were to realize lasting change, he would have to let go of old logical reasoning.

Out of no way and out of nothing, a way will be made

A Fresh Routine and an Old Friend

The party was hyped out to the max. It had all that was expected. Kevin and the guys spent all day building the stage, right off the back of the house in the large backyard. Several kegs already stood at attention on the concrete patio. Cold River would play the prime third slot, as it was their party. Crazy Jane and Cypher warmed up the crowd. There were stacks of speakers and piles of partiers. Someone concocted a less-than-brilliant idea to hang a motorcycle from a nearby tree and sell sledgehammer blows for a buck each. A bat was also offered at no additional charge. The more booze they drank, the cooler that became.

The band had a great set. How Kevin loved pounding the drums in tribal rhythms and sharing in music he helped bring to life. This had its own kind of seduction. It sure was different sober. He liked it this way; it allowed a more innate sensitivity to be found. Kevin made it through the night without drinking.

In the morning, partiers were crashed out all around him, empty beer and booze bottles spilled about. Staleness permeated the air. Someone hurled off the back porch. It was disgusting to listen to, as he shot up and awake off the gross couch. It was all too familiar - this is how all the past years had been, party after party. He was sick of it. Something else in him, now, longed to be nourished, to be set free from the chains that had always bound and constricted to find him waking up just like this. The only difference this morning, he was sober. It didn't fit like this, not anymore. He tried to ignore the nagging feeling: *Something has changed.*

Take the booze out of the equation and suddenly it doesn't make sense … this whole sobriety thing was cultivating a fresher vision, bringing a better world into focus. Something was guiding him toward another way, and it was awkward and wonderful at the same time it was frightening. There were the screaming monkeys begging for another drink and then there was that still, soft voice, gentle and nurturing.

Stay the Course

He felt out of place in the band house. He did not belong here. Crashing on the couch was getting old. A propitious interjection came by way of an odd little fellow who came by often to hang at the band house. "I have a room for rent, if you guys know anyone looking." Maybe Kevin could move there.

"Could I pay you in a couple weeks?"

"Sure," Evan said. He sounded like a nice guy.

The room was decent and only two hundred bucks a month, in a quiet home on a large secluded piece of property and close to everything. "It's a converted garage," Evan said upon entering. "You can move in right away."

The placid white walls felt sterile, but it had a good heater and was surrounded by cedars and pines and plants of all kinds. He wouldn't be here much, just a place to crash for a bit. It was perfect.

"I'll take it."

***

Providing the greatest peace and freedom were the meetings, group sessions, and being with others that were working to change their lives. Nature and being of the Heart was so nourishing. The work was toward a spiritual life, a looking inward for Truth. It was not religious, dogmatic or oppressive. This was about finding one's own Spirit, through direct, purposeful inquiry. A treasure was here, deep within, so favorable and intriguing that the old life paled in comparison. It felt like an eternal solution.

But still: *You are not good enough. Changing is too hard. Just give it up. You know what works to bring relief - to hell with this other crap. This time will be different, you'll see. You can handle it now. C'mon. C'mon!* Damn screaming monkeys.

Around the band house and parties and practice, there was too much pull backwards and down. Something was out of alignment in this old place. Expecting circumstances to change by exerting more self-will held little promise of real change. This was always the case, and the results were all-too obvious. He was white-knuckling it again, trying to force something to work, and with the stark contrast, was in a state of confusion. There did not seem to be a place to pray and meditate in peace with the river and birds and trees, like before. That sanctuary - he longed for it now.

One day was shared the story of two wolves fighting inside of a person. Which one wins? The one you feed more, it had been said. That story rang bells. Working on honestly looking at himself (more accurately, who he thought he was) and getting into action toward the more spiritual life, he was nourished from the inside out. Trying to make it all work in that party-life atmosphere felt like going against something – there *was* fighting inside, and this was only one example. But he also loved playing the drums and the music … maybe he needed to feed both the wolves so they each were happy and stopped fighting?

There was much to learn. For now, it caused him to *question everything*, his actions, where he was choosing to place his feet. In this was the new awareness growing. Here, no one was doing anything *to* him, or forcing. Nope, it was his choice. Maybe this was free will.

***

"Dude, we're sounding great. Cold River is winning this showcase, be sure of that," Jimmy exclaimed after a ripping run through of the set.

"Yeah, band's sounding awesome," Shack chimed.

"Yep, we're coming right along, vocals are sounding killer. I'm gonna take off, see you guys." Kevin wanted to go write.

The groove of calling the color line each day, going in several times a week to give a UA and engaging the group sessions were falling into a copacetic rhythm. The two often coincided and he liked the accountability, the intimacy of communing. Inpatient treatment had been a great introduction to this way of living, but was not nearly enough for lasting change; being accountable felt necessary now. Resisting, this treatment plan would surely be difficult and intrusive. Conversely: Being willing, letting people in and sharing honestly brought relief and ease. Especially with a UA - it felt good not to worry about failing the test, *to be sober.*

He made the conscious choice to *see* these people, and not just the counselors, but each of them - from the overworked woman that answered the phone to the quirky fellow that did the original intake interview to each person at the meetings and even the judges. Looking at it this way, his own reflection was changing. Today, he sat and wrote about all of it.

As you see others, so will you see yourself

Still, he had not been able to get back to the daily rituals as in those first precious months. The results were missing, and he was missing them. There was too much diversion right now, and so the mandatory nature of the drug court requirements along with a *personal choice* to attend as many meetings as possible kept a forward momentum on the path. One particular noon meeting someone suggested fell right into place after Group. Several members already went there. It was just down the street, fondly called "The Nooner." He began attending regularly. The big silver coffee pot sat on a long, narrow table with tasty pastries.

At this meeting, the readings were different and broadened the focus, including narcotics and other drugs. The other noon meeting focused on alcohol, but each addiction was still talked about in both. No matter which it was, he belonged, and always made friends. Besides, he was addicted to *everything,* not such a big secret anymore – like it ever was outside of his head.

~ 173 ~

Everyone was always hugging each other at the meetings. Kevin began to like this part quite a bit, strange as it was at first. Some didn't like the hugs too much and that was all good – but once they let go, they became the greatest huggers. Funny how it worked.

***

Living at Evan's was mundane. It was only a place to crash and keep his few possessions, relax at the end of the day and have some peace and quiet. It worked well for just that over the next few weeks. If it was boring, it was about to change fast.

30 Days Off

Evan and some pal of his were drinking and smoking, Kevin found upon flinging the front door opened like Kramer from Seinfeld. "How's it goin'?" He was restless.

"Oh, good, man. Just chillin' watching some TV … we feel like having some ice cream but we're vegged out, man," Evan said. His eyes were bloodshot and the TV was way too loud. Evan's friend, whose name Kevin had already forgotten, sat there placid and nodding, smirking and agreeing with everything. Both of them looked like stoned zombies.

"I'll go get you some," Kevin offered, even though he did not know why; maybe to be helpful, maybe just to get out of there for a few.

"You will? Awesome." Evan was overjoyed, in addition to being cotton-mouthed.

"Be right back," Kevin replied, leaving out the front door, oblivious to the ensuing adventure. He would not be coming back for a while.

With the frozen goods on the passenger seat, he waited to turn onto 128th and head for home. The thoroughfare ran east and west. A cop car sat and preened at a stoplight just to his left, waiting to pounce on the first opportunity. He always noticed the police, from those days not so long ago, on the run and hiding.

No warrants now, he thought, still nervous as he shot a look over at the looming black and white. "Nope, been doing everything right. Go ahead and eyeball me," Kevin whispered nervous through gritted teeth, practically making eye contact with the officer, who was staring. Crossing past him, Kevin made the left turn toward the house.

Why is he eyeballing me, anyway? I'm not doing anything wrong. A glance at the dash found that the headlights were not on, and it was long after dark.

~ 174 ~

"Shit!" he blasted, flipping them on and completing the turn. Too late; Officer Unfriendly flipped a cookie with the same intensity as if someone had robbed a bank and Kevin was driving the getaway car. "Freakin' cops – whatever." Oh well, he had a license, but no insurance, *again*, and that was a fat ticket in this state (still had one from a few months ago - unpaid, of course). "Damn," Kevin cussed, pulling over. He decided to remain calm and just tell the truth, hope for a little street mercy. But this guy, this cop, had a hard on for trouble; Kevin could tell just by the way he got on him and how he walked up to the window now, hand on gun, with that self-righteous *I'm gonna get you* look about him – rigid, programmed, right.

"License and registration, proof of insurance." The officer insisted. Kevin dug around, found the registration and license, and began stuttering, "My insurance ... is ... umm-"

"Wait here," the officer interrupted, going back to his car. The dude was rude.

Kevin kept both hands on the steering wheel, something he had learned over the last few times of being arrested. Cops get very nervous when they cannot see your hands during a traffic stop, and somewhere he'd been told that it is best to keep them in full view. After an unusually short time in his cruiser he noticed the officer suddenly get out. Pistol drawn, he approached the car practically screaming at him to get out and assume the position.

"Now!" he yelled as Kevin tried to ask what the hell was going on. "You have a warrant for your arrest!"

"What?" Kevin's stomach dropped into the transmission. He was aghast! Been walking the straight and narrow, in a court-monitored treatment even, surely they would have known about a warrant.

As the over-cuffing ensued by the less-than-charming officer who was using more than enough force to do so, he calmly asked, "What is it for?"

Perhaps it was this calmness and letting the officer do what he had to do without resistance that caused the man in army-issue boots with too much testosterone to loosen up a little.

"No-contact-order violation out of King County," was all he said. Now Kevin was scared. The judge had said any *hint* of another one of these would be a ticket straight to prison.

His gut fell all the way through Andromeda, two-and-a-half million light years away. "What? ... No way!" He said, simultaneously realizing it sounded a lot like "I didn't do it! I'm Innocent. You got the wrong guy," and every other unfortunate cliché the bad guy likes to say when they are caught. Caught! But for what?

"That's all I know," the cop said as he walked his fresh cargo back to the cruiser for a nice evening drive. In this moment, Kevin realized there was a choice:

Struggle, or thrive.

Obsess, or let go.

What could be done about it, anyway? One thing was for sure, he was going to jail, and couldn't do a damn thing about that. The ice cream ... it would melt everywhere. The officer had calmed down considerably now, as if satiated by the thrill and now basking in the glory, a jungle cat whipping his tail. Through the Plexiglas, Kevin watched him filling out paperwork from the backseat.

"Could you *please* pull my Explorer into the parking lot below and off the street so it won't get towed, and make sure the stuff on the seat won't spill everywhere?"

And, to his amazement the officer agreed and moved the Explorer, (hopefully up-righting the ice cream), came back to the cruiser, got in, and drove off. But first, *he* turned on the headlights. On the brighter side: No tickets, anyway.

***

It was a much different experience, being booked while sober. No one could answer what the warrant was for in any more detail. Since Marie lived in Seattle, they'd transfer him to a jail way down south. Continuing to trust the process, he told himself, *this will work itself out, somehow.* Time would tell. For now, he had a worthy ally: *Acceptance.*

He practiced it going into the cold, cement and stainless-steel holding cell to await whatever was next.

The show was still a few weeks away, on the night before Thanksgiving. Surely there was enough time to fix the problem and be home in time. Besides, there was the safety of the drug court team; he had been accountable to the program and felt they were behind him. Everything was going to be OK. *Just relax, stay calm.*

After the transfer, they moved him into a temporary cell. Still, the warrant remained somewhat of a mystery. What they did say was that it was a "no bail hold" – that is, no bail was set, so no getting out that way. Acceptance began to give way to fear. What was the arrest for? The warrant? Was he going to prison? Was there a screw up in the system? Did they think he had been seeing Marie and issued another no-contact-order (NCO) violation?

There was someone who may have had a part in all of this: Selena. She had also been on the brink of filing an NCO against Kevin on many occasions. Only nine months ago she'd told him, "*Never* contact me again."

Selena was a strikingly beautiful Sicilian woman, with long dark hair and piercing blue eyes. She was an Alpha, and from witnessing her crazy driving and burning rubber the night the two had hooked up a couple years back, he was "in love." He had put her through hell also. She helped him, loved him, and even ran the business with him in its heyday. She was very good at it. This only lasted about a year until it became ugly, with his buying and using as much as he could get his hands on, day in and day out. Same story again. Guzzling as much vodka at any bar most every night on the way home, even throughout the day oftentimes, mixing any and all drugs and then driving:

"Be home in an hour," he would slur, and then stumble in the front door in an awful condition many hours later, often causing a scene with Selena and her kids. And she always cleaned up the mess, just like Mommy.

When they were first together it seemed a great match; he needed a good woman like that and certainly needed the help, even though she was to be yet another enabler to use up and throw away. The honeymoon months were great. He even thought he might marry her, but those heavy demons were writhing within, dominating. Selena would bear witness to their rising up on many occasions.

Hiding in this kind of self-delusion, and then trying to run that racket on another, especially one close to you, apparently required an awful lot of heavy duty sedatives, which were indulged at every opportunity. Somehow along the way, Marie and Selena had become friends even though he often ran from one to the other. They both cared for him a great deal while he could not even care for himself.

Many times after violating the NCO with Marie, he would bolt before the cops got there and call Selena. Sometimes she would come get him, but oftentimes the cops would show up instead. He'd been too polluted and diluted then to make sense of it, but it had been the two women who had corresponded and had him arrested. Shack even helped at least one time.

To all of them, Kevin had become a drug-crazed lunatic, unsafe, and a public nuisance in general - but to himself, he was in pure agony and just needed help. No one understood.

If they would just do what I want, I'd be OK!

Why won't anyone help me?

These voices had screamed from every corner of his tired mind from behind bars - but they always *were* trying to help: Marie, Selena, Mom, Brother, Sister, cops, judges - and, even though refusing to see it, jail was always the very best place in such condition. Mom said this more than once when he called from there asking for bail. Her enabling was coming to an end.

But this arrest, now, was different – he was sober, keeping his nose clean, and walking the line.

It must have been her that did this. Damn it, Selena! He pictured her treacherous blue eyes deviously squinting as she dialed the police. She was connected, too, having been a paramedic for many years, knowing all the cops and emergency workers. She had turned him in just to get even. But even if she had, he probably deserved it for all the hell he had put her through.

Unsure steps plodded toward the phones. *How can I talk in a way that is not implicating?* His gut was in knots trying to figure it all out. The phones in jail are monitored, officialdom looking for some good old incrimination. Who would he call? Well, first, the Explorer was in danger of being towed – he'd call Shack who just might know what was going on. Shack would let Evan know why he had not come back. They probably all thought he was on another drug run. Oh well, he deserved it.

Gotta let 'em know I'm hemmed up, away for a minute. He hated jail lingo and couldn't help using it at the same time.

Six phones were next to each other in a hexagon kiosk, a few had chairs and some didn't. One dude with dreadlocks and arms-full tattoos talked loudly on the horn directly across. Kevin felt like a jackass trying to talk in code and coax out information about the arrest, about Marie and Selena. He wanted to just blurt out what he was thinking and feeling as this anxiety-ridden insanity ran through, but thought about the dozens of other fools that surely sat in this very seat and condemned themselves to additional time in the clink, not able to hold their tongues. Instead he just sounded stupid, and knew it. After all, his innocence was not fully intact.

"Please, please, go get my truck," Kevin implored Shack. "The keys are here at the jail, and I will send a request to release them to you. If they impound it, I'm screwed."

"Oh I will dude, don't you worry." Shack voiced it with the same exact subtext as when he said, "Don't worry dude. Your gear is safe." It felt uneasy on top of uneasy. In fact, Kevin's gut, which he thought had sunk all the way, sank. He *knew* he was screwed, knew Shack was not getting the truck, just like he knew there was no uncle, and no more gear. His life was a mess. But, delusion is *powerful*. Shack promised he would do it, so he will do it. *He'll do it.* Kevin was helpless here in this damned jail.

Please take it!

***

"It's November anyway, the weather is turning, gettin' cold. Not a bad time to be locked up," Kevin rationalized to a guy next to him at breakfast. The other inmate did not even look up from his bland cereal, just gruffed an agreement -"Yup."

The oatmeal wasn't bad, even if it was only a cold 6:00 a.m., and someone had given him an extra two pieces of wheat bread. Someone else taught him to put water in his milk because the little carton wasn't enough. It was good that way.

He'd call Mom today and try and make some sense of what was going on, what the warrant was for, why the arrest even occurred. But she didn't get up till noon if she got up early. His faux calmness was forced through agonized nerves, feeling the guilt of what he had put her through – and everyone else, for that matter.

That damn shop. Mom had given him his inheritance early for the down payment for the loan on it, over a hundred grand, and with the best of intentions. Maybe she could see her son finally realize peace, some solidity in his life. But the screaming demons ruled, and no amount of money could buy them away.

However they had come to be, eradicating them was now an inside job.

Mom had been put in the position of having to facilitate the sale of the very same shop at a significant loss. All the vultures had come out at the sight and smell of blood, horrified her with their petty battling each other for position and sickening manipulations as they moved in for the kill. "It's just business," one man had told her. The whole thing left a bitter taste in her mouth. Kevin had become numb about it, unable to even deal with it.

The next few hours were tormenting until it was late enough to call. After the irritating, automated, "You're receiving a *collect* phone call from your *again* incarcerated son," stupid interface mechanized recording played and she, probably reluctantly, pressed the appropriate key to accept the call, he heard a groggy and less than enthused "Hello?" which he interpreted as *"Now what?"*

Clumsy and struggling again for the words to extract information without sounding guilty of anything, Kevin again felt like a total moron. What the mother and son conversation boiled down to was that no one had a clue why he was there and he would have to just wait it out. Wait it out! He heard the real meaning of every word she spoke, too: "Now can I just get off the damn phone?" It was clear he had used his mom up, that she had no more energy to put towards sorting out *his* messes, let alone any desire to do so. He was sad, but didn't blame her.

In a defeated voice, he said goodbye. Then, off to the book rack and found something decent, back to the cell and cracked it open. He would likely be placed today with the "extended stay" inmates. Maybe someone from the courts would shed some light on this whole mess.

Too Many Days Later

"Apparently you missed a sentence review hearing," the lawyer-type 30-something woman in the business pantsuit said into the telephone. Her image was obviously distorted by the two inch-thick Plexiglas, but even without it she'd be no beauty. Two agonizing weeks had gone by with no answers as to why he had even been arrested. Now this?

"I never got any court date!" It was the truth, too; if he had, he'd have gone to it. So this is what all the commotion was about. He would have breathed a sigh of relief except that it was not yet resolved.

"Yes, obviously," she said. A hint of *that or you just didn't go, probably out on one* hovered in the air. His mind started playing blame games. Anyone scrutinizing his attendance record for court dates over the last year wouldn't have to be a math whiz to see a pattern there. The realization caused him to back off. She continued: "They sent it to an address in Yakima."

"Oh, dammit. I moved … I, well … so now what?" he waffled, opting to not explain the debacle further.

"Well, it doesn't matter why you missed it, but it *was* a sentence review hearing for your no-contact-order violations, in front of the sentencing judge," she said.

Missing this was bad.

You don't mess around with the sentencing judge. Some people in the program joke about this guy being their Higher Power. Those judges are busy, so getting in front of them is not easy. And, you can only go before the one that sentenced you, as she told him. As fate would have it, this particular judge was on vacation; the very judge that had said if Kevin so much as projected a *thought* toward Marie and he found out about it, it would be off to prison for at least a year on a felony charge. He was probably guilty of more than that.

On the other hand, he had been doing what was required by the courts, staying clean and in another treatment program, all of which were good. But was there something else threatening freedom, lurking in the shadows?

The big show was just over a week away, and so was Thanksgiving. He longed to be home for both - sick of being under the microscope, *sick of being in trouble.*

She went on. "We're working on getting you the earliest court date possible and the judge being away is what's taking so long." Explaining to her all the reasons why he simply had to get out, she said they would do their best, but couldn't promise anything. It felt like the court's mantra was, "We reserve the right to be vague."

Back in the cell he got to his knees. Many prayers over these last two weeks were for patience. Praying for patience had not suddenly brought a bolt of lightning and *Pow* he was so endowed ... nope. It was more *Pow* and suddenly he was gifted with *situations* in which to *practice* patience. Hence the bars, perhaps.

By comparison, thanking this Mystery of Life or whatever it was for patience, it was often simply realized. It already existed as potential. All needed is to acknowledge in faith and trust anything desired. Guidance always comes for any situation. Gratitude is a powerful and respectful way to practice this. It works with all principles. In the very infancy of learning this art of allowing, what came by way of it was astounding.

Thank You for Patience

Desperately asking for patience or acceptance or prosperity, for circumstances to change or whatever it is, just brought more situations and opportunities in which to seek, find, and practice those very principles. Could this be the actual purpose of the arrest? Was the desperate pleading only an acknowledgment of a lack mindset rather than one of abundance? But what if either could simply be claimed, *was* being claimed?

What if we are loved so much that *anything* we desire is available, and the access is simply true faith?

Thank You, for everything

***

Kevin tried to call Shack about ten times, and every time, no answer; a most hideous trait.

"Damn it. He better have gotten that freakin' car." He pushed the expletive out through gritted teeth, using every ounce of restraint not to slam the phone down. Kevin needed to talk to Shack, tell him he would be out in time for the big show.

A heavy set guard with a giant belly hanging over his belt approached. "You have a visitor," he said, offering a welcome diversion.

It was the tightly wound lady lawyer from the public defender's office, in cheap high heels, with perfectly straightened hair and monotone voice. She had promised to get back to him as soon as there was an update. There was good news, and bad news. The good:

"We got you the earliest possible court date and you'll likely be released at that time."

Wait for it, wait for it …

"The bad news?" *Who is this woman? Is anyone even home?*

"The Judge won't be back until several days after Thanksgiving," came the nasal reply, with no trace of emotion.

This meant he would not be able to do the show, in addition to missing the holiday.

"Can't you get me an earlier date?" He was insistent, trying to remain calm while his roller coaster gut flopped around like a fish in a blender.

"It is the earliest available option, and you're lucky to even get this one," she stated matter-of-factly, sliding a piece of white paper with the December date through the small stainless-steel trough under the thick glass. He felt defeated. Only now, through it, came that same voice of solace, carrying with it another offering of help and acceptance. That simple core choice presented itself again - struggle or let go. Everything would work itself out, somehow. The choice of surrender felt good.

Still, the being in trouble was sickening, thought he'd been doing everything right over these last few months. *There must be some reason I am here; something beyond what I can comprehend is working here.* The thought came slowly, gently, and like some mystic beginning training, it gave way to a better choice: "I will be here now."

He said it aloud, deciding to do just that. There was instant relief, just as exercise time was announced. Outside the pod which held about 65 inmates was a courtyard of some 60x30 feet, and the sole opportunity to get outside. He'd go walk. There, he found his friend, Tim. They had run together.

"Hey dude, what'r you doin' here," Kevin asked, stepping out as a cold wind shot through the open door and whooshed upon him.

"Duh." Tim was cool, a likable guy, except that he loved talking about using and glorifying all that went with it, and Kevin wanted to stay sober. He hated that drug-world and yet loved getting high. It was a tragic conundrum, and talking about it felt treacherous.

"Yeah, dumb question." Kevin shifted the conversation to starting a business again, flourishing and living sober. Tim appeased him only after telling everything he felt about how good it was going to feel to get high, and that it was the first thing on his agenda upon release.

Kevin understood. He had been in jail many times over the last year, and this was always the prime directive: Get out and get loaded as fast as possible and stay that way - no matter the cost. But now, something had changed.

The fresh air was crisp, cool and delicious. A pull-up bar and some benches beckoned from next to the grooves worn in the concrete around the perimeter. He quickly created a workout routine of fast walking, pull-ups, and a series of various push-ups at different angles along the benches to tone the old pectorals. There was also basketball going on which he respectfully avoided interrupting during his evolving regimen, and sometimes joined the game. The natural endorphin high felt so good, the working out bringing relief in many ways.

Strange, to Kevin, was that he had choice in these matters. Choosing to believe that everything was right where it was supposed to be - even being here in jail and missing events he could not miss - the easier the time went by. Choosing to think about how tragic it all was - wishing it was different - caused suffering. And he was the only one that could choose one or the other trains of thought. He'd been plopped right into a unique classroom, everything in it a teacher if only he allowed the lessons.

Where were these contemplations coming from? Why had he not had the ability to think like this before? Something strange was indeed happening, and he liked it, a lot – it felt like magic that was always there but had just been obscured, until now. Even the books, which called him to read them, brought great comfort. They, too, had been placed by sweet synchronicity, just for him. The information they contained simultaneously validated lessons he was being taught in other ways, like how a single raindrop hanging from a leaf reflects its environment, the world around it. It was fascinating. Whatever was going on, it was so welcome.

And with that, Kevin settled in for the next two weeks until the court date, reading, sleeping, working out and learning how to just be - instead of struggling. Praying at every opportunity, this prayer happened deep within, instead of pleading to some external god to change circumstances. It was accessing the highest expression of what he really was, some part of him he had always suspected was there but could never let flourish. Everything was transforming, even again.

The only constant thing in the universe is change, and, nothing ever changes

Freedom

Court day, 7:15 a.m. Old frozen snow crunched under the chain gang's bright orange sandals, cold steel shackles heavy on legs and hands.

The frigid air tasted good, even though taking it in too fast only doubled the trembling. The gang was loaded onto the bus bound for the courthouse. All the inmates wore were short sleeved shirts and thin pants, socks under now-frozen slip-ons, and inside the bus was even colder than outside. Their breath came out in generous puffs of cool clouds. Shivering, they looked ridiculous. Kevin felt ridiculous, but he'd be *free* soon ... it was worth it.

The bus clambered down a few side streets and found the freeway to Seattle. The inmates chided each other about who was getting out and who wasn't, between small outbursts of *"BRRRR!"* in attempts to buffer the bone-chilling, biting air. The loud engine rattled freezing ears, its stinky-diesel power reverberating throughout the steel shell of the bus. Cold vinyl seats finally began warming some. Then the bus did. Kevin gazed out the window to see the King County courthouse come into view.

"You're walking a thin line," the judge growled, "and if you don't get it together I'm gonna lock you up again, and for a long time!"

Deciding not to answer with more excuses, Kevin agreed with an obsequious "Yes, sir," even if recently he had been fairly honest and following through. But over the past year he had been a complete ass, and realized that from the judge's perspective he seemed just another doper loser. After all, the last time he stood here, there had been helicopters out looking for him after one of the many NCO violations in the depths of a gnarly coming-down.

The court set another hearing date and Judge Grumpy released him. *Free at last.* It took a long time to get home and several busses, but it felt so sweet to be *anywhere* but jail.

Back at Evan's, he learned that Cold River had found another drummer and won the showcase, took first place in the battle of the bands competition. He acted happy for them as Evan spoke it, but was disappointed, more with himself than anything. After Evan delivered that news, he added, "Oh, you have to move out, we need the room for ..." and went on and said a bunch of stuff that sounded a lot like "we just want you to go." Completely understandable.

Great, now what? At least Evan gave him two weeks.

Shack finally answered the phone; must not have recognized the number. "What happened with my rig?" Kevin asked, hopeful that somehow he'd handled it even though he never came and got the keys.

"Oh dude! It was... uh... I mean ... ummmm ... I couldn't find it where you said. They must have got it before I got there." Kevin would have been disappointed if he hadn't expected it. Just more proof that he was the ass, not Shack, not anyone else. Just him.

Shackey quickly changed the subject and told him how killer the show was, how the fans ate them up and loved it, how excited they all were, and then, realizing it probably made Kevin feel bad, reassured him that he was still their drummer. This was good, right?

The ambience in the band house felt like everyone was talking about him, probably bad mouthing the jail bird-loser-now-homeless drug addict-alcoholic. Band practice was awkward. He could feel contention and condescension, thick in the air like a humid southern day. Except that it was dead-winter. Somehow, he would find his way. Somehow.

***

The impounded vehicle was finally tracked down, the bill a little over a thousand bucks to get it out. The date of impound was several days after he had begged Shack to get it. His band mate had likely just never even gone there. It would have pissed Kevin off, except it was his own doing that got him locked up. It was not anyone else's responsibility to clean up the mess. He did, however, begin to feel defeated. He called the only person that could possibly help.

"A thousand dollars! After all that's happened? You've got some nerve!" Mom *was* pissed, and let him know it. After a ten-minute tongue-lashing she said, "I know you are trying to do the right thing, and you need a vehicle for treatment, damn it." She had given so much - if she didn't help him with money to get the rig back, it might be better in the long run, and he knew it. She caved and did it anyway, one more time.

All these ways of being were old patterns: Putting trust in others that he knew would let him down, breaking the rules and Mommy bailing him out and of course, playing the helpless victim to all of it. Yet still, awareness of such things was progressing. There was a light at the end of the tunnel, and this time it wasn't the train coming. The alcohol and other drugs had indeed been the glue that held these ways and such thinking in place. Without it for a while now came a new sort of disturbance, a welcome disruption of patterns. As one older-sober said, "You can't coast uphill." He had done some work, but it really had been only scratching the surface.

Like an iceberg, that which is seen sticking out of the water is only a very small portion of the massive hard-ice that lies beneath.

You are not aware of what you have not found

Mom had made EMI and drug court privy to the situation, and they had been surprisingly accepting of it. He would have to write a letter of explanation around the circumstances, which was done and turned in promptly. Missed group sessions would have to be made-up. Friday, at court in front of the audience, he explained briefly what had happened, even though

~ 185 ~

they already knew from the letter. Since it was a documented, honest mistake, they did not throw him back in jail, although they did give him some community service hours to perform as a reminder to stay accountable. All participants had to be reminded that no falter goes unanswered.

A list of choices was available for where to do the community service, places like the local food bank and Goodwill. He would need to do eight hours. At first, it seemed excessive.

"What's 'The Farm'?" Kevin asked the coordinator, concerning one of the places listed.

"Oh, it's a youth outreach center in Snohomish. Great place. You might really enjoy it."

He did. There were goats and geese and rabbits, even a pig or two in various pens. An aviary full of parrots and other birds was built behind the main building, heated and full with large plants in which the feathered creatures could hang out. Kevin entered only to get dive-bombed by what seemed a hundred of them! One on each shoulder now! He laughed with shocked surprise. It got so loud from all the squawking he almost could not believe it. Maybe they would have to get used to him. He ran back outside, where dogs and cats roamed around – a little safer, it seemed. There were other animals, too. He wanted to know them better, to love them and be loved by them.

Bruce owned and ran the place, with help. Like Kevin, he had been in the body shop business. "Well, the doctors told me I had maybe a year left. Rough living, probably. Anyway, I said to myself, well, in the time I have remaining, I'll give back … to the kids. Grandmother had left me this one-acre farm, and I turned it into this …" Bruce slowly waved his arm through the open air, palm facing up, a gesture inviting Kevin to gaze over the open fields of corrals and huge tents where events were held.

"We help underprivileged families, have them come out and enjoy the animals, throw birthday parties for kids of parents that can't afford such a thing, bring Christmas gifts to those that won't get any, and so much more. Most all the animals are unwanted or rescued."

Bruce's far-away look embodied the quality and treasure of living great purpose. Kevin pondered it all with great longing. He could feel Bruce overflowing with joy and love and gratitude. It was a peaceful, contented feeling.

"It's been ten years, now," Bruce said, watching the questions in Kevin's eyes.

***

Kevin began volunteering at The Farm. Eight hours was not nearly enough time there. Something about the whole of it nurtured a small, broken child within. A lost part of his soul was being called home. What at first glance seemed another nuisance turned out among the most epic of blessings.

Realizing lasting change would require a daily renewal of willingness. Taking new actions again and again was becoming easier and more rewarding. He had no idea what would be found in staying the course. The God he had all but mocked in the conversation with Christian was becoming real. He needed someone to help, guide, teach and show him how to continue. Relapse is a process, not an event. Going it alone was too treacherous; would he attempt it or ask for help, even again?

~ Chapter 16 ~

Tom

A New Home

Silver bullets, cold and dense, poured from the dark grey universe through a hollow sky, a million-man army drumming pavement and attempting the annihilation of rooftops. Gutters overflowed like rivers flooding. Hot coffee felt good going down, the warm cup soothing to hold. Cozy and warm, the little café was bustling with others with the same idea – keeping out of the rain. Kevin found an interesting little apartment advertised, near EMI and court, complete with a small detached garage. He reached inside the dry pocket of a wet coat, found the phone and dialed.

"Yeah, we're working on the place right now, just doing some finishing touches. Come by if you want," Rick said, and gave the address and directions.

Honesty had worked well this far, and he told Rick, who owned the place, the truth about his situation - minus the little piece about just getting out of jail, of course. Rick was a generous man, and the apartment was perfect - a one bedroom with a good sized living room, and one bathroom with a bathtub. Hot baths on these cold winter days were indeed a treat.

The first of the month, three hundred and thirty nine bucks was added to his debit card, and a couple hundred was leftover – didn't use much money in jail. Still, it wasn't enough for the six-fifty rent, let alone the damage deposit of two hundred.

"I love the place," Kevin exclaimed immediately upon entering. It was the Taj Majal - versus the band couch or a cold cell, anyway.

"I don't quite have enough right now to move in, but I do cars, and once I find a place to work out of, I know I can make up the rest of the money.

"I'll give you five hundred now and write a check for the other three fifty," after a quick calculation, he finished his hopeful offer, "post-dated for two weeks." Rick thought about it … since it would be nearly halfway through the month, the rent pro-rated would make it …

"Five hundred and you can move in," Rick said. Kevin could make that happen right now. In the time it took to blurt out "Thank you!" a check was scribbled out.

"About ten days 'till you can move in, gotta finish up some repairs and painting."

Perfect. Evan had given that much time.

"You know what?" Rick queried with that tone that says, "Here's what I'm gonna do for you."

"You can use the garage for your work until we find a renter, no charge. Go check it out." He lobbed a single key through the air.

Kevin caught it with one hand as his eyes bugged out. "Sweet!"

A tall fir had shed its once-green needles all about the cement stairway which led down to the garage. A craggy old cedar branch blocked the path. Kevin moved it, trudged through piles of brownish, soggy maple leaves – these steps hadn't been used much. Two walk-in doors led into the workspace – more of a shop than a garage, and no bay doors. A car wouldn't be able to come in. Not a whole car, anyway. But it was free, and it was his, for now.

It all caused quite a feeling. It had been a long time. If he didn't count Castle de Chestnut, not since Arizona had he a place of his very own. Another new beginning within a new beginning. The gifts were flowing, more grace. The last several months had been clumsy. He felt like a baby bird that just pushed out of the shell, with eyes that could hardly see, and had subsequently fallen out of the nest. But he'd been picked up from the mud by something, and soon enough, he would learn:

You can fly …

***

Owning little made the move-in easy. There was a mix of emotions about the whole thing. Would he be able to make it on his own? Would he be *OK* alone? Could he make it with no woman? Now, he did not have to answer to anyone, no grumpy roommates, maybe he could even get a kitten or something. Fear was quelled by the newness and excitement of it all. Instead of letting a relation-slip divert the path before him, he would turn his energy toward the huge commitment to the court and the new treatment program. Living close-by was key to holding up his end of the deal. Between group sessions, UA's, and court every Friday, he was required to be there almost every day, at least for this first phase. Band practice three times a week was only a few miles away. Placing one foot in front of the other and doing what was in front of him, the days began to flow more smoothly.

Inside the hot steamy shower, a little window offered a view out over the garage, through the trees and down across the main highway. A few business signs of a shopping center glowed blurry through the frosted glass. Tile work around the little one foot wide and three-finger's taller window made a shelf for the bottles of shampoo. But the bottles obscured the latch. Moving the stuff to the edge of the tub instead, he slid the latch up and pulled the window open. A cool gust shot onto his hot-watered skin. It sent a shiver through him, just like the gaze out upon a new world. Each day, he read one of the signs out loud: *"Pedigo Piano."* Even this was a prayer. It became a daily ritual, and ended with a smile. The silliest little things brought happiness and contentment.

Living here was a great blessing. Being in treatment again, *engaging*, was proving to be more valuable than he even imagined. Being arrested and found in possession of narcotics had been a gift, even though it certainly did not seem so at the time. Now, he was surrounded by people, places, and situations that were all there to help. Taking the ten days in jail, the easy way out, not only would be a felony on the record, but he may have been without this whole world of help. He may even be dead, or worst – slowly dying a selfish death of endless suffering. Staring off into space, contemplating for a while such notions, his heart burst with gratitude. Something was guiding. It had been all along.

Everything is a gift if you let it be

The Sage

Every Saturday night was the speaker meeting at the Alano club. Just two people shared their stories. These were different from the regular meetings where people would be randomly called upon and share for several minutes each, for the duration of the meeting. Sometimes there was a podium and each person would get up and speak from it, but this was rare. Normally, it was just from their seat, pretty laid back and informal. Some meetings were even had by candlelight, which Kevin liked best.

The Alano Club was a safe place. It was almost always open, with various meetings throughout the day and night, as well as sober dances and other great events. Most entered through the back door, closer to the parking lot. Tonight, a blustering cross-wind shot rain sideways, pelting Kevin as he slammed the door shut behind him. "Geez!" he shivered, shaking off the wet chill. First thing inside the rear entrance were the two bathrooms, and a bit further an open door led into a deli.

"Jessie!" One of the guys seated at a table called to the server busting her matronly butt on the floor. She didn't pause in her hustle, delivering and picking up dishes as if her own sobriety depended on it.

"I'll get to it, Gene," she tossed over her shoulder, blowing a sandy strand of hair out of her eyes with an under-lip whoosh. "Back in a minute." Her smile warmed the room – and Gene – as she raced to the kitchen through too many bodies with her tray of dishes.

His nose told him whatever Gene was waiting on was sure to be delicious. The espresso machine was loud but the stout aroma of the coffee was worth it. A few steps later the hallway opened to several children running crazy around a pool table; a few video games blipped and whirred beyond it, played by happy kids. Along the walls were benches, tables and chairs where people often came to meet and do step work together, or just hang out. The clatter of pool balls, mechanized lasers and blasters, voices and squeaking shoes faded as Kevin proceeded down the hall into the next room. It was big and open. Three men carried a podium to the front and dozens of other men and women milled around tables and chairs. Still others poured in through the front entrance. Smoking was not allowed inside, a fact for which Kevin was grateful. The coffee which was free for the taking along with a platter of chocolate-chip cookies was so inviting.

Kevin had been attending regular meetings here, had even made the daily noon meeting his home group. But tonight, there was a different vibe in the air than any other time he had been here. That feeling of impending good was dripping off the walls.

The speaker usually had at least a year of sobriety, and often much more. They did share their story from the podium, or at least the front of the room. Each spoke for 30 minutes or so, enough time to give an ample "what happened, what it was like, and what it's like now" summary of their own journey from alcoholism and addiction to recovery. Where he was, in this infancy of a new life, wide-eyed and shell shocked, he could not even imagine getting up in front of people like that … how did they do it?

As 7:30 rolled around and the speaker meeting was about to begin, Kevin grabbed a good seat (along with a coffee and plenty of the sugared treats, of course) and settled in. Accompanying those entering through the front double-glass doors each time was a shivery gust. Best show in town for a buck. Even though dues or fees were not required, they passed a basket for contributions. He always put at least a dollar in along with his court-slip. The collection was called the seventh tradition, but he did not know what that meant. A lot of the people knew a great deal about this thing, how it worked, and all the particulars. There was much to it, even if they did call it a simple program. He was just happy to be here now, safe, and with the show about to start. There were several pretty girls that distracted him and, of course, he attempted to make eye contact with each of them.

The loud buzzing of voices and chatter, shuffling bodies moving and scraping chairs on the linoleum, quelled to near silence as the readings began. Three readings, one person each, at the podium: *How it Works, The Traditions, The Promises.* Soon after, the first speaker was introduced. "Please welcome Sandy P."

Respect and compassionate attentiveness was given to her sharing. It was almost like a play, her story. It captured the imagination and engaged the audience, suspending self-obsession if only for the while. Listening, he was catapulted into someone else's world. There was always at least one golden nugget in the sharing that resonated, some piece he could borrow and use. Here, the suffering the story-teller had endured became useful. Sandy talked a lot about looking at her part in every complaint she had about the world, after she talked about once blaming the world for all her shortcomings. Then she talked about forgiveness.

A tall, thin woman brought a glass coffee carafe around, filling anyone's cup that was willing. She looked like she was enjoying herself as she poured the last drop, walked over to the machine and inserted a new filter-full, pressed the appropriate button to brew, then grabbed an already full and waiting carafe and proceeded from where she had left off. Kevin flashed a smile as she filled his cup with the steaming hot stuff. Returning the geniality, she was off to the next taker.

Sandy finished sharing her story to a grateful round of applause from the audience. In this place, people looked for the best in each other, much different from how he had been living, the circles in which he usually roamed. Kevin was looking for the best in the blonde two tables over, who was doing a good job of acting uninterested.

They announced the next speaker. "Please welcome Tom O."

Applause filled the room again as a man approached the podium.

Long, tightly-woven braids fell right out of either side of a black Stetson, almost reaching his waist. Their pure white color gave away his age, which was probably late 60's. He wore an intriguing, clean, button up shirt, with a Native American feel to it. In fact, Tom had a Native American feel to him, altogether. The colorful shirt tucked into blue jeans, which landed on a pair of worn, brown-suede cowboy boots. He had a calm and soothing and patient presence. *So patient.*

Two traits in particular stood out before he even spoke: The depth of his eyes, and a smile that warmed the heart.

"Hello …" Tom said, removing his hat and setting it aside. What came across the room with that word? It whispered to Kevin, offering something difficult to comprehend. He could only feel it, and did. God, he felt this man. "I'm Tom and I'm an alcoholic." Tom spoke with a softness and gentleness, which added to the grandfather-like comfort emanating from him. His words stirred something in Kevin, as if reaching into murky waters that had long been stagnant. This Tom was warm, comfortable, *trustworthy* – and it was not only his words.

Exactly what even happened over the next forty or so minutes, remains a mystery.

A Great Mystery

Each word felt like that first "hello." Every utterance carried thousands of years of ancient wisdom that coursed through Kevin like good medicine. Tom talked about living in the great emptiness, sharing *his* story. He talked about what was true for him, and in this could Kevin see his own similar truths. Tom put words to what Kevin never could. At the podium, Tom talked about his own struggles and where they may have originated, how alcohol and drug use perpetuated the extreme selfishness and damaging behavior to others which Kevin identified with all too well.

"The alcohol and drugs *were* my solution. They act like cement and mortar that holds these old, small, stifling ways in place." Kevin had heard similar sharing before, but coming from Tom it just plain sounded different. It was, strange as it appeared, as though something was speaking through him. "Alcoholism is a disease of perception."

As Tom continued, the monkeys were silenced, and Kevin was allowed to be present. He was so present that it felt like he had been laid open, split down the center, and was in a state of pure receiving. He was certain he had not felt this way before, ever.

Whatever had happened, he tried to deny the very minute the audience began applauding Tom. The monkeys immediately began their shrieking –

You're an idiot. You don't need this. Let's get out of here. There is nothing this silly man can do for you. You are just fine the way you are. You don't really have anything in common with him, anyway. Surely there's a redhead or brunette we can talk to. What about her? Her! We've got big things to do, damn it. These losers can toil here while we continue with the plan to take over the world. Go to the bathroom. Leave, fast, go. Go!

Endless, much less important thoughts swirled around like storm clouds but could not displace the precious purpose of this moment.

~ 194 ~

Providence allowed Kevin to just sit there for a minute, a feat of which he was somehow capable. He watched the crowd disperse. Others approached Tom and Sandy to chat with them, thank them, shake hands or offer a hug.

A cerebral argument thundered. He wanted to go and talk with Tom, but the monkeys! *There's no way we're talking to* that *guy, let's get the hell out of here. Besides, you cannot achieve what he has. You are not good enough.*

Instead, Kevin froze. It felt like a great length of time had elapsed, and then a sudden surge inundated him.

It must have been a tractor beam. It literally seized him, like some kind of alien abduction. Kevin's body rose and began moving toward Tom, one step, then another. The mind was telling the feet to stop, but they would not. Helpless to cease his approach to the compelling man, he found himself within twenty feet. Tom lifted his head and his eyes found Kevin's. It was a mysterious, inviting look. Kevin would *never* forget it.

Like the first word Tom had spoken, the look had a quality to it, bringing all that had ever been and what could ever be into the very room in which they now stood. Going straight through him, it seemed a very different look than Tom shared with the others. It was a strange, permeating, sideways glance. This beholding said, "Ah, we have been expecting you."

In this moment, their spirits saw each other. It was a visceral feeling, pure light energy infusing like stepping into bathing sunlight, only from the inside out. As if they had spent many lifetimes together in myriad dimensions and had found each other again, they greeted one another. It was reunion unnecessary of words for acknowledgement. This occurred in one instant devoid of time, before Kevin had physically reached Tom. The room had all but cleared, and the ones who remained were a million miles away. Within earshot of Tom now, he introduced himself.

Back in the head now: "Really appreciated your story ... I'm Kevin." His eyes, like two pinballs, darted around at everything but Tom's, at them, then back around again.

Tom kept looking *through* him with eyes that were every color. Unwavering, he answered, "Thanks, don't know what I even said."

Whatever had seized Kevin blurted out, "So are you working with any new people?"

The monkeys went wild!

NO! What are you doing? The freaks countered with a harangue that left an adrenaline taste in his mouth. What Tom heard was:

Will you help me? of which Kevin was somehow aware. Just how he was aware of this was as mystical as the whole evening.

Tom simply answered; "Yeeahhh," the word drawn out with that same gentle tone that spoke volumes beyond it. He paused, then continued, "Love ta' get together."

In this way, around the meetings and working the program, it is highly recommended to have a sponsor. A sponsor is usually someone that has gone through the steps, has done the work and is willing to help guide people who have not, or that simply need assistance. Kevin heard to seek someone that "has what you want." But he did not even come close to knowing what he wanted, aside from peace.

There were all kinds of people with all kinds of ways to work the program. Some professed one way to be the only way. Yet, here he was finding his own way. It was such a different path. A more permeable force or power was guiding, leading. It had to be. This was all so … ambiguous. Maybe all the prayer had something to do with this? Subtle shifts in thinking and action were bringing change, helping him *listen* from another place.

Kevin had slipped from his daily prayer ritual lately. When he did pray, it was usually for guidance and for help, and now something had moved his feet toward Tom, spoken words right out of his mouth even, in spite of the berating primates' insistence to keep quiet and bolt out of there. He was beside himself and alive with inspiration, as if the old control panel had been commandeered and a more capable power flowed instead. Whatever it was, it felt like moving forward, and it felt good. Perhaps it had been invoked.

Be careful what you pray for

Tom wrote down his number. "Call me, anytime."

"Thanks, I will." Others milled around the room but were not interrupting the two in the now nearly deserted meeting hall.

"I'm not a *traditional* sponsor the way you may have heard around these rooms it's done. But we'll work together." Kevin had no idea what that meant. Still, he felt this new man, now in his life, had opened an abstruse doorway, further awakening a vitality long entombed.

***

Day to day, chaotic life settled into routine. Life at the apartment, the treatment program, and the daily commitments began to coalesce. Even band practice was better when recovery came first. Kevin called Tom the very day after meeting him and had a wonderful conversation, and of course did most of the talking. Postulating to Tom all he knew about alcoholism and addiction and recovery and spirituality in his whopping six months of experience, he almost forgot to breathe between sentences. And Tom, in his infinite patience, let him go on until he was finished. Only then he answered. "Well that sounds great, you have a good start at this thing and have found a way that seems to work so far. Nice going."

With Tom, he found a willing audience to share what was burning inside. This elder had an extraordinary capacity for listening. Kevin felt his caring and attentiveness. Yes, he liked this new man in his life.

During the conversation, Tom again said he was not a traditional sponsor. He told Kevin, "I'll be your *spiritual sponsor.*"

A spiritual sponsor? thought Kevin. *Great, I haven't even been praying much.* As if chops were necessary. Turns out, prayer works far beyond linear methods.

"Alright. I'm willing to try anything," Kevin replied, and he was.

When Tom spoke, it was often supernal. A soothing warmness came with the words, between them, through them, and, through him, all at once. Some timeless power effortlessly moving as a vast sea was revealing itself through a growing awareness. Kevin was drawn to Tom in ways that defied definition. He had not known anyone like him before, except his own father.

His dad had this way about him, too, this ability to genuinely listen, to be a true friend. Again he recalled how this connection between him and his father was beyond form and matter, an ethereal bond. Often he shared with others this notion: Though they were separated in human terms by decades, they shared an ageless connection. The countless phone conversations into all hours of the night, discussing nothing and everything; how he loved, too, those hours-long conversations at Dad's smoky little apartment. The once-white walls had a perfect tobacco-brown overlay, dusty piles of books and magazines on the multi-use table shared space with a well-used typewriter. He would sit just left of Dad, who was seated in a chair that could lean way back. Dad would push it back to its limit and raise his hands palm-up in the air as if receiving a large gift, like a giant globe or something, fingers out-stretched, and expel a hearty "Right. Right!" Maybe he was acknowledging some divine gift commingling in their meeting, just for the two of them. And it was.

Yes, Tom was a gift much like that.

~ Chapter 17 ~

Slippage

Monkeys are extremely intelligent creatures. They are crafty and cunning and demanding and love to get what they want. Maybe there was some way to satiate them by exerting just a little more of their own attributes against them. But what if real belonging could abate the endless seeking of domination?

The meetings and treatment were helping, though engaging life seemed to vacillate back and forth from the head to the heart; from self-will to trusting; from control to allowing; from fear to love. The sickness was still there, buried, threatening. Tom and others, meetings, groups, step work, and this Higher Power could only help to the degree which Kevin would allow.

Shack was an extraordinary fellow, and to his credit was an ability always to be creative, find little niches, ways to maneuver through life. Spending a lot of time together, the music was pouring out of them, which happened every time they got together. Shack with his guitar and Kevin behind the drums always led to new songs - good ones, too. This made it easier to look past their individual dishonesties and shortcomings.

They had also dabbled in business dealings together, and discussed possible schemes. Indeed, they just wanted to have fun and enough money to get by. Yes, that would surely do it, money and fun. Kevin was grateful they had let him stay at the band house on the couch. During this short time, Shack had introduced him to Craigslist's "Free" section. The new apartment was furnished for next to nothing. The universe easily showers inspired beings with plenty.

"Dude! I found a couch in Everett and a bed in Bellevue. All *free* - Let's go grab this stuff." Getting the goods was a whole adventure of its own. Kevin developed a near-addiction to the free section, and daily perusing

~ 199 ~

usually bore fruit. It was always good for entertainment, too – some of the unwonted items people attempt to give away!

And, now that he had this new garage to use, the wheels started turning again. Cameron owned a local car lot for which Shack had done some work. Visiting the place, it turned out Cam was an old high school buddy of Kevin's. And, he did have some jobs - small enough ones, in fact, that the damaged part of the vehicle could be taken off and brought into a shop that had only walk in doors. He wished the garage had a bay door, but it just did not, odd little building as it was. At least, he could do the repair and repainting inside, and then bring it out and bolt whatever part back onto the car. It was more work, but it was work.

Having few tools was another stumbling block. Another fellow who lived right next to the band house had a small compressor, a sander and a paint gun. He was willing to loan it to them, and did. The cold little rectangular shop had one interior wall dividing it into two un-even sides. On the smaller side went the tools, and on the other, the work was done. It was a decent little set up, and the price was right. The doorway faced east. Here in this humble garage, with only meager funds, a way was being made. Kevin's only part was taking small, consistent action. The rest was being supplied by some invisible source.

Providence will always meet every need

It was humbling starting over. Kevin had always identified himself as his possessions and sought worth externally. During the last year before the epic shift, the pawn shops swallowed up most stuff of any monetary value, and much had been stolen. When Mom sold that big shop, the upstairs still held all his personal items in boxes: Trinkets and memorabilia from childhood, possessions held dear, including one letter from Dad which he most treasured. The stuff had been in a couple dozen or so boxes, stored there because he had no other home - only the big, lonely shop. After Group, Kevin called the man that bought the place. Rob and he had done plenty of business over the years.

"I had a bunch of personal items in the upstairs," Kevin began. "Any chance I can get that stuff?" His voice cracked as he choked back tears. The humiliation of all that had transpired! Grotesque things had taken place in that very attic, and Rob surely had to clean up the horrific mess.

Rob was precise. "We took everything to the dump." Kevin heard rigidity and resentment in his tone.

It probably came from having to deal with that atrocious attic, Kevin thought. *Not to mention watching me go under with that gross addiction and alcoholism.*

By the time Kevin had abandoned that damned attic, it looked like some vagrant with severe mental issues and no respect for life had lived there. And that is just what had happened. He felt like an even bigger biggest loser in the world. Kevin paused with the recollections, mixed with the news, for only a tragic moment. But then, surrender. What could he do about it?

"OK, thanks," is all he replied, choosing to let it go, but with a bitter aftertaste. Just like that, all those possessions, reduced to fading memories.

A lifetime's accumulations, gone - *in an instant* - and taken to the dump, even.

Well, what about the damn gear!

Shack finally divulged, yes – the ebony, fine-shelled drums, the microphones and amplifiers, guitars, the speakers and racks of audio components, all the wires and plugs that connected all of it together: *Vanished.*

Yes, there was the grandiose story about how it came to be gone, but it was only capricious ranting. Ten thousand dollars and countless hours of work, evaporated. Though he figured Shack was probably lying and wanted to blame him for everything, the point-in-fact was that his own doing caused it, just like everything else. He had the biggest part in all of it, and for once in his life, was willing to own it.

This collection of band gear had taken more than a decade to accumulate, the stuff in the attic a lifetime. In one swoop it was *all* ... just gone.

The whole of it was a blessing in disguise, for it was all laced with an energetic residue of the very ways of thinking and being that had brought him to hover at the threshold of death's door, even *inside* for a feel.

The disappearance of these symbols of what once was - this was among the greatest of blessings. It only required a perception shift to realize. Retaining any of them would only be a weight and a burden, and would impede destiny unfolding.

Yes, it was all in perfect alignment, and more eternal doorways were certainly opening now. The Lotus flower grows from the mud and muck, indeed. The jewel is within. Practicing simple acceptance, he chose to let it all go, chose to forgive Shack (to the best of his ability) and move forward on the unfamiliar path. Lighter now, without the false idols and misguided material identification, these clearings made easier the next step on the Great Journey. Dad's letter was the only valuable thing he had lost.

The sweet voice of the Heart spoke again, saying only:

Through Me is the treasure you seek

***

Hanging out with Tom was always a lot of fun as well as nourishing; the man was calm, generous and eccentric. Many times, they met at the Alano club for the noon meeting, and when Tom got called on to share, his words and his voice were medicine. He had been coming around these rooms for more than twenty years, and his easy going approach helped Kevin see that struggling was only one possible option. Tom had also struggled in extreme selfishness. Now he rarely did so, simple as that.

Let go and allow

Today was especially nice, one of those winter days where the sun is out and visions of early spring beckon from afar. *A perfect day for Green Lake, skate along the water.* Slumbering trees lined the trail, standing still as the frigid lake. In the summer these friends were full with leaves of myriad greens, so vivacious. In the fall, their own transformation exuded an especially beautiful plethora of reds and yellows that faded into orange-browns just before detaching and returning to earth. But it was frigid now. They had let another season go and gone to sleep.

The jet-black knit hat snugged over Kevin's ears kept out the blue-cold air. If that biting wind got in there it nearly froze his brain. Sometimes, people would dart out in front of him, especially kids on bikes. It was wise to be diligent and careful. On days like today, after weeks of blustery and wet weather, the place was busy with people lured out-of-doors by the enticing sunshine. *It sure is beautiful today,* he thought, skating cautiously down a hill. Suddenly - "Watch out!"

He screamed at the careless couple who darted sideways directly in front of him. "Move!" Were they purposely trying to wreck him? The couple, instead, froze at his shriek.

Bam!

As they collided, going down promised to be a painful landing. Kevin did a sort of spastic maneuver, ridiculous and completely unnatural, arms flapping for balance, miraculously staying up on the clumsy skates - but drastically tweaking his lower back and an old injury.

"Sorry …" the girl called out, meekly. He barely maintained his balance and skated on, throwing only a scowl backward. At least tasting cold pavement was averted. "Damn it," he expelled, skating toward the car in pain.

The vagary messed him up, more than he realized at first. Over the next couple days, the pain got worst. And it was always pain alone that drove him to the doctor - always in hopes of procuring some opiate. Old injury, old solutions, old habits …

He told the doctor what had happened and described the nasty wrenching he was having, which had now somehow shifted directly to his balls. Doc figured it was a hernia, and recommended taking it easy – and narcotic painkillers.

The truth was - there was a great deal of discomfort. It sure did seem like it was all from the injury, and that the remedy was numbing it. That old diversion. But he was also in the treatment program, going to many meetings, and had a good support group. Treatment allowed such medication so long as the hospital filled out a form the court supplied, letting them know the prescribee was an addict, and – *it was taken as prescribed*. The doctor had no problem filling out the form for the the bottle of little white, chalky, bad-tasting relapse-enhancers.

At least a hundred pouncing monkeys with whipping tails grabbed at the little brown container with the childproof cap. He went into the first bathroom and read the label: *Take 1-2 for pain*. The craving writhed like snakes in a pit. His mouth watered. A wave of expectancy shot through in anticipation of the rush, chicken skin rising up the whole spine. Every hair rose right from the tailbone to the back of his neck. Even if he wanted, stopping himself now was not an option. Shaking and sweaty hands finally fumbled the lid open, popped two into the mouth like old times. He ducked under the running faucet for a gulp to wash them down. Coming up, he caught an uncomfortable glimpse of shifty eyes in the mirror, wiped his mouth with his sleeve and turned quickly away.

When the all-too-familiar sensation the substance entering his system caused, he changed. There was only temporary relief from the pain. This early in recovery and with as much of this crap as he had taken over these last few years, he only wanted one thing, even if he would not admit it: *More*.

On the way to EMI to turn in the form, he called Tom right away and let him know what had happened. Tom said it was OK, it would be all right. "Next time, call me *before* you take them." They talked about taking only the prescribed amount and Kevin emphatically maintained that he would - and did, for a long three days. In meetings he talked about the allergy, the obsession, the compulsion. But still, he knew he was in trouble, hated being on this crap! It felt like standing on thinly-frozen water. Again, he was caught in the dilemma of not wanting to take it and always wanting more, all at the same time. Not one minute went by free of thinking about it. The demon engulfed him, easily.

***

Tonight, the band would be tearing it up at a sleazy rock club he and Shack had played many times before - right along a run of boozing bars located within walking distance of each other. Lots of Kevin's drunken binges had occurred here on this strip, and tonight he was especially nervous. Being on the as-many-as-needed-as-determined-by-me meds schedule for over a month now, he was in a weakened state. Shack and the singer, Jimmy, found him.

"Hey. We're going to have a shot down the way." Shack pointed across the street, out the window of the venue they were playing. They were going to have the shots - Kevin was going to just come along. Entering the lounge, its ambience had all the beckoning of an old, reliable lover. Mentally maintaining he would not have any alcohol, they went in. That atrocious spring day when he'd guzzled those last three warm beers was just so far away.

The trio sat down at the bar. Neon lights glowed in the windows, dimly lighting the dungeon. People were having a good time. Kevin was plain nervous, but with a plastic smile to hide it. At one table, a man sat with his wife. Kevin knew them. Gary was someone he had fixed more than a few cars for over the years. He, also, had watched Kevin's decline.

"Hey Gary, Samantha, how are you?" Kevin said, acting real cool. "I got a new shop, been working. Need anything?"

"Sure, I always got a job for ya'," Gary said. "Give me a call."

"OK. Have a good night – Oh. We're playing across the street if you wanna check it out." Kevin was eyeballing their cocktails.

"'K, we'll talk soon." Gary was always smiling and happy. It felt awkward to see him here, but then all of it felt that way – the bars, the band, the pills; this whole night was just weird. It was all still too foggy coming through the eyes of pain-medicine-monster to put anything together.

Gary was relaxed and loose. He and Kevin had tossed back more than a few together, many times. Kevin recognized his friend's warm, sedated buzz. It was enticing. He suddenly became thirsty, kept swallowing dusty and dry. Such an uncomfortable dichotomy … what to do?

Before, he never hit the stage without attempting the perfect buzz. Sometimes he would drink too much and miss beats and wreck tempos and the like. Often, in fact. The more he drank the better he was - if only in a distorted mind. A perfect blend of pills and booze was always sought, chasing the right combo, fleeting as it was - for as soon as the razor's edge buzz was there, was it gone again. A horrible feeling: *Always wanting more*, and too much never being enough.

It had been some time since he had indulged, and the forgetter was working well tonight. Many taunting diversions dotted these slippery slopes. Everything was melding to justify the inevitable.

Jagermeister was among the stuff he had been drinking the night he flat-lined. The guys ordered their booze - the same thick, black licorice liquor of which he'd drank *way* too much in his guzzling career.

The shots came to the bar in front of them. *Three* of the little teasers.

It was like some haphazard test: There was the color line, he could roll the dice here … maybe his color would not come up. Probably wouldn't, besides, one shot. Who's gonna know? He could keep lying to the counselors, could hide from this as well.

The guys guessed the bartender accidently brought the extra little one-ounce demon. Might as well have it, they figured. "We don't wanna mess you up, dude," the boys said, practically in unison. He got the feeling they wanted him to drink. Maybe he was dull sober, maybe they missed him drinking, maybe he was too serious, maybe he needed to loosen up – a thousand leading thoughts danced in disarray.

Screaming Monkeys!

The plain truth was that he was an alcoholic and needed a drink. Blood for the vampire. Then he thought about the program, the clichés about people going back out: "It's that first drink that gets ya'. Try getting drunk without it." He had heard it said enough times.

The shot stared at him.

He remembered something else he had heard. If you doubt you have a problem, go out and try some controlled drinking, see how it works for you. Any excuse would do. All the suffering heretofore was suddenly cloaked from memory, a stealth fighter now. The dangling decision: *I can have just this one, that's all. This will* prove *I can handle it* …

And with that, he took the shot. It was warm and soothing and he hated it immediately. Shack perked up a little at Kevin's audacious toss-back. "Been a while, huh, bro?"

Kevin replied, morose. "Yeah." The somber tone spoke a world that did not match the word.

The very same thing occurred instantly, as with the pills - he wanted more. More! He wanted to maintain that perfect elusive buzz and nothing else mattered. Another problem was his tolerance. The tortuously puny doses of pain medication he had been punishing and teasing himself with in the beginning – this had recently turned into taking way more than prescribed, buying the stuff from dealers, and *constant* obsession. Mixed with one lousy shot, no way was this going to come close to satiating anything - so down went another, in spite of telling himself: *Just the one.*

He hated himself right now. The truth was, his Spirit did not want to be here, and yet here he was. *Powerless.* Right now he just did not care. Again at some damned turning point, scared and alone, except for the new life, which seemed ten thousand hours, a million miles away. A rush of longing for the peace of nature again near the river trail felt sinking. The band was on stage in only a half-hour, and this battle raged within. Drinking monkeys and rabid demons toasted each other in a burning hell.

He hated the pain pills, hated the bars and what was here, hated these castigating, vicious thoughts! Torture ensued as he walked across the street and back into the venue club. The music blaring off the massive stage was too loud. In this skanky place, all his abysmal focus was on fighting a thousand screaming monkeys. Still, he put on the "cool and together" act, flashing false smiles at hungry takers.

Be quiet, he longed to yell out loud. *Shut up!*

But instead, he could only approach the bar as if on auto-pilot and get yet *another* shot, as if another would quell the agony. He put two more pills in his mouth, swallowed them down. The woman that poured the monster - he swore her eyes sang with satanic delight as she handed over the thick black syrup. This time it was in a much larger glass. This bartender knew him well. The hand-off took place, free of charge, for such a long-time loyal customer. Then, another, another, another

And this was enough. *Enough!*

Kevin went purposefully back to his drums, loaded them on stage, and played the show. He might have cried if acting cool was not of paramount importance around these parts. Cold River had a decent performance, which was for him only forgettable. This whole night was. The booze did not work to produce any effect he truly desired, even if he had thought it would, once again. The pills had failed, too, even the combination had. Old solutions no longer worked. Something had changed. There was a dark cloud over this night, and it rained on him all the way home.

***

A gentle intimation came, sunlight breaking through the gross haze. Sanctuary called from not far away.

It is possible to live a life of Love

This life had been tasted, and not long ago. It felt wonderful to be free like that, released from the anaconda chains that bound and constricted again, tonight. No, not so far away ...

The still, small voice proffered once again:

It is possible to change

~ Chapter 18 ~

Ancient Ceremony

Surely the coldest February wind that ever was shot through thick outer layers, clear to the marrow of his bones as two scurrying feet crossed the meager cement porch into his barely warmer domicile. A gust of extreme loneliness came, too, as a shiver shut the door behind itself. Kevin longed for answers: Would he ever find his purpose or forever be stuck in a plane that was going *down?* Could that grievous night possibly mark the last drink he would ever take? Would sporadic serenity ever find its way to true peace? Would the burning questions within ever be answered?

The guilt was so unbearable he flushed the last of the pain killers. His face turned red as his vagus nerve fired, burned through his chest and pushed at his throat and eyes. He was hanging off the edge of a cliff by one hand and even those fingers were slipping.

Tom let Kevin's discourse about the drinking roll by like passing rain clouds, the same way he did about the pills and about most small-minded complaining. Tom acknowledged the admissions, yet let another remedy work, providing guidance in a much subtler way than a reprimand might bring about.

Tom had a way of acknowledging without inserting much, if any, judgment. Often it was done with one particular sound, which he uttered in his own special way. The sound offered with it the soothing medicinal quality and timeless wisdom. He was sharing a much older remedy. It might come after Kevin gave an ear-bending rendition of why the world had wronged him, or after sharing that Jesus himself had made a personal visit. It was, simply:

"Ohhh …"

He lied to Tom about the amounts, about the depth of despair, but even telling anyone he had slipped was progress. Kevin knew it was not clean, knew he was abusing the pills and knew he was in trouble. His own will to not use had failed again, even being in treatment and doing the meetings. There was still the gnawing pain in his lower back and lower, and a thought began to percolate that perhaps it was more than only physical. Maybe this had something to do with losing the battle in the bar that night. Kevin just did not know.

Onto the knees in the little apartment. He swore his heart quivered as he entered it again, as the tears spilled off his cheeks once more:

"God, whatever you are … please help me stay sober. I'm sorry I messed up and fell, please help me do better. I cannot do it on my own, from whatever I have been until now, I need you. I feel so empty without you. Teach me how to see what I cannot, how to live. Thank you. *Thank You.* I know you can hear me; I will listen with everything in me. I trust you. I love you so much … Please help me."

***

Tom and Kevin met up at the noon meeting. Sometimes, Tom would mutter "… dog and pony show." Today was one such day - someone would get on a soapbox and preach instead of sharing. There was a distinguishable difference, though Kevin could not tell half the time. It was baffling how one person heard a totally different thing than the person sitting right next to them. During one man's sharing, every word irritated Kevin to the core. Even his tone, maybe especially. This guy, *so* irritating to listen to his ranting!

He *finally* shut up and the meeting ended. Kevin was sure Tom must be thinking the same thing, and turned to him: "Can you *believe* that guy? Auuggghh."

Tom responded, "Yeah, that was *awesome.*"

Kevin's jaw dropped, though he kept quiet. No, he did not think it was so awesome! Maybe this pointed to something. With the profound respect that had been developed for Tom, he decided to try and deepen the listening next time, see if he could maybe hear some of what Tom must have heard. Maybe something important was missed by way of the thick judgment.

During the meeting after the meeting, Tom extended an invitation. "Hey, we're having a sweat Sunday if you want to come by."

What was a sweat? He had no idea. "A sweat? Whad'ya mean?"

"Oh." Tom said. "Sweat Lodge Ceremony, you know what that is?"

"No, what is it? Like a sauna or something?"

"Well, kind of, I guess," Tom said.

Then he explained in a very general way. "There's a structure … maybe, like a tent, kinda' dome shaped, holds about 25 people."

"We heat up some special stones in a big fire and then bring them inside, sing some songs and have some prayers."

Sounded strange. But he liked being with Tom, and there was just something about it that was intriguing.

"Lots of people come. It's good." Tom spoke in an easy, inviting way, like having someone over for tea.

He went on. "We hang out around the fire, have the sweat, and then there's a grand feast at the big table up in the house; everyone brings some food. There's always lots of food, and great fellowship."

That word "fellowship" kept coming up, too - made Kevin think of the Knights of the Round Table or something. Such a medieval word, it was to him. Some of the meetings were held in what were called fellowship halls. He figured it pretty much meant a group getting together in a good way, and that reminded him of Dad. So did Tom.

"You don't have to come." Tom's kind glances were always comforting. "But you're welcome to. If you do, bring some shorts and a couple towels. If you don't have any, we have a bunch of extras."

Sunday was several days away. He didn't know if he might go, or not. Even though he had no idea what this "sweat" was, he trusted Tom. Plus, he liked food, and was beginning to love this sober fellowshipping. In fact, fellowship became his new favorite word. And, especially now, coming off the relapse he needed to pull close. Tom said the sweat was physically detoxifying. At the very least, a big get-together might be nice. In a way, the sound of it reminded him of the ones that his family used to have, when Dad would come over and they would all have a big meal together. Difference then, he was always loaded at those get-togethers, loud, and boisterous - maybe to shut up the turmoil in his own head. Maybe, if he talked and laughed loud enough and told enough raunchy jokes and drank enough, he wouldn't have to listen to those damn monkeys …

Kevin's brain momentarily flashed back to elementary school, angry and loud even at ten years old, chubby and uncomfortable in his clothes. The teachers and counselors decided he was hyper-active, which was no stretch. They gave him a watch to wear, but it was not for counting time. It counted instances, instead, by way of a manual clicking. They said, "Every time you feel like yelling, click the watch." He found it difficult to ever get out a sentence, because all he ever did was yell over everyone. He would have to interrupt himself mid-yell to click the damn watch. In only a couple days, the watch broke from over-clicking. Seemed like everything he touched broke.

But here, now, he was making so many friends and enjoying this new life, even though he had cheated lately. The guilt from using and hiding it brought that sick feeling. He hated how every aspect of the lack of control made him feel! Tom mentioned the sweat was cleansing in many other ways, too. Kevin was curious, but more – he was desperate. Tom sure was vague about the whole thing, and was not one to try and force anything upon anyone. Rather, he tended to let things be, work themselves out.

Tom reflected life as a great flow, uncontainable and uncontrollable. You can simply flow with it or fight and resist. Each way brings a distinct set of results.

Yeah, he would go to this sweat thing, see what it was all about.

Inipi Ceremony

The Explorer squeaked to a halt in front of the double-garage doors of a massive home. Tom's place was in a beautiful neighborhood with expensive homes boasting large yards and magnificent sweeping views, much like where Kevin had been raised. The house was like Mom's, too, with its huge deck. The several levels must have at least ten bedrooms and who knows how many bathrooms. About the property were copious trees of all sorts, various plants and shrubs. Rolling lawns began at the top of the yard and terraced down, all the way to the bottom of the shy-acre. A small creek which fed a pond below huge cedars trickled along the southwest side of the home. In the moment it came into view, he felt it.

Above the waterway on a clearing of bare earth a large fire raged. Beyond this fire place was the sturdy-looking dome shaped structure. It had a small opening, which if one was to enter, would have to be on the knees and crawling. The height of the door was less than two feet. The sight of it caused a mix of emotions. The earth was cold and damp.

A few of the faces in the wood and plastic chairs around the fire were familiar. A community, family atmosphere filled the whole space, emanating outward like ripples in a still pond. It was a calm, peaceful, warm feeling. Interwoven into it all was a palpable presence – a focused *Intention.* There was great purpose to this gathering, and Kevin's being was stirred by it.

Tom welcomed him first with a long, compelling gaze, which pulled at Kevin. It came again in the timelessness. Ten other ancient souls were also witnessing through his eyes, or it could have been ten thousand. The very same look and feeling present the night of their meeting lasted only a flash – milliseconds of measured time, lifetimes in pure consciousness.

Just as quickly, Tom spoke. "Hello. Glad you could make it … here, meet some friends."

Kevin peered, confused, at the small doorway of the dome. Tom relieved him of having to ask. "That's the *Inipi.*"

"The what?" Kevin had never heard the word.

"Inipi. Sweat lodge," Tom clarified.

Kevin's imagination chugged as he recalled the mental picture he had painted of what a sweat lodge must look like. This was not it. A weathered, greenish canvas of some sort covered the whole thing. It appeared as though the covering lay upon a crude stick frame, by his ignorant summation.

Tom's whole heart was smiling as he watched Kevin's process. They were student and teacher, only the student had no idea. Maybe the teacher didn't, either. Time would tell.

Between the Inipi and the fire a raised mound of about three feet in diameter had handful-sized stones around it. *Volcanic rocks?* Whatever they were, they had been carefully stacked to form a circular, raised border. Oddities decorated this mound, one of which was a painted, feathered and beaded buffalo skull.

"That's the Altar," Tom said with a humble respect. His speech was easy and gentle.

"We heat up these stones in this Sacred Fire …"

Kevin looked into the center. How was this fire any different from a regular old fire? Underneath the neatly stacked burning wood he could barely see the stones, ranging from the size of small bowling balls to much larger ones. 25? 35?

"Then we bring them into the Inipi. In the center, there's a pit dug into the ground … we place 'em there, and sit around them in a circle."

"In there?" Kevin said, crouching down a little and peering in from a safe distance. He could not see much, no pit, and, not wanting to appear too concerned or anxious, he only nodded.

"Yeah. We'll bring in some stones, close the door, sing some songs and have some prayers. There are four rounds; after each round we'll open the door, take a small break, then bring in a few more stones and have another round. There's a lot more to it, but that's basically it. You'll see as we go."

So many questions. But not wanting to *look* ignorant, he just nodded his head again and found a seat. He was drawn to the peace at this gathering. The people sitting calmly having small talk … they were content just being. There were no agendas here, no rushing or urgency for anything, no specific start time, or end time. But there was *something* here. It was awkward, too. So much so, he thought about just getting back in the Explorer and leaving. At the same time, the whole of the gathering was awakening something inside of him that wished to be recognized.

Quieter now, most of the people were crafting small pieces of colored cloth and tobacco into mini-bundles as the fire warmed them. Intent on their work, some were obviously meditating and others whispered prayers as they finished each one and tied it to a red string of many. Some even breathed their prayers right into the colored little things.

"Prayer ties," Tom gestured. "Would you like to make some? You can put your prayers into them and take them into the Inipi with you." One woman had a stretch of blue, yellow, red and white ties, each some two inches apart. It was a long strand, must have taken some time.

"Oh, no, that's OK," Kevin declined, overwhelmed by the whole thing in general and intimidated by the powerful energy altogether.

His mind raced: *What am I doing here?* How had he come to be here? Did he really want to be going inside this dirty old thing with these rocks that were sure to be extremely hot, and how did that work, anyway?

When Tom had first mentioned the sweat lodge, Kevin's mind saw a big YMCA or a public gym or the like, a regular sauna with glass doors and benches, where the steam was hot, but controllable. He had done these before, and had liked them enough. But this was nothing like that, not at all. It rattled him.

Here it was again, the trying to appear as though he had it all under control. But he really felt less than, scared to be here – though he was curious. And, he knew he longed for something. Maybe this something had brought him here.

A giant of a man tended the fire, going at it like killing snakes, but with great respect for the intensity of the heat and the flames. The man worked with the pitchfork, arranging the flaming wood around the stones, anxious to get it to his satisfaction and get away from it, which he finally accomplished. Sweat dripping off his brow, huffing and puffing as if between rounds of a wrestling match, the fire tender sat down with a thud in a green plastic chair. It trembled but held him.

"This is Big John," Tom said. Kevin shook the massive hand. Big John looked him up and down, the huffing and puffing slowing as he did. Big John wiped the sweat across his brow with the back of his wrist.

Kevin breathed the peace and wood-smoke odor of him. John had heard Tom sharing a little about the basics, and wished to embellish:

"It gets *hot.* If it gets too hot, pray harder," he said with a distant gaze, surely recalling too many times he had practiced this very thing he was sharing. The flames of the fire reflected off his glasses. Or maybe the flames were in his eyes instead of pupils as he recalled the heat, like dollar signs when someone thinks too hard about money.

"It's not a tough man competition." Big John gazed on, not at anything in particular. "In fact, the tougher you try to be, the harder it is."

Big John went on to share more about the way it is in the lodge, his version at least, which did not help Kevin feel any better about going in. But then, something difficult to grok began to make Itself known. It came from within, the feeling. It was as if everything was vibrating.

What was this badgering of the brain? There were two parts, one that said "be afraid" and the other that said "just be." He chose to listen to both of them, and confusion threatened to reign. The Something was seeking to emerge through the fear, the whole scene. He juggled the possible scenarios:

He could just leave, but how would that make him look? The thousand screaming thoughts went to work. Yet, the warm nurturing undercurrent waited patiently and with great stillness, effortlessly overpowering all of them - *if only he would allow it.*

A glance up, over the deck rail and into the kitchen found a few women bustling about, surely preparing the feast. He could only imagine the aroma of home cooking. Most who came showed up with some kind of a dish or dessert. One man brought Tom another gift. Extending a long, meaningful handshake, the pouch of tobacco in between their palms, his other hand gently upon Tom's shoulder, their eyes locked. An exchange of great respect was taking place. Tom said a word in a language Kevin did not recognize, as the handshake turned into a hug.

For the next hour or so this was the scene: Various people tended to the Sacred Fire, some gathered more firewood and placed it around its perimeter, splitting it and making sure there was plenty. Others sat patiently and finished their work. The stones in the center of the fire grew increasingly hot. More people arrived, bringing gifts and food, finding a seat near the fire's warmth, preparing the prayer ties, making small talk. Tom made sure each person was attended to, doing his best to introduce everyone.

It felt good to be a part of this family right now. At the same time though, that fear buzzed in the back of his mind like nagging mosquitoes: Fear of the unknown, fear of the heat, fear of being revealed. Again, the Voice:

Trust, you will always be safe ~ All your needs are met right now

A couple of the women brought down generous stacks of blankets of Native American design. They took them inside the Inipi. Kevin could see them through the small doorway being carefully placed upon the Earth. The energy of the people began to shift, their attention now more inward but also directed toward the Inipi and the Altar.

"Time to get changed up," Tom announced. Some already were; the others went to do so. The women wore loose dresses, and the men, shorts or

~ 213 ~

something they did not mind getting sweat-soaked. Tom had everything in that huge house. Plenty of towels, extra dresses, shorts and shirts, more blankets, all of which sat upon a rack of shelves inside the sliding glass door of the downstairs big-room. The room also served as a changing room for the men.

Kevin stripped to shorts only and then squished his way down the slope toward the Sacred Fire. Soggy grass and mud tickled between his toes and the earth beneath bare feet felt good. *Too late to turn back now.* Everyone gathered round Fire and Altar, coming together for the ceremony. All the elements were coming to life.

Tom held a large, flat head shovel with a pile of some kind of dried plant in it along with a braided strand of long grass and some cedar on top. In the center, he placed a good sized, hot coal from the fire. The blend began to smolder thick white smoke, the aroma pleasant. He called it, "Smudge - sage, sweet grass and cedar."

Tom brought the smudge around, each person wafting it over themselves in slightly different fashions, turning around and letting the smoke touch each part of them, as if they were bathing in it. Tom then walked around clockwise, smudging the outside of the Inipi, and then inside. He set the shovel down carefully, next to the Altar, still smoldering. Kevin loved its sweet and appealing scent. All attention turned toward Tom, the Altar, and the Lodge.

An older man with long grey hair rested a hand-made drum against his leg. He was lean and muscular with darker skin. The stick he held was a crooked branch, polished from many uses, with an animal hide bulb tied on the end with rawhide strips. As the steady rhythm commenced, he and several of the people began singing in the alluring, primal language. This drum and song stirred even more of what was waking up in Kevin, enveloping and moving him in some familiar, far-off way.

Everyone was now standing in a large circle around Tom, who was beginning another ritual. From a colorful, long and narrow tan leather pouch decorated with beads, he removed a pipe stem, and then a red-colored T-shaped bowl. He smudged each piece with reverence, holding them in prayer a long while before putting them together. Tom held the assembled pipe with great respect, offering it toward each of seven directions, still praying. Then, opening the drawstring of a smaller leather pouch, he removed a pinch of some concoction, held it up, smudged it, and put it in the pipe. He repeated this many times until the pipe was full.

Kevin did not know what Tom had put in the pipe, and wondered if it was anything he should not be smoking if invited. If it was, he could simply pass on it. Something told him it was safe, had to be if Tom was doing it.

The drum stopped, as did the singing. The air was calm and still around the synergy. Kevin could feel the trees watching as they swayed gently in the living breeze that surrounded the gathering. The sweet stillness was only enhanced by the crackling wood and gurgling stream.

In the enraptured silence, Tom rested the pipe with great care against the skull at the Altar, and only then spoke:

"I'd like to thank each and every one of you for coming here today; it means so much to have you here to share in this sacred way.

"We come here today for ceremony, to sing and to pray, to suffer some, and to honor the gift of life."

Here it was again, this suffering thing. He did not like the sound of it, and with what Big John had said he wondered if he would be able to go through with it. He only wanted to *look* like a tough guy, but closer to the truth, he was scared of everything. Maybe this is what Big John was talking about; maybe he could see right through Kevin.

But, as Tom continued to speak prayers aloud, the voice again soothed him, accompanied now by a symphony of spirits, all here to help him find another way. The message was inside him, part of him and part of every living thing.

Let go ~ Everything is all right

The message allowed another choice through the fear. It came as trust and total respect for, with and by pure Love. Beyond time and space itself, it was so powerful that for once, he did not feel the need to argue, to listen to a thousand reasons why not to go through with this. His thinking mind had been easily suspended by this omniscient power, which each one here, now, helped call forth.

The spirits were dancing for him!

Beyond even emotion, only One Presence was flowing now, unobstructed for this instant. It was Love. Had it been there always? It felt eternal. As Tom went on speaking, Kevin could see and feel that this gathering meant everything to him. He loved what he was witnessing, loved being invited, and loved that he was a *part* of it.

It was time to go on in to this strange Inipi that might just swallow him whole. Dread and fascination did silent battle within. With no idea what to expect, he would continue on blind faith. The others did not seem scared, so he just acted cool. One by one, each person knelt in front of the small door and touched their forehead to the ground. Several spoke in the other language. Tom had told him for now to just say "All My Relations" when he entered the lodge, acknowledging just that: The relationship of all living beings.

Each person crawled on their hands and knees, barefoot on the blankets upon the cool earth, and found a seat around the center - most sat cross-legged. The dirt smelled good. It was cold in this Inipi and he could feel the whole earth. The people finished entering, forming a fairly tight circle, shoulder to shoulder. Now, he could see the pit better, around which the blankets were neatly placed. Above, boughs neatly tied together formed the branch-frame of the lodge. Other blankets were between them and the outer canvas. From the vantage of his spot, he could also see the fire out through the door, just past the Altar.

"We will now welcome in the Grandfathers." Tom motioned out to Big John, who then broke the fire apart and removed one stone from the fire with a pitchfork, which looked … challenging. Then, he held up the stone, and a woman with a brush made from fresh cedar branches dusted it off, until it was perfectly clean. This would be repeated for each and every one.

The stone was glowing red-hot!

Tom again spoke for the benefit of the newcomers. "We use this cedar, this powerful medicine, to clean the Grandfathers. One, it blesses and purifies them. And two, it removes ash from the fire, which is not good to breath, especially when the water mixes with it. It takes care of us in both ways."

What did he mean, "Grandfathers?" And what was this putting water on them?

As if Tom heard these questions, he went on. "We call them Grandfathers because they are so ancient … these stones have been around for millions of years, have seen *so much*. They are *wise*." The way he said this, along with the pause, caused Kevin to listen even more intently, find a keener attention. "Wise like grandfathers, they carry with them this ancient wisdom. In this way they can help us."

Kevin liked how this sounded, and it made him think, *really* think. More than that, it let him feel. *It's true,* he pondered; *they have been around for a long, long time.* He imagined the life of one of these Grandfather Stones. Yes, it made sense that they embodied millions of years of patient, profound wisdom. Different from the stones in that old backpack? The contemplation felt so good. Why did it resonate *so* much?

It was still daylight out and the darkness inside shifted as Kevin's eyes adjusted. But that was about to change. People were also shifting to find a comfortable position, and he wondered how this was going to work, hours of sitting in here with some fifteen other men and women. How hot was it going to get? Would it break him? His knees already began to ache as he squirmed. Would he make a fool of himself?

The first Stone came in. A man just inside the door respectfully took it with a pair of deer antlers, and set it gently off to one side of the pit. Heat radiated from it. One woman leaned forward and placed a small amount of sage directly onto the glowing red Stone, which immediately began to smoke. People whispered "Welcome, Grandfather," as the smoke danced around, its pungent odor finding their nostrils. Some leaned in and wafted this smoke over themselves. Then another Stone came, same thing. Then another, each time carefully placed in each of four directions, each time having only a little smudge placed on it, each Stone venerated by the whole group. The temperature in the Inipi continued to rise.

Acknowledging Life with great reverence was the foundation of this ceremony. As the Stones came, sweat beads trickled down and down.

When there were enough by Tom's cue, the fire tender covered up the remaining ones in the fireplace outside with more wood, carefully. Big John crawled inside only after handing in the drum and a bucket of water to Tom. Swirling heat waves from the Grandfather Stones closed in.

Tom spoke again. "I'd like to thank each and every one of you, again, for coming here today and being part of this family," his voice gentle and quivering with happiness. It was obvious this day, this moment, meant the world to him.

Kevin had never known anything like this, did not *remember* ever being around such honor, total respect and tender care. It was thick in the air, all-encompassing. Time now slowed. He felt as if he were floating. The nameless fear still loomed but here, it felt out of place. Was it possible he could actually *choose* it or … not? This thought was a blip on the screen. It went by so fast that it was more visceral than an actual thought. His mind held little with which to compare it. Choose or release? Could it be that simple?

"This ceremony has been around for a very long time. Inside this Inipi is the womb of Mother Earth. We bring the door down and it becomes dark, representing our ignorance."

God, it made so much sense in some curious way.

"Here, we can become like children."

Tom nodded to John, who then pulled down whatever was to cover the door, adjusted it, made sure no light was coming through, and then became still again. The darkness left only glowing Grandfathers; it was looking into the core of the earth. Heat disseminated from them like rapid growing vines wrapping legs, arms, bodies.

"At any time if it becomes too hot for you, it is all right to call for the door to be opened, and we will help you out and make sure you are OK. But first, you might try to pray deeper, go within just a little more … also, Mother Earth is our helper, she is cool, and we can come closer to her. She will help us. If this does not work for you and you need to get out for any reason, just say 'All My Relations' and we will open the door."

Kevin hoped he would not have to call for the door, wanted to stay. He began to feel some hiding child within. This child was wounded, tender, and vulnerable. The nurturing made his throat tight and his eyes swell with tears that threatened his façade. It was like being home in a place he had forgotten. He bowed his head in one final attempt to hold back, but the tears began to flow down his cheeks, commingling with bullets of sweat as he trembled. But these tears were not from pain or fear.

Tom said more words. Just what they were is not as important as what came between them, around them, and through them. As he spoke, verbal affirmations from the men and women acknowledging agreement and receiving came, the most common being the sound "Aho." Kevin remained silent, trying to hold it together, dumbfounded at the whole of the ceremony.

Tom poured water on the Stones. Hissing with delight, the powerful Grandfathers easily turned the water into steam, which danced around the lodge and coated and penetrated each one's skin. Then more water, the heat rising each time. It felt good. Honoring the directions, Tom spoke about the North, the East, the South, and then the West. Tom spoke eloquently of Mother Earth, Father Sky, and of Creator. He talked directly to Spirit as well as the people, while spilling water upon the Stones. Deep seated longing within Kevin continued to open and come alive, a bubbling volcano brought forth by the depth of Tom's message. It was a message of the integral connection of all living beings, and everything is alive.

"We will now sing a Four Directions Song to honor each direction and welcome those good Spirits into our Lodge." The drum began and soon after, most of the circle was singing in the other language. It was here the ancestors came and fully revealed themselves. They danced around the lodge and became visible as Kevin's Spirit joined the ancient dance. They told Kevin that not only is his living body interconnected with all form and matter but that his Spirit is eternal. It is part of them, and they of him. This essence is the fundamental connection of the Spirit of Life itself. It is a boundless ocean. It is a web that stretches throughout the entire cosmos, connecting everything.

The drum, the harmony of voices, and all the elements reflected in and through each other as the Spirit of the ceremony integrated with each soul attending. The world itself began to collapse inward.

The physical temperature was penetrating, but the song was access to the inscrutable strength, the whole of it taking him within, where the heat had almost no effect, just as Tom had suggested.

When the song was over, everyone said nearly at once, "Aho." Again in the same uncanny way, as if the language and its words were second to the greater eternal truths they carried, the Spirits spoke through Tom, took him over. He had allowed them, asked for it even. After a couple more of these pervading songs, the door was opened. How much time had passed? Kevin was nowhere and everywhere.

As light filtered into the Inipi, he looked over at Tom. Sitting with one knee up and one down, drum resting gently on his leg, drenched strands of white hair crawled down the front of his body. The smoke and steam were dancing wayward gypsies. Tom became an ancient portrait in the light and shadows. Kevin did not know what was happening. This whole captivating process … just did not know.

More Stones were brought in. Hotter than the first ones, glowing close to molten lava, each one welcomed in and smudged in the good way. One woman lay on her side. Outline curves flowed along her entire length, past hip and over soft shoulder, dipping and rising hills and valleys. Long dark hair curled past her breasts and spilled onto the ground, one delicate hand outstretched toward the Stones. This da Vinci masterpiece sang the sweetest melody. The lone, tender, female voice … must be Mother Earth herself singing a song at the Altar of Love.

The door came down again, and this time Tom said he was going to put some medicine on the Stones. What did that mean? He sprinkled small cedar bits on them, which crackled and popped and hopped on the glowing Stones. They provided just enough light to barely see, illuminating only nuances in the Lodge. Kevin swore one Stone was the face of an elder who had come to him in a dream. Smoke swirled up and then back down again. "Breathe in this medicine, it is good for you," Tom offered, and many wafted the smoke over their bodies again.

He poured more water on the Grandfather Stones, hissing and sizzling as it instantly turned to steam. When it hit the skin, it was almost too hot to bear now. But then the drum and another song began and it somehow soothed the rapidly increasing heat. Now began an even stranger mix of elation and fear - and this odd, surreal power was intensifying as well. It was through and around, commingling the entire lodge and all in it, swirling, dancing and permeating.

The Spirits had been called and welcomed and they were here, dancing everywhere!

Here, in the dark, with the heat and the songs and the intentions set from the beginning, the material universe disappeared. They all became only One: The people, the grandfathers, the drum, the medicines, the earth, the air, the fire and the water, stars and planets and galaxies. All One, all related. Everything, interdependent: One living breathing whole.

Would this last song of the round ever come to an end? The heat was reaching a nearly intolerable climax. It was certainly beyond physical. Kevin had never endured anything like it, and vacillated between fear and love, feeling awkward between them. The steam that could only be felt in this dark place almost burned his skin. The water continued to hiss as it transformed upon hitting the Grandfathers, sheets of punishing heat testing him. He flew between dimensions, wanting to cry out and yet not wanting to look like a fool or seem to be afraid. But he was both; this thought not able to be completed as he shuffled around trying to find a position that would let him stay even another second.

The door *finally* opened. He gasped in a breath of wonderful cool air, as quietly as possible - in this moment, realizing what it felt like to be truly grateful. At the same time he wanted it closed again - to go back into the surreal meditation that could take away the fear, that nourished every part of whatever he was. Even though there was suffering, it was far beyond worth it.

As the light fused in, he saw bodies glistening with sweat. Some were lying down, some sitting up, some suffering and others calm, even serene. Tom spoke in a taxed breath: "This water." Even the pause between the words spoke.

"This Sacred Water is the first medicine. Without it nothing lives." A more primordial voice now uttered just two words in the other language. The words were unclear, except for their humble, full respect.

Kevin thought about that … without water, he realized, there would be no life. He suddenly became grateful for the water, simultaneously realizing how thirsty he was. What a gift his next drink of water would be! Why had he not ever realized what a gift was this water he'd always taken for granted?

"We will hand this around; take a drink if you wish … pour it on any part of you that needs healing … it will help you." Tom scooped some water out of the bucket with an apparatus that looked like an animal horn attached by rawhide strips to a foot and a half long branch, adorned with various dangling trinkets, attached with more of these strips. All natural. The trinkets looked to be animal, too, and sounded alive as they rattled together, singing their own song. This represented something, too – even a fool could see this, feel it. Tom purposefully spilled just a little onto the Stones which let out a quick sizzle, easily transmuting water into steam. Now visible, it flitted up and away, disappearing into the ether.

Someone giggled as the first person Tom handed the water poured it on his head. This aroused Kevin's mind further. Everything here was challenging the very way he thought and had walked his whole life. Only, it did so in a good way, helping him to see with different eyes, eyes he *did not know* he possessed. A rush of gratitude filled him as someone handed him this contraption that held the precious element. It was animal horn, handmade, and what Tom had been pouring the water with, and from which they were now drinking.

He took this horn, half-full of Sacred Water, and prayed with it. With the new found gratitude, he raised the horn just slightly in a show of acknowledgment to the Source, just as Tom had done, contemplating the gift of it. Raising it up with both hands, purposefully, he poured just a tiny splash on top and to the back of his head. It trickled down the length of his spine. Then he put it to his lips, and tipped the horn back. Never had water tasted so exquisite, never had he felt it cascade just this way, through him, into each cell. Never before had the water been alive, for never before had he cared to listen, to consider, beyond only taking from it. Careful not to drink it all, he handed it to the next person. As the water made its way around, Tom talked about the next round, the third round. He called it the prayer round.

"These Grandfathers, the ancient wisdom they embody ... they are *powerful.*" He paused to allow a moment of contemplation before going on. "They will take from us that which we no longer wish to carry. Maybe you are having trouble in your life, many of us are. Maybe a loved one is suffering or sick, or has passed." A woman sobbed, and Kevin's heart went out, opened even more as he approached tears, memories of Dad almost painful. The others seemed to absorb the pain, as he was doing with the woman. "Maybe you are struggling with addiction, anger, jealousy, hurting ... or are stuck somewhere you do not want to be. Maybe you just wish to share your gratitude. We can release anything onto the Grandfathers, and they will take it ... we do this with *Intention*, speaking whatever it is and letting it go unto the Stones."

It was palpable now; Kevin could almost hear the people contemplating what to let go.

"Then we pour the water onto the Grandfather Stones, which turns to steam, mixing with those prayers and intentions. When we open the door, it all goes out and away, and we no longer have to carry these things we have named. *If we choose.* Great Spirit will take anything we ask."

Another pause let the meditation set in. "Our only job is to let go of them, to trust, and not pick back up and shoulder them again when we leave, trusting Creator with them. We can just let go."

This was staggering to Kevin, and it made so much sense. Was it possible? He thought about that fourth and fifth step he had done not even six months ago and how they had burned the paper upon which it was written. Watching it burn, as the smoke and the ashes drifted off, he had experienced a similar notion. Same with the backpack full of stones.

Was being here connected to all that by way of some metaphysical extension? Just how powerful was this spiritual way? This could be the greatest discovery ever made!

Tom continued: "Pray about anything you wish, this is a safe place. What we hear here and what we see here, we leave it here." Kevin had heard this before, at the meetings. "We will bring some more Grandfathers in, sing a song and then have the prayers, starting to my left and going clockwise. You are welcome to pray in silence, too, if you wish."

Kevin swallowed hard. What would he pray about? Since he was several persons from Tom's left, he would be able to see how the others prayed. This was a relief. Tom's voice changed now, even again. "Before we begin with the prayers, we will bring in the Chanupa." Big John handed in the long-stemmed pipe Tom had so humbly prepared. Could this be the famed peace pipe? What could possibly be in it? What was it for?

When Tom accepted the Chanupa, taking it in his hands, it was as if he had known it throughout many lifetimes. He held it with deep respect and tender loving care.

"This is the Sacred Pipe and with it we share our prayers." He allowed for contemplation again before going on, as he did so much, taking a few purposeful breaths. "The bowl represents the feminine, and the stem the masculine. When you hold it, you are holding the world. Left hand on the bowl … with the right, the stem. This pipe opens up direct communication with Creator. Be careful what you do ask for, it just may come to pass and not always in the way you think you're asking. You can also use it for very personal prayer or meditation. If you wish not to smoke from it for any reason, that is OK, too. You can still pray with it and then pass it on." The Chanupa represents the connection of all Life.

Invisible and tangible energy came through everything. Golden threads of soothing respect and gratitude filled the Inipi. Tom talked about what was in the pipe; it sounded like he called it "chin-shaw-shaw." It was mostly red willow tree bark, Tom said, and it caused no physical high or anything like that. Kevin was relieved, for too many pipes he held contained substances that were only for taking. This pipe was for connecting, for giving and forgiving, to honor and to share.

Tom lit the pipe, arm almost fully extended to reach the bowl. He drew in with care and intention, blew some smoke in each direction, wafted some over himself in a purposeful way with his right hand, and then lovingly blew out the rest upon the Stones before passing it on. Each person handled the Chanupa in a slightly different way. Then it came to Kevin, who awkwardly did his best to mimic what he had seen. He passed it on quickly, after a clumsy puff and an internal prayer only for help. It felt weird, having a pipe in his hands again.

The Chanupa made its way around the circle and then Tom emptied it. Upon the Altar it was now placed in the opposite direction. More Stones were brought in, easily as hot as any they had experienced in the first rounds, then the water bucket and horn, and the drum. The door was brought down, and then a song.

The first person began his prayer by saying "Aho." Many made this sound, usually when they heard something they agreed with or that touched or moved them. It was some kind of acknowledgment.

The man praying also spoke a few words in the other language, and Kevin began to recognize some of them from repetition. This man prayed for his family, for that which he was grateful, and for help with humility and various other challenges. His prayers had an authenticity that caused a cleverly-hidden place within Kevin to continue welling up. What to do with this? A sinking in his stomach was eased by the safety of the ceremony. He felt much closer to the man now than the judgments his first look at him had allowed. The intimacy of his prayer had done this. He ended with more words in the other language, and others echoed those words. It all came in a sense of togetherness which made Kevin uneasy. This was somewhere he had not let himself go, hardly at all. Here was the threat of uncovering things long ago buried.

Then on to the next person, a woman; since it was dark, he could not put a face to the voice as he had with the last man. But it was not necessary to know the person's physicality.

Her voice so caring and tender, and by it was she surely a being of profound beauty. "Grandfather, please help my Aunt Gracie … her surgery is Thursday, and she may die from it. She is in tremendous pain with this disease; let me help her somehow, some way." She sobbed in a great wailing that tore at Kevin's chest. Surely her connection with Aunt Gracie was a life-long story. Her tears brought his, and her caring made him care.

We are imperfect beings suffering together.

Her plight was no more or less than his, but a part of whatever he was. Kevin was reeling from a great cavern of pent-up emotions and fears. It was always so lonely pretending his problems were paramount to anyone else's. More present than any other feeling was the Unity of the moment. Caring about this woman and each person present made him care about the world instead of seeking to dominate it. This brought forth something of great value, always sought but never found in all his selfishness.

Tom had said we come here to suffer for others. Being here and feeling this caused a tightly barricaded fortress within him to open. A great deal of empathy poured through her every word and from and through the people sitting in this powerful circle. It was staggering. Then another man, his turn to share and pray. The prayers were in every direction and with so much love and gratitude, along with the suffering and the powerlessness.

It came to Kevin's turn. What happened will remain as much a mystery as anything he would ever experience.

Kevin began his prayer, clumsy, trying to look good and say the right thing. The heat was lashing serpents at every pore of skin, monkeys punishing from the inside. "I'm … happy to be here, and I umm … so much to …" His throat all but closed as a flood of emotion burst from his very center. *Damn it!* He clenched his mouth to stop it from purging. Surely everyone heard it snap shut. Full darkness threatened and thick silence dared him continue. He could feel the attention on him, in the heat and fog and uncertainty. "I …. I … can't….." Then, his floodgates burst open:

Like a petulant child *bawling:* "Please let me stay. I want to *stay*, I don't want to go. ... I don't wanna GO! Help me stay with you." Over and over he said it, pleading, crying, imploring.

Something in his thinking mind yet outside of awareness had been at a standoff to get *out* of here from the beginning. His gut twisted as he curled up, monkeys gnashing, demons lashing, writhing in the fetal position, clutching his chest, screaming these cries for help. It was the most affirming prayer he had ever made, save when he prayed and cried on that jail floor curled up in the exact same position: *Please Help Me.* Each instance carried the same exact intention, beyond any conscious thought and emerging from an unknown place. But here, now, *HE was accessing it*, daring to voice this excruciating prayer. No one else could have done this for him. The ability to do so was not something of which he thought he was capable – the ability came by the very essence of the ceremony itself, *through* the people, the Stones, the heat, the directions, the ancient and timeless Spirits that had been revealing themselves over these last months, and now here in full view – yet, it came through him.

But not *from* what he had always thought himself to be. The sincere invocation gave way to a much Greater Power.

"I've hurt so many people! Caused so much pain! *Damn it.* And now my life is in ruins, I am so ashamed. How can I ever …" He could feel the people envelop him with inexhaustible love and compassion. "Please take this from me. I … I don't know who I even am, what to do, where to go. I just want to stay *here* … please let me stay, Grandfathers, *please let me stay."* Kevin was held with invisible hugs and embraces. The whole of it lifted him up, even as his prayers turned only to sobs. He felt them all praying *with* him, felt their empathy for this newcomer's revealing of lifetime suffering.

Tom uttered … a sound. He did this a few times, and it somehow said "I understand your suffering and I am suffering with you." It was nearly a groan, as if Tom willingly absorbed some of what Kevin emanated, but not without toll. Tom's intervention, the Inipi and its Circles of Souls, the Grandfathers, had all become a ground for the charge of Kevin's guilt and shame. He would never be the same.

Kevin's prayer was simply a cry for Love. Ancient Stones absorbed it as dancing Spirits stomped away corporeal residue under celestial feet.

The rest of the ceremony was pretty much a blur; as the prayers continued he went back and forth from relief and then feeling foolish and stupid for revealing himself. How could he? And where had it all come from? He had spent a whole lifetime hiding all of it and from all of it, at any cost. He certainly had not planned on this, had not intended to have *these* atrocities come out, *they just did.* His only intention from the beginning was to be as honest as he could, as Tom had suggested - pray what was on his heart, and he was willing to do that much. He had no idea what would come. Should he feel backwards about it?

But then the other prayers took his mind from himself, if only in spurts. There were others suffering, also – and flourishing. Much more than his own plight was going on in the world and being prayed about, helping him see that his own personal battles may not be as important as the credence he always gave them. Tom had suggested listening to the people, praying *with* them. Setting aside the self-obsession allowed compassion to emerge. Caring about other beings brings purpose.

The heat helped Kevin get out of his mind. *Battling* the heat was like battling these screaming monkeys every minute of every day. Accepting it instead and going within, he suffered less. The timeless round went full circle back to Tom, who prayed in both languages: English, and then this other more native tongue. The strange language stirred flashes of untold lifetimes.

The fourth and last round was blistering. The hottest and last of the Grandfathers were brought in and another song. "We're going to send the Spirits home now," Tom said, and with the end of one more song the remainder of the water was poured onto the Stones at once, causing one grand finale of saturating heat and steam, bubbling, hissing, singing and singeing.

Purification Ceremony

Every limb was limp with exhaustion, the heat at its apex. On cue, everyone exclaimed "Aho! Mitakuye Oyasin," and the door was flung open.

Depleted bodies crawled out single file, many still shaking away tears of grief and of joy. Heat and steam rolled out with them. A short, plump woman tugged at the steam-and-sweat soaked muumuu that clung to her skin as she came up off her knees. An older man needed assistance to stand, and when it was accomplished he raised both hands in the air, fingers outstretched and let out a huge "Ahhhhh!" Kevin could not help but think about the prayers being mixed with the dissipating steam, watching it pour out and away and integrate into anything and everything again. A few sweat-slathered participants exchanged a hug or handshake, and then dragged themselves to the cool grass and surrendered their bodies to the earth.

After several minutes of curiosity getting the best of him, Kevin asked Tom what that last prayer before opening the door meant, clumsy again trying to pronounce the words. "Ohhh…" Tom said in that gentle way that never grew old. "Mitakuye Oyasin? All My Relations," he imparted, far and away. Others listened on nodding their heads, as if pondering a great truth. *Feeling it.*

Even though there were a thousand new questions, Kevin let it go at that.

More will be revealed

For a while, everyone just took in the luscious cool air, imbibed some water, and slowly began to collect themselves. Tom said there would now be a *Wopila* feast. He translated in a whisper toward the newcomer: "Thanksgiving feast."

Everyone had brought something for it. Some prepared a dish of their own, while some had gone to the store. Everyone except Kevin. He had brought nothing. He chose to keep quiet about it; maybe no one would notice. Lessons anew certainly abounded here at this wonderful gathering. Next time he would be sure not to come empty-handed. He thought about all the get-togethers over the years and how almost always he had shown up empty-handed, only able to take.

Tom invited everyone to clean up in the downstairs rooms. "Take a shower if you like, there's one in the back bathroom." Each made their way to the house, found their clothes and changed. The aroma of what Kevin could only imagine as the finest array of cuisine lured him toward the upstairs kitchen. A huge table was set: Fried chicken steamed on giant platters, rolls in bowls lined with plaid cloths, pasta dishes and green salads, fresh fruit, cornbread still hot in baking pans. Found! What his nose had promised.

On the stove, a huge pot of bubbling bliss. "Buffalo chili," Tom said, answering a silent question, chuckling. "My own private recipe." He stuck his nose in the pot, sniffing as he stirred. "Mmmmm."

"Buffalo chili!" Big John's voice echoed, affirming a stew of the highest order. And there was *plenty* for all.

Between the kitchen and dining room with the feasting table some fresher faces roamed. Hustling about on task, these two women had prepared the feast, but had not sweat, save over a hot stove. Kevin recognized one woman from the noon meeting. "Hi Janice, looks excellent."

"Thanks," she said into the oven as she retrieved a glass baking dish of piping hot roasted vegetables. "I love doing it," Janice said, and then carried her steaming burden into the dining room. Kevin followed her, floating a full two inches off the ground, propelled by the sweet aroma itself right into a seat. Two fat pies and another plate of chocolate chip cookies summoned from a table against the wall. His eyes tasted everything.

Soon enough, everyone came to the table. They looked different now, lighter, calmer and serene. Many had bloodshot eyes from the sweat and crying. Kevin was sure his were. The energy between them had changed. They had shared the most intimate prayers and Kevin felt closer to all of them. Still, he felt awkward about revealing such a fragile and hidden-away part of himself. He wondered if anyone else did. He would let it go, for now, and *trust* whatever was this purification process.

No one was taking any food yet, so he sat still, hungry and waiting. Tom went around with a small plate in hand, placing onto it various selections from the cornucopia. As he did, silence came upon the room while gracious swirls of sweet aroma filled the air, begging to be indulged. All attention went to Tom, who held the plate up the same way he had done with the water horn in the lodge. He said a prayer again in both languages, giving thanks for the ceremony, the people, for the food and for this gathering. Then he took it outside and placed it on a ledge of the deck, nearest the living trees.

"What was that?" Kevin asked a woman next to him.

"Spirit plate," she said. The intimation caused a landslide of new thought to cascade.

"Let's eat!" Tom spouted on his way back in.

Everyone dug in at once, and the feast commenced. The room came alive, and the seriousness of the ceremony shifted to lighthearted conversing and storytelling, with lots of laughter amidst chiming silverware and clanking dishes. There was so much fine food he almost couldn't decide what to go for first, but the minor problem gave way to a soon full plate. From the first bite, it was the best he'd ever had, tasting it now with a more purified body. How closely related are suffering and bliss.

Big John was quite a comedian, the gentle giant with a huge heart. Kevin had liked him right away. It was a new family. The love in the room was obvious as a full amber moon. Tom sat at the end of the table. It truly was a thanksgiving feast. Everyone gratefully indulged to their delight. The crowd eventually began to thin, but Kevin, inhaling every word and recording every sound, lingered to the end.

So much had happened. It did feel like being reborn. Finally, Tom walked Kevin to the door. "Glad you could make it; you are welcome here anytime." Tom's arm around Kevin was warm and guiding. "Thank you for sharing yourself in such an honest way - that took a lot of courage." It made Kevin think about the serenity prayer he'd said hundreds of times by now, especially the part, *"Courage to change the things I can."* Did it have anything to do with the whole of what had moved through this day?

"Thank you so much for inviting me here to your home, to this beautiful ceremony," Kevin replied, wanting to speak a thousand words, excuses and reasons stirring within why he'd spoken the prayers he had, why he'd allowed those things to pour forth. But it would have been back-peddling, attempting to control; it would have been picking up the backpack stones again. Instead, he followed Tom's suggestions. He left those things with the Grandfathers, with Creator. And at this doorway did their eyes meet again in a silent exchange of true understanding. Somehow, Tom already knew. Something had cracked tonight, given way, and there could be no turning back. The door behind him clicked shut, gently.

Frosted steps led out to a cold, clear evening. Stars dangled in a midnight-blue sky. The door of the Explorer creaked open and the seat let out a huff as his full two hundred and fifteen pounds sank into it, nearly limp. After a few visible breaths, Kevin slid the key into the ignition.

***

An invocation had occurred – a direct invitation to the Greatest Power available to any being.

How had he gotten here?

Who were these people, and what this surreal ceremony he had just undergone?

He saw through the physical world tonight, with some other vision. Glazed over, bloodshot eyes sore from too much sweat, steam and smoke stinging them for hours were now only for a smaller world. Ancient lifetimes coursed through this night. A thousand drums beat sweet cadence, calling the deepest dream. Ancestors danced around fires in ten thousand realms. Imagination, dusty and rusty, drove something else, transcending this world, and saw past the mundane. He *was* something else now. But, how was this possible?

How had he gotten here?

It felt like remembering

~ Chapter 19 ~

Abundant Universe

A harsh season was swirling into something else; the frozen soul's shivering began to subside. New worlds of opportunity abounded. Cold and wet, spring was a pretty pondering on a gloomy day. Clash of the seasons was evident. The old days were long gone, what was once considered success let go and a new definition was forming. An entirely different pathway had made itself known. Kevin would not trade today's journey for anything.

Yes, winter was nearly over, and he was outgrowing these walls.

With anticipation and humble respect, many more sweats at Tom's were engaged and so many meetings it was hard to keep track. Several months had now passed since the night in the bar and the pills and booze. It felt good to be truly sober. The band was preparing to record its five-song demo in a world class studio. Treatment was progressing nicely.

As part of the court requirements, Kevin needed to complete a 12-month domestic violence treatment program. EMI administered one, into which he enrolled, concurrent with the drug and alcohol program. This program had its entirely own workbook and step-work, requiring much more writing, more sharing in Group, more painstaking honesty. But, the more honest he was, the greater the relief – and transformation.

Phase One of the outpatient program had gone well. All this treatment and introspection was confronting, to say the least. What at first seemed an impossible and unwelcome process was instead proving to be most enlightening. Was it the choice to allow help? To *listen?* To take action on ridiculous suggestions?

On an early, sunny and soggy May morning, Kevin phoned the color line: Red and blue. He was blue, they'd just changed it from red. Either way, it meant a UA by noon. Today was also a 2:00 p.m. meeting with the new Phase Two counselor. That left enough space to do The Nooner again, if he hustled. Just like in Yakima, he looked forward to seeing the growing number of friends, even if they didn't know.

But, somehow they did know. Intimacies were discussed and shared - many of the people were in great transition, scared, unsure and needed to be heard. Even being there and just sitting in the chair was being of service to others, and their being there, the same for him. It worked both ways.

Sometimes just a smile, a kind handshake, an authentic, "Hello, how are you?" helped so much. Maybe he could help someone else with a simple greeting, the way they helped him. Maybe someday he could even take someone through the steps, share the process. By choosing to give was he also allowing himself to receive a once hidden treasure. Altruism is the antidote to egotism. Rather than rational thoughts and postulations, it was more experienced by doing. Showing up, open and receptive, and willing to share.

How you look upon others is how you will see yourself

It felt good to be accountable, be doing what was asked, and to be a part of something. Today, blowing into the breathalyzer and peeing in a cup were only an excuse to commingle with the staff. Sober, there was nothing to worry about. How he had managed to give up resisting was a mystery, but the results were so favorable that he just kept doing it. The feeling of being lost and alone was fading.

In the meetings, oftentimes he practiced being present and making a conscious effort to connect with the people, *to listen*. In this listening was an unexplainable essence that could only be felt. Many did try to explain this presence, and even though words usually fell short of accomplishing a feat of such magnitude, it was still there. Especially in the story.

The meeting was like that today, uplifting and inspiring.

***

Within a few minutes in the cold vinyl chair in the dank lobby of EMI, another guide appeared. "Kevin? I'm Paul." The light spirit invited Kevin, but to what? Modern dress and above the shoulder hair could have just as easily been long blonde strands flowing down a medieval wizard's robe; the sparse goatee, a decades-long beard. What had these considerate blue eyes seen? Surely worlds, lifetimes, universes, said the swirling oceans within them. The man, who'd been maybe a half a century in this body, smiled and squinted as he stood, sure, of who and what he was. Just one glance was his scepter; easily it cleared any obstruction that could have been between them. The invitation spoke.

The two men walked, past the UA bathroom and toward the back of the building, into a darkish, 12x14 office. Paul did not shut the door; he left it open. He was still smiling. "Looks like you did well in Phase One," Paul said, eyes still on the paper in his hand.

"Yeah, I like treatment ... I really do," Kevin said, honestly. The part he was not as honest about was the pills (or the night of drinking), but he purposely did not mention it and neither did Paul. Besides, he wasn't ready to change his sober date.

Instead, a different kind of conversation broke out. It was like two regular old guys talking, not a counselor above a patient, or some kind of a "here's how it is" conversation, but more of a heart to heart. They just talked about life - Paul leaned forward, elbows on the desk between the two of them. "Tell me about *Kevin*."

So, he shared briefly about what a tragedy life had become, out there using, about the great torment. He shared the relief experienced at The Sanctuary, told him about Tom, about his feelings as he progressed on this new and unfamiliar path.

"I've been working out of this little shop below my apartment, but it's cold in there. I need a new shop, and I'm ready to start looking for one," Kevin said, realizing it was time now.

"Oh, what kind of work?"

"Cars. I fix cars, trucks, whatever. Body and paint mostly, but whatever needs done I can do. Been doing it a long time." It felt good to say it like that, felt good to know what he was doing - with cars, anyway.

"Well that sounds excellent. It's a good skill to have, always plenty of work. You'll find another shop." Paul's encouragement was infectious. It caused Kevin to feel capable.

"Yeah, it's good ... I'll find a new place to work. But lots happened at treatment, and one thing was that I figured out what I *really* wanna become - an actor. Did lots of writing, and thinking. It's what I want to do."

Paul's eyes filled with a charge that had not been there in the beginning of the meeting. There was a sudden shift. Something changed; the *feel* changed.

Paul lit up like a football stadium at touchdown time. He easily became a whole foot taller as he blurted out, "You need *The Secret*."

"Yeah!" Kevin said, almost snorting, matching the intensity now filling the room. The very mystery of such a thing was tragically enticing.

It came down a notch when Kevin realized, "What is it?"

By this time Paul was already at the computer, googling. "Well, it's a new movie, but much more than that - have you ever heard of the law of attraction?"

"Nope," He hadn't, but had the feeling he was about to.

Instead of trying to explain it, Paul handed him a piece of paper on which he had written a website address: www.thesecret.tv

"Watch it over and over until you get it," Paul instructed with that sparkle in his eye that was intriguing enough to capture the imagination and ignite it. Kevin accepted the challenge.

He took the paper and thanked his new counselor. Paul went back to the original reason for the meeting, which was only the excuse the two had gotten together, but not the real purpose. He explained Phase Two of the program - details, just minor details.

"Sound like something you're willing to do?" Paul said, referring to the schedule and requirements. "The program of recovery comes first."

"Absolutely. I will be here, willing, honest and open." Kevin walked through the open doorway, "Thanks, Paul. I'm looking forward to knowing you better."

Breadcrumbs on the trail

If Kevin could witness these past several months from a macrocosmic view, he would see every step was guided, each person and every encounter part of a grander symphony. The great web of life is interwoven like a fine song. For now, he could only experience it, and the music was so sweet.

"The Secret"... What was it? *Is it really a secret?* Was he about to find hidden treasure that would open even more unseen doorways? It sure felt so, the way Paul had risen out of his chair and become angels singing the path alight. Paul sensed something in Kevin that was *worth* attending, and had engaged that task.

With sails full set, Kevin left the meeting. *Can't wait to check this thing out;* the thought itself was enchanted. This high felt better than any fleeting drug high. Invisible winds swooped eager sails, whisking another seeker unto the Sea of Adventure. Uncharted seas, even again, budding senses continued to be nourished and awakened. Every day brought gifts once deemed unattainable.

These guides and way-showers, the seas and pathways, had been there the whole time. Only, Kevin had put his ability to *see* them to sleep, and only Kevin could allow the awakening. His whole life he had blamed others for doing this, for blinding him. Beginning to see his part in all of it now and that no one can *do* anything to you without your permission, once bedrock old foundations grew feeble and trembled.

If you wish to know your true savior, you need only look in the mirror

***

On the way to Café Zippy for a morning java-n-journal session, Kevin contemplated his gratitude list, the new focus of journaling. Third pass through his now favorite movie and some of the *"Secret"* notions began to sink in. Taking new action always produces new results.

Writing, he acknowledged gratitude for his sobriety, for the apartment home, the current shop and work, his hands and eyes and beating heart, then all his organs and limbs, even his breath. Each person he could think of that was so much help, treatment, the counselors, his family, the meetings and the steps, water, fire, earth and air – it all was written down. Each thing he was grateful for led to something else, and pretty soon the gratitude list was huge. It felt good to write them, and changed his focus to positive, every time.

Pushing the journal aside, he sank back in the old wooden chair and let out a hearty "Oh, yeah." Sipping hot coffee and drinking long glances, he absorbed the 100-year old building. Creaks in the old floor boards and walls and rafters alluded to vintage spirits that refused to leave their home. The entire eastern wall was an old, blown-up black-and-white photograph of the street and shops outside; must have been from when the place was near just built. Ghosts in strange clothes hustled down streets that had not so much changed. Kevin peered out the window to contemplate the progress since the effigy. For a long while he imagined living back then … walking the streets, breathing the air, engaging the contraptions of the era.

After enough time, a refill was in order; a fresh coffee sounded good. One sip later his cell phone rang. He fumbled around in his pocket and found it. "Hello?"

"Kevin? Don here … you emailed about the garage for rent?"

"Yes." He had, sent one this morning before leaving. "Tell me about it, please."

"Well, you close? Why don't you just come by and have a look?" Don explained where it was, only three short miles from the apartment. "I'll be here all day."

Kevin put the phone away and thought about it while nursing the lukewarm joe. The rent was just over five hundred a month, he could make that easy. But he had next to nothing right now, again. Whispering under his breath as he stood up, "Oh well, just go take a look, what can it hurt," he placed a wrinkly dollar bill under the half full ceramic mug.

The Explorer pulled in, past a house with the proper address, crunching gravel as an older garage came into view. Both bay doors open and lights on. The spot was fairly secluded from the main road.

A well-groomed man in a grey suit swaggered up to the old Ford. Kevin judged him near 50 by his greying hair and telltale crow's feet. He stretched an arm out, quickly. "Hi, I'm Don."

"Hi, Kevin. OK to park here?"

"Sure, sure. Glad you could make it," Don answered, pleasant enough. "One guy came and looked at it, said he might be back. Go ahead, it's open. Check it out." Don adjusted his blazer and swaggered right back to his house, moving with purpose, as though he had several tasks that were pressing and needed his immediate attention.

It was a larger two-car detached garage, a pair of eight-by-ten foot doors on the front and a walk-in door on the north side. The would-be humble shop was about sixty paces from the house. All of it sat on a shy acre in a good spot, close-in. In a time gone by it had surely been residential, but now it was commercial property. Nearest the street sat the house, the garage set back a ways. Hedges high as the roof all but covered two sides of the little shop. The peaceful seclusion of the place was attractive. Before, he always thought it was necessary to have frontage and a big sign and be as busy as possible. This had changed.

Keep it simple

This place did have a special something; it called to Kevin in addition to feeling right and, one could actually pull whole cars into it. Two of them at a time, even. He thought about the possibilities ... but there was the money problem. Don returned. "What do you think?"

"I love it," Kevin replied, feeling once again the need to be overly honest with him. "I'm going through a major life transition and am in a treatment program. I don't have much money ... but I know I can make the rent as soon as I get working." The now-old sing-song statements. Oh, well. If it works ...

He shared with Don some developments over the past year. Overall, he was abundantly honest, the new ability being cultivated over these last few months. He still offered way too much information. It worked better than creating some fantastic story based on lies, though.

Don was a good listener. He asked, "So, what do you want to do?"

"I want it. I know I can come up with the rent. How much would you need to hold it for me for a few days?"

"A dollar's all that's required by law."

Being that the house in front was a commercial real estate office, and Don was the owner and operator, Kevin figured Don probably knew what he was talking about.

"Really? All right!" Kevin reached in his pocket and pulled out a crumpled old bill. "Here's a twenty."

Don smiled. "Tell you what … I'll hold this until Friday, and if you don't come up with the first month's rent, which is all you need to move in, I'll give it back to you."

Kevin was beside himself. "So you'll hold it for me?"

"Yep, let me know what happens. It's all yours if you want it."

Don narrowly avoided getting spontaneously hugged, and watched the Explorer drive off.

Speeding and weaving traffic all the way home, Kevin's mind raced with potential schemes for procuring five hundred bucks. The law of attraction! He'd just attract that money right to him. Then, just as quick as that thought had come, in slipped an old pattern. Show an alcoholic a rut, and they'll move in.

He dialed the familiar old phone number.

"Hi Mom. How's it going?" Of course, he only wanted something from her. The question was merely a courtesy.

"Oh, OK I guess. Collectors have been calling again, all the time, for you. I'm just kind of … well, down about the way it all turned out, with the shop and all, dealing with these vultures." Mom's answer came in a depressed tone. "It just makes me sick, ya' know? Here I thought this was the best thing, getting that place, and now … well it's just such a mess."

Kevin's bubble burst. "Yeah, I hear you. I'm trying to get it together, repair some damage." His focus was on the rent money, but it began to shift in realizing … Mom had been through enough.

"I just want to put it all behind me and move on. I know you're trying hard, but what about this *damn mess*?"

As he listened, he realized again how much pain he had caused her, the damage he had done and the way he had affected the people around him, especially the ones close. His family. Marie, Terra, Alisa, all their children. Countless other failed relationships he'd only sought to take from began to seep to the surface. Could he ever make amends? His stomach turned in disgust.

The part of him that wants what he wants when he wants it started to become pissed off. He could hear through her words, too, that she did not trust him, and could feel her thinking he would easily do it again given the chance. And here he was.

~ 235 ~

A chippering monkey with a sandpaper tongue licked him dryly from his jaw all the way to his forehead before smiling ear-to-ear.

"I don't know, Ma. We'll work it out somehow." He was somber now.

This very phone call's purpose was to extract more from her after she had already given him everything. It did feel like sliding backward into a sludgy old rut. He knew this wasn't right. Shifting the intention now, to the best of his ability, he attempted to *genuinely listen*. Guilt was heavy and thick to match the shame, and there was not much he could do to change the past. What was done *right now* did matter. If she was not the source of his well-being, then who or what was?

Cheating never begets a sustainable level of prosperity

The choice of having a real conversation with her barely won out over asking for anything. Still, their goodbye held an uncomfortable mix of emotions. The best thing he could do to show up for his mom or anyone else right now was to learn how to show up for Kevin first.

Providence

It was an easy May morning, fresh and pleasant. Things were warming up and waking up. Sober nearly four months now, Kevin awoke charged and inspired. Less than a month and it would be a year since that first day at treatment. The small apartment was set up in a way he felt the least lonely; the TV and computer helped him feel connected to the outside world. Putting them with the bed in the fairly large main room made it like a studio. The one bedroom remained empty, for now. *It sure is quiet here.* Something still seemed to be missing.

He thought about the prospective shop over a cup of coffee, and began a kind of contemplative prayer, a new habit forming now. Instead of thinking about all the reasons it would not work, he instead *imagined* working there, felt his hands working on the cars inside of the place, heard the tools clanking, smelled the products and tasted the dust from sanding. He imagined handing to Don the amount of money agreed upon, felt the handshake of a done deal. All of a sudden, inspiration on-high and overwhelmed with *feeling*, he blurted out loud:

"I'm doing this!"

Not going to do it, or maybe do it - *am* doing it, now.

I AM

With fresh enthusiasm, it was onto the same website where he had found his shop and furnished the apartment for next to free. He placed an ad for his new business as if it were already in operation and accepting new work, and released it to the very Universe itself, knowing the results were already so. Corresponding keys were clacked to post the ad and complete the task, a prophecy fulfilled.

Then, *let it go.* The very next day, he had to put down his razor to answer the phone.

"Hello, my name is Karl, calling about your ad. My truck got stolen, taken for a joy ride, used to rob a house, and banged up pretty good. It's at a tow yard and they're charging me sixty bucks a day for storage. I'd like to get it out of there as soon as possible. I don't want to pay the overinflated costs at the big repair shops, and there was just something about your ad … anything you can handle?"

"Yes I can," Kevin said with complete confidence, took the address and set up a time to meet.

"She's hurt, but I can fix her," Kevin said as Karl inspected damage behind the rear wheels.

"Good. I have towing insurance to get it to your shop. How much ya' think?"

"It'll be at least twenty-five-hundred," Kevin announced, picking a reasonable enough number out of the air.

"Twenty-five it is then, better than I thought. Half to get started?" Karl offered. "I'm in no hurry to have it done, it usually just sits."

Kevin almost could not believe it. Just like that. He was part of an unlimited flow of pure potential just waiting to be claimed. A great omnipotent ocean of possibility of which anything one wishes is available.

Depositing that check was sweet. He withdrew enough for the shop, went and handed the money to Don, shaking his hand and taking the key, just as he had seen in his imagination. There was enough for this and plenty left over to get some tools he'd need. Something was acknowledged this day, a new trust developing inside a new way of life, and he was sure this was only the beginning. So much had changed. Or had it?

Today a new power existed, which did not need vices to survive and could not be usurped. It could only be allowed, and in the allowing did the real miracle take place.

The stillness from which all emerges

***

Busy as he was, there were dreams to pursue. A small ad was placed with clear intention. *"Beginning Actor Needs Help!"* It produced a phone call.

The young woman's voice was sweet and soft: "I don't usually do this, but I know this woman, a coach, who helped me so much. Maybe she can help you …"

~ 237 ~

Kevin took the information and called right away.

"Call me cp," the voice of another angel answered. She was confident, pleasant, and it just so happened that her car had a large scratch right down the driver's side, which she'd like repaired. A fair trade for six hour-long acting lessons, they agreed. It would prove to be much more than that.

***

The little shop came alive. Cam brought in a repair on a car that would need to be done inside. Today there was a garage to bring it into. Some inexpensive products which had the exact smell imagined, a skilled hand and an artist's touch, would make the damage disappear. A price was agreed upon which would cover an entire month's rent.

Doing the work was fun now. What a sober mind can do. He could not help but think how much more difficult the work *seemed* before, all those years. Yet it was the same work, which was now simple. Instead of obsessing on getting high or escaping life, *being here now* was proving to be much sweeter. His focus began to change toward the very processes that were bringing about all this newfound joy and wonder: The world of prayer and imagination, of intention and spirit, of being, seeing beyond, and practicing *inspired action*. Here was a far more favorable world of conscious manifesting and co-creating a brand new life. Was this what he had been searching for? Were there even greater miracles beyond *this?*

The little car turned out great. Cam was pleased with the work, and happily paid. He even brought Kevin another job. Karl's Dodge was on hold since he didn't need it back for a couple months, and some of the money had gone to tool up and for supplies. Profits from the incoming work would easily pay for the repairs to Karl's truck. With two weeks until rent was due again, another job, tools and materials for doing more work, it was going well. A new confidence was emerging that was not forced from a confused mind.

The Universe is always conspiring favorably, indeed. All needed is to get out of the way and let it flow. There was plenty of time to fulfill the treatment requirements, do meetings, band practice and now acting lessons. In fact, these days, time was variable. Today he was free, and by his own choice. The more he allowed, the softer a day went.

However, back bills were looming: Court fines for all the no-contact-order violations racked up trying to control Marie, restitution, the ambulance and hospital stay back in Montana, speeding and no insurance tickets, plus paying for treatment and rent at the apartment. There was more step work to do, too. There were amends to make, which scared him most.

Do the next indicated thing

~ 238 ~

When he set worry aside, followed direction, did what was in front of him and maintained faith, things always worked themselves out. Both treatments were going well. Being completely transparent and honest proved to be the best way. Trusting the process of consistent action resulted in incremental yet profound changes. *Everything one ever needs is right here, right now.* Each day is indeed a new adventure. With so much less, why is there so much more?

***

The second phase of the three was just a few weeks shy of complete. Wreckage of the past was being cleaned up piece-by-piece, but there was so much shrapnel. Tom liked him to come over, sit and chat over coffee, and always offered a tasty treat. They would sit in his huge house and idle chit-chat about nothing and everything.

"I'm happy you stopped by. People don't do that enough nowadays … why do ya' hafta call? Just stop by, I'll be here. We can talk. It's good ... *Wastelo*," Tom postulated, one elbow on the small round kitchen table where the two sat across from each other, gripping a mug with the serenity prayer imprinted upon it. Tom liked to speak Lakota any chance he got. Kevin had nothing to do that could be more important than sitting right here, right now, with his brother, friend, guide, and grandfather.

Today, Tom handed him something that would blow him away. "Here, this is a great book, read it if you want." It was likely inspired by their conversation. The book was *The Seat of the Soul* by Gary Zukav. Many more would follow, and each would be another breadcrumb.

"Wow, thanks." Kevin was not sure what to make of it, but open enough to receive it.

"I think you'll like it," Tom said, and then gave him a hug. Kevin did like it: The conversation, the book, and the hug.

He was getting to like Tom and their relationship, a lot. He could not help each time feeling like he had just left Dad in some strange yet familiar way. It was a surprise, this feeling, and it began helping him let go of some of the anger he harbored around his father's passing.

Time takes time

This was the most compelling walk Kevin had ever embarked upon. Turning back now was an easy no. Where went the rabbit hole?

Dad loved books and learning. He dropped out of school way early and instead haunted libraries, learning much more than any regular education might have taught. His rich life, a school of its own, was laden with quantum lessons. He loved sharing his wisdom in many of their late night phone conversations and get-togethers. The greatest thing Dad ever gave was his

~ 239 ~

time. Kevin cherished this today. Back then, steeped in self-obsession, he could not see past his own "knowing" long enough to become open to any other way.

But even in spite of this, during these conversations there was some presence beyond just the two of them. Father and son became lost in what felt like a conversation having itself. It often bent time, going on for hours that seemed only minutes. When Dad passed, Kevin had *believed* that "death" severed this connection. But now he was beginning to feel his father's presence as if it had never left - through the whole world.

The very Universe itself was divulging hitherto unknown pathways. He wished he had spent more time just *being* with his father, and wished, too, that the time he had been with Dad, he had been more present. Maybe it was possible to do this now. Like retro-presence or something. Was time just another illusion? Maybe the whole world was.

Kevin cracked open Tom's gift, reading each word slowly, taking care to attend it fully. He ingested each sentence, and then each paragraph. Where had this idiosyncrasy come from, especially in one who supposedly suffered from an inability to keep focused attention? He was not any speed reader, but the information was much more potent when engaged in this manner. The book opened yet another fast-closed portal. The eternal notions crackled as a wood fire on a cold winter's night. Anticipating eyes, wide with fascination, took in every word.

Reading in such a way before bed always made for interesting dreams. Of course - doorways to other realms were opened. Tonight, it was just a few paragraphs. Heavy eyes drifted off, imagination free to roam, treasure map upon his chest, thumb still between those first few pages.

~ Chapter 20 ~

Unity

One thing, at first glance, seems separate from another. Perhaps a great number are trained this way. Some forget. Many choose not to remember. *Can I call to You, Great One, and ask to be awakened? When I do, in sincerity, I know You are here; You never left. Can I seek the goodness within myself with all that I am and find my purpose, my true calling ... what am I for? Must I have this human body and not know how to use it, or learn only how to use it devoid of real Love, and then pretend this is who I am? Have I sought only to grow thoughts of separation when evidence of Your Love is at the center of all being? I do call out, now - show me how to live! Is there no one out there, is this the answer? Am I the maker of a world that does not exist while only You are real? Please, show me what to do.* I forgive you. *Thank You, for this day, this moment, this ability. Thank You for everything*

Reborn cells soaked in golden rays of sunlight as Kevin awoke in a cat-like stretch. These contemplations danced in resurrected vision long since discarded and buried under mountains of misperception. The sun on this morning spoke of giving and sharing, healing.

Paul's group sessions were easy to love, and Kevin engaged them with complete abandon and lightheartedness. More and more he enjoyed sitting in these groups and being a part of instead of separate from, and doing all that was asked. Paul always had cool stuff he brought in and talked about, and the conversation was always engaging and down-reaching. Similar notions came through both Tom and Paul. Today they were talking about anger, and Kevin remembered something Tom had offered and repeated it:

"Anger is unresolved fear."

Paul lit up as he so often did. "Yes! Where did you get that?" His question was enthusiastic. Kevin only smiled as if he had been aware of this his whole life ... maybe he had.

Whatever was going on, he always felt better being with others. Today was a one-on-one with Paul. Newfound happiness, the growing fondness of being in the groups and meetings, and the massive expansion from the inside out was all Kevin could talk about.

Swirling spheres of living oceans, Paul's eyes became bright as ever. "What are you doing Wednesday night? I go to a church, but not a church like you may be used to. It's called, *'Unity Center for Positive Living'.* You're welcome to come if you like."

What was it about Paul? It opened channels in Kevin, activated something, even if he could not quite put a finger on it. Either way, right now he knew where he'd be, come Wednesday.

Another Sanctuary

"It must be a hundred years old," Kevin whispered, walking between two pillars under an archway, "and so well cared for." Not only his eyes scanned the room, reminded him again,

Listen

Welcome filled the air in the light and beautiful space. It was a surprise to see Paul up front facing the gathering of people.

"Thank you all for coming. This is my wife, Miriam. We'll be leading you through tonight's events.

"I've prepared a little lesson, and we'll sing some songs ... but first, let's begin with a meditation." Sitting still for several minutes was at first, challenging. Kevin had never been very good at being quiet and not fidgeting. But tonight, it felt good to just sit, relax, and follow directions. Paul led them in the meditation, which brought the quality of a more internal focus. The twenty-some souls sat a few minutes in pure silence. Kevin swore he could hear the walls breathing, children of generations long gone-by giggling, and his own heartbeat. The gentle strum of a lone acoustic guitar filled the room just before a human's melodious lyric danced upon it, a surfer riding his perfect wave.

After it fell to silence once more, Paul slowly opened a book, with intention and care, as if he himself had been the author and knew it so well. "Phineas Quimby," he said. *That name!* "He lived in the 1800's ..." Paul read and shared about the man, of that to which he dedicated his life, and again what came forth fell in perfect alignment with what was engendered by way of the meetings, the sweat lodges, in all the treatment programs – and in

Kevin's own contemplations. In the book Tom had given him, too. Were all those that had dedicated their being to something greater than themselves coming to teach him now? It didn't seem to matter if they were embodied or not, they came. Yes, they were here now. Whatever was happening coursed through his Heart, the Heart of the world itself, which again felt like it was growing, expanding in every direction simultaneously. Everything was indeed helping to keep the momentum of relearning living principles.

Golden Threads of Love run throughout every molecule of the cosmos

Paul attended only what was right here. He was fully present, and did not talk from a soapbox, or preach. He was simply part of the Circle. Dad would have called it a bull session.

Kevin's mind flashed to his father. He was well-loved in the martial arts world for his keen teaching style and gentle manner. A student and friend of the legendary Bruce Lee, Dad taught out of his little apartment in North Seattle. A handful of guys and gals would come together on Tuesdays, Fridays and Sundays. No mandatory attendance and no rules, no belts or levels; it was just a get-together, where the first order of business usually consisted of catching up and sharing. Connecting? Then, they would move onto some martial arts stuff. In fact, Dad called it "The Stuff."

The name for his school pegged it well:

The Ed Hart Literary and Social Club, Gung Fu Also Taught

First and foremost, the Ed Hart Club was for getting together, always beginning with a bull session. It was for community, and strongly resembled the get-together he was at tonight in that way; same with the sweats. And, that light in Paul's eyes … very similar to the light in Dad's eyes. Hmm … and to the light in Tom's eyes.

There was a gathering each Sunday morning at this church. He would come, without an acknowledged reason. Church experience thus far had been OK, but with a sort of shroud of oppression. This place was different to him. Vibrations of lightness and offerings of peace called out to him.

***

Sunday, there were many more people in the arced rows of wooden pews. Morning sunlight filled the room, beautiful through the colored glass. Open windows let a flowing breeze through the place, peaceful and inviting on this picturesque spring day. A lone wooden frame behind a pulpit encapsulated just three words:

Peace ~ Be Still

Sunlight glistened off the finely-polished hood of an ebony piano in the northeast corner at the top of the room. A woman, surely another angel, played the sweetest melody, and the melody filled the space. Her smiling face, kind eyes behind round glasses, peaceful swaying side to side while mastering the keys, all seemed to say, "Welcome, come inside." Kevin took a seat. The piano stopped, started again with another song.

The soothing, powerful baritone voice of a man caressed the air, delicately interwoven with each note. The music coursed through Kevin. Many in the room were in a trance-like state; others sang along. No applause followed it, just all attention forward. A man and woman stood at the pulpit and greeted everyone. Their Aura was visible to Kevin, but this was so new he had nothing with which to compare it – or did he? They welcomed new-comers, and spoke to the people as if they were brothers and sisters. Bob and Charlotte were pleasant and magnetizing. So much was happening inside Kevin, it was overwhelming. Everyone was invited to stand and sing together; the man with the resonating voice, who seemed familiar, led the song.

Bob then led the room, at least 75 people now, in another meditation. Peace filled Kevin. There was a connection with not only the whole room and all the people, but by an unseen Essence that was bigger than all of it put together. Here it was again, this all-permeating Spirit which Kevin was beginning to recognize in and through everything.

Divine Love, once found within, reflects in and around all things

Amazing that this many people could create a silence that was so palpable. It was a thundering stillness, which became a soothing peace. Bob led everyone deeper with a soft-spoken voice. "Let your attention go, from your always thinking little mind, to your heart. Here you will find a light. This is your light. Let it encapsulate and surround you, in peace … then the whole room and all in it, our country, the world, all planets and galaxies. Expand this light as far as you wish …"

Bob let the room rest in a soothing silence for what could have been a minute or a thousand more lifetimes.

This time of quiet was only broken at first by the piano, then the haunting baritone voice. The song that ensued brought tears to many an eye. A supreme power rippled through the lyric, the dripping melodies, the piano and the people. He looked again at this man singing and turning songs into pure Love. It was *Peter*, the kind man who did his intake at EMI. And now *his* eyes sparkled with the light.

Loud, happy applause filled the room as the song ended. Silence fell again. Kevin was overjoyed to be here. Bob began a lesson. He did not preach about things Kevin remembered hearing at every other church in his life - heaven and hell, sinning, devils and doom, right and wrong.

Bob spoke of our part in the world we have made, the world in which we choose to live. He talked about projecting out a particular view of reality, seeking out evidence to support that view, finding it, and living right into it - and then blaming others for being the cause of it. It made so much sense! And it connected to every other teaching that had come over this whole undulating year.

I am only reminding you of what you already know

"We're either living from memory or from inspiration," Bob said, holding his hands out, palms up and open, shoulders raised and cocking his head sideways in the "you choose" gesture. "You are both so very special and not that special at all."

After the service was social hour, downstairs, complete with coffee and snacks. Kevin had a wonderful time, and liked it so much he decided to come back. This place and the people felt like even another family.

He thought about this Sunday all throughout the week, and came back again for the Wednesday "mid-week boost," as Paul had coined the evening. Again he loved it, and as Sunday approached Kevin was curious more than ever. He could not wait for the meditation. This time he would pay attention so he could begin to meditate on his own, as Bob had suggested.

Everyone is a teacher, all are students

Bob's lead brought Kevin into a transcendent meditation. It was a moonlit evening upon the warm shore of an ocean ... so much magnificence. Waves came and went as each breath. *So much Love.* He stayed in, all the way through what came next: A song of angels, which sang to his soul. Not until the people applauded the performance did he snap back into his body and the room. His shoulders softened now, his whole face and every limb, even his skin felt right-sized. Radiance was preeminent.

Today, Bob spoke of a Spirit of the Universe, connecting all of the cosmos and beyond, of the hundreds of billions of galaxies, and the life that surely exists in, through and around all of it. Waves of awareness far beyond consciousness were stirred, rippling all the way back to notions of the big bang itself. Again he could hardly fathom it. Was it beyond his current abilities? It did not matter.

Let Me move through you

The social hour downstairs found more connections. During a bit of small talk, someone directed his attention toward a small store of books. Did he realize how much the ten steps to the little wooden bookshelf would change the path of his life?

On it was a small tag: *Community Bookshelf*

It must have been mislabeled. It should have said *The Rabbit Hole* as he would soon come to believe. And this, too, called by way of the new communication.

A woman had directed him toward it. "Anything on it is free for the taking. You can also leave stuff on it you would like to share." Her eyes were glowing pools, as all eyes of those guiding him toward something worthy. There must have been 40 or 50 books, and various recordings on the lower shelves.

As he grazed through the shelves, picking up one book and then another, some kind of vortex or wormhole began to pull him into another reality. Awe and wonder in anticipation of the next bestowing via the unknown swirled and spiraled, flew far beyond the place he stood. The whole room was sucked into some other dimension - he alone floated in this odd experience with the bookshelf which had a life of its own. The attention was unwavering.

"What's this?" He whispered under his breath, catching a book that practically jumped into his hands. As he held it wide-eyed, staring at the cover, the oddest interaction took place. He read the title with the same quiet breath: *"Patterns for Self Unfoldment,"* as he gently stroked the cover with his fingertips.

He opened it and began to read. Whatever the words were was not as important as what came between them, the very energy that surely created it. Were the pages made of magical paper? The cover, some extraterrestrial composite? In this subtle language that was unfurling through everything now, the book spoke.

Take me ~ I am a gift for you

Leaving the church, he could not wait to get home and start reading. The same way as with the others: Read each word carefully, from the very first one, including the dates of printing. It was an older book, but that did not matter. He was supposed to read it.

Like so many other traits of the thinking mind, he'd always lived inside that pesky set of limiting notions. Especially with prayer, meditation, the confusing definitions of God, religion and spirituality, and the plethora of judgment and opinions around all of it. Never having sought a personal relationship with any of this until recently, he had always lived by a phenomenon he had heard called "contempt prior to investigation."

"That won't work for me."

"Oh. Well, have you tried it?"

"No."

"Then how do you know?"

In this world of contempt, it was stifling and confusing. Up until now.

The Way is open

It felt good to let go of the old ways; everything was so alive now! *Everyone* was there to help guide, even seeming strangers at a strange church. *I would have never considered any of this, would have stayed stuck in my arrogance.* The new, old book made him contemplate these gifts.

Instead of hearing the deafening clang of steel trap doors of his once narrow mind slamming shut, he now felt them continuing to open. Beyond, where he had never before been willing to venture, this new path was revealing *itself.*

And with all of it, his Heart continued to open.

This book was not one only to be read. Rather, it was a guidance manual and suggested action. It was also, coincidentally and to his astonishment, a book on meditation – no wonder it had asked Kevin to take it home. He had requested just such a thing. It spoke of the nature of meditation and outlined a process for learning. It was another breadcrumb. Abandoning himself, he began to take fearless steps on the outlined trail.

Take the next indicated action

***

Clean and sober only six months. Already a whole new world, new realms of existence even, had opened up. But he'd been sober nearly this long before and it had been dark and miserable. And then the relapse. What was different now? As the willingness to literally hand over his will and his life to this Higher Power each day grew, so too did opportunities to do just that: Tom's sweat lodges and the ever down-reaching personal conversations he and Kevin were often having, all the writing with journaling, step work in both treatments, even the meditation book required it. Both treatments also required community service and making reparations. There was the honest sharing and listening in meetings and in groups, which was becoming easier to do. The gift of true sobriety is so much greater than what just not getting loaded brings; maybe one day he could realize this.

Changes were occurring so rapidly there was no point of reference, nothing with which to compare them. Had ever he known such Love? There could be no turning back. Who would want to? Once a single ray of the Sunlight of the Spirit graced his awareness, he knew he had stumbled upon much greater purpose. Was it only this, sought in every bottle and pipe, every diversion and manipulative move ever pulled, never to be found? All of it, hidden from awareness, until now.

And here, the fabric covering the windows and concealing Life outside the stuffy dwelling which had always confined him continued to unravel and fall away. The Light touched his skin, warmed him, and filled the once darkened space.

It beckoned him to come into it and play, that it was safe and beautiful. And he could see that it was.

The Way Emerges

When one begins to awaken, miracles become commonplace.

When one calls forth the essence of their being, of Being Itself, a shift occurs that easily washes away the misgivings of conditioned existence.

Life comes into view in a way that seemed impossible before: People, places and things change before the very eyes. The function of the world morphs.

Once concealed pathways are revealed, subtle and mysterious wonders begin to emerge through every molecule, delicately woven and detectable only through direct experience, presence, metaphysical observation.

Calm and acceptance begin to develop as one sees and experiences the Universe itself with a trust that was before too tenuous to suffice.

True Power comes through letting go ~

Allowing finds your greatest potential

***

Months passed. Living the new design manifested unparalleled contentment in a world of belonging. Why had he not allowed spiritual help until now? If he had, he may not have found himself in such precarious situations, and may have even been able to avoid much of the suffering, but this had not been the case. In fact, through the new work, something was coming into awareness: Always knowing too much about too little had manifested the *illusion* of a small, claustrophobic world that *he made real -* and then lived inside.

This was not his fault, for he had been taught much of this. And it was not the fault of the ones who taught him, for they had been well-educated in perpetuating these lies … and on and on, for how many centuries? Using positive imagination and intuition had somehow fallen into atrophy. He rarely sought there for any answers, too enamored with his own false idols and rote ways of seeing and being – even defending them unto his own destruction, which had nearly been accomplished.

He was breaking the cycle now.

It was only he who had accepted limitation and self-deception. But now, by another choice, some Greater Mind whispered true, pure direction; in surrender It could be heard offering harmony, bliss, joy and real love.

By declaration and invocation, the choice was made to seek here for the key which could release these chains that had bound countless generations.

The work done by way of the various treatment facilities was a good beginning. Much still remained to be cleared away, but so did the willingness to trudge onward. The work always continues. The journey from the head to the Heart is an ongoing, gradual process, which requires daily nurturing and maintenance. It is also a sudden awakening. Life is a paradox. He may never arrive or be cured, but that was OK. Today, the joy was in the journey.

Sanctuary is but a state of being

Daily Ritual

"Thank You for this beautiful day, Thank You for Life."
Kevin's first words were spoken aloud and set the pace for another day. Careful not to disturb the pair of just-weaned kittens sleeping next to him. The little white puff-ball girl with crossed baby-blues curled up even tighter into her tiger-striped brother. Penetrating emerald eyes opened wide as his yawn and then, back to sleep. Kevin made his way to the kitchen, straight to the two-cup coffee maker.

He could not wait to go into the little meditation space, the once dismal and empty bedroom. A sturdy knee-high tan table with stout black legs sat below an East-facing window. It had been given to him for an Altar. Upon it was a gift from Tom - an abalone shell and some fine-smelling sage and sweet grass. Prayer and meditation had become the core focus now. The meditation book was nearly completed. Each step as suggested, nearly a three month undertaking. Beginning each day anew in sweet surrender, he was learning how to live from the Heart. Life was anything but lonely now.

First, he stretched his body in a series of movements, in ways that it asked him to, and that just felt good. These stretches enhanced and grew into broader and deeper postures. It allowed him to be more relaxed and comfortable. He loved the way his body was feeling these days, and it loved to be moved in these ways. Every part of him loved the precious gift of sobriety: Mind, Body and Spirit.

Some days, prayer and meditation was done on the knees, but often times sitting cross-legged. In deep internal prayer, he thanked the Great Mystery for his life and for all life, then for each gift:

Please guide my day. Thank you for my sobriety, thank you for my work, for my home. Thank you for this body, this mind and for my health. Thank you for these precious little kittens, for the food we receive. Thank you for the treatment centers and the counselors and workers. Thank you for my family, for Tom, and all my new families. Thank you for taking care of us. Thank you for the guides and way-showers you have placed upon my path, both human and beyond. Let me be of service to someone else today. Please help me with my shortcomings and selfishness.

He ended with something he had learned from Bob during church: Ho'oponopono, ancient Hawaiian healing prayer.

I Am Sorry, Please Forgive Me, I Love You, Thank You

Then, holding both hands out in front of him, palms facing up and not quite together, he imagined his entire life in them, as if it were a globe or something, a sphere containing all his own self-will.

"Here is my will and my life, I willingly hand it to You, to do with as You wish. I let go of it."

Then he did let it go, gently releasing both hands, palms down onto the ground on either side of him, bowing his head slightly in humble respect, feeling the surrender. The sphere, falling through the air and into the earth, disintegrated and vanished into everything and nothing. Kevin trusted that the God of his understanding would take it and turn it into the best and highest good. He did not know just what that would be, but believed he'd be allowed glimpses as more was revealed. And it always was.

Thank You for taking it

Abalone shell in the left hand, a small pile of sage and other medicines in the center of it, he circled his right hand over it in the direction of the sun: "Earth, Air, Fire, Water," he whispered, contemplating each element and its gifts.

Then in both hands he offered it to the North, the East, the South and the West, down to Mother Earth, up to Father Sky, then to Heart-Center. "Thank You, Creator." He imagined each of the Seven Directions expanding infinitely.

Lighting it, he smudged himself, letting the smoke clean and purify him as he'd been shown and taught. Then, he settled into silent meditation.

***

It felt good to be in a constant state of gratitude, and throughout each day now, he became increasingly aware that each breath was indeed a gift.

Practicing gratitude and mysticism even with the morning coffee: Holding it up, it became sacred substance in a sacred vessel; cupping it with both hands, arms outstretched toward the sky, smiling; feeling the radiating warmth, imagining how good it will taste; thanking the plant and all that had brought it into existence; slowly bringing it to anticipating lips, the golden elixir that right now cures all ailments. Accompanied by invisible beings, he imbibed a slow, nourishing sip, feeling it cascade through.

Time seemed to stretch and then melt away. Even though there was more to do than ever, the Universe always allowed enough space for these daily rituals. Throughout any day, each event connected to the next in some chaotic, yet perfect order. Doorways were opened with an invitation to simply walk through, if the choice be made to do so – only, his hand had not had to open them alone.

Could it get any better? The traffic and court fines were nearing completion, as were drug court and the anger-management treatment. The obsession to use had gone. A court date came, but it was not for doing anything wrong. It was in front of the same sentencing judge, but this time Marie had asked for it. Without fear, he went to the court date.

There was Marie, who he dared not even look at, just ten feet away at the other table facing the judge. Judge Smith appeared different, softer. "Your reports are excellent, looks like you've been doing quite well. We don't usually do this, but considering what people have been telling me about your progress, I've decided to lift the no-contact-order, at the complaintant's request."

Kevin would have replied if he hadn't been choking back tears, and could barely squeak out a meek, "Thank you."

Outside the courtroom, he and Marie exchanged a long, strange and wonderful embrace. Much had happened between them. She was one of his divinely placed guides. She had been responsible for keeping him alive, at least in this incarnation. She answered this calling, whatever the reasons. It was another gift among so many.

More books came, and with each, so did more guidance. These books would not have come in the old ways, for he would not have seen them. Neither would have Tom come, or the ancient ceremonies, or the other guides, the daily practices or any of what his life had now become. It had all come by way of the new circles in which he now roamed, and he would not have found these circles without awakened sobriety.

And for him, true sobriety was not possible without finding the Source of Being.

Could it get any better? Well, now it had been revealed …

All is possible through forgiveness ~ Forgiveness is the miracle

Extension

It was late October once more. Along with a growing chill in the air, a warmer feeling was an old friend. Something good was going to happen. Tuesday night, great eight o'clock meeting at the waterfront. Tom was going, too.

Along the beach, the giant orange fireball reflected off a whipping sea as it disappeared over the horizon. It was a gift for grateful eyes. A ferry blasted its arrival, around which dozens of seagulls blew in the wind, shrieking and singing their welcome. Kevin sat, silent as the sun set, before making his way toward the door.

Inside, voices echoed off brightly polished white-tiled floors in the huge, open room. Twenty or so round tables with some eight chairs around each were over half full.

Through the double doors walked a man that seemed ... familiar. This man had a defeated walk, surely encumbered by the weight of the world. His head was hanging, trying not to be noticed. Shaking hands came out of his brown coat's pockets, clutched and slid out a chair from an emptier table toward the back of the room. He fell heavy into it. After a few moments, the man raised his head just enough to reveal bloodshot, pain-ridden eyes.

The meeting began. Tom came and sat near Kevin, who was only watching the troubled soul now; he could feel the man's suffering. The readings finished, and a topic was chosen: Acceptance. When it was announced, the man winced as if he'd been poked with a cattle prod.

As each person shared, Kevin listened but continued attending, with silent support, the man who could not sit still. Something inside was stirring. Halfway through the meeting, the man was called on: "Would you like to share, the guy in the brown coat?"

There was a long silence before he spoke, and when he did his voice was quivering and broken.

"My ... my name's Sean. I ..... I'm ....." He fell to tears for a while, not a full minute, before he spoke again. Now the full attention of the room was upon him.

"My life's a mess! Lost my job ... my wife, she ..." a few sobs thick with guilt were all that was heard for a few more moments.

"She hates me. I'm kicked out, and there's a restraining order! I got violent, so much, I ... What do I tell my kids? I've been drinking every night, in the basement. Can't get up in the mornings... My kids hate me, too. Damn it!

"How'd it get like this? How did I ... I feel so lost, so out of control." With both palms he wiped tears out of sore eyes, pushing too hard to try and stop them and hide from the world at the same time.

Tears welled up now in Kevin's eyes as he sent his Heart field out, even more, to fully encapsulate Sean. He could feel it blend with every other soul in the room, could feel Real Love envelop this man, extend through each being, the sea just outside the window, the planet, and then beyond all of it at once.

"I just don't know what to do, so ... so I came here. *I need help ...*"

Sean paused in contemplation for a few strained breaths, before finishing. "That's all."

Everyone thanked him for sharing, and the rest of the meeting carried depth and weight.

After it was over, several people greeted Sean and gave their support. Eventually it cleared out, save a few people cleaning up. Sean and Kevin sat, one with another one.

"It's OK, I've been there. I know what you're going through," Kevin said, softly, and he did know.

Sean went on and talked about all the destruction and the guilt and the shame, the feeling trapped and the anguish. Kevin let him go on, until he was done.

Then he took the meeting schedule which had been given to Sean and circled some meetings, sharing a bit about each one. Sean seemed to perk up, even if only a little.

***

"Give me a call if you need to talk," Kevin said, as they made their way outside and began to part ways.

A perfect crescent moon hung against the backdrop of the Universe, her two points could have easily punctured the fabric of the cosmos if she were not such a peaceful being. A ferry again blew its horn through the dark night sky as it approached the nearby dock. Stars danced overhead, sparkling and watching. One particularly bright Star bore silent witness as waves crashed into the bulkhead only a stone's throw from where the two men walked.

Kevin stopped. A pause took in all that had come and gone and changed. The Star nudged. Purposefully, he turned toward the man. "Hey Sean ..."

"Yeah?"

"It is possible to change"

~ 253 ~

Epilogue

Many events have transpired since the writing of this book. All have been beautiful gifts, even if not always easy to accept. I write this note to you now, sitting here on a fine fall day in October, 2014, at our little Snohomish lake cottage. The days are again growing cooler, but the sun is golden upon the evergreens across the way and upon the water that is now too cold for swimming. I have not had to drink or use anything else since shortly after the time in the bar, that tortuous event midway through the book. My sobriety date is February 14th, 2007.

Sometime in 2012, I asked another very special man I had known for a short time to be my sponsor. He was always carrying around a certain big blue book and saying things that spoke to my heart. He told me, different from Tom, "That means we will go through the steps." And so, we met every Sunday (often adding another day, too), at a local hospital cafeteria for at least a couple of hours. Over some seven or eight months, we went through all twelve steps together. We also hung out before, during and after meetings as well as frequent get-togethers and long conversations, where he showed me what living the principles meant. Duke was willing to share his time, as Tom had done, which I was soon to learn was more precious than I knew. When we were at the fifth step, Duke was diagnosed with terminal cancer. Knowing Duke and being close with him for the time he had left was, for me and many others, among the greatest of blessings. A true connection to life and to others at the essential level is no small thing.

As I wrote this book, I realized along the way that it was not a book about any one program, or concerned with only the twelve steps (which I have come to learn are one of the most effective ways to realize emotional sobriety). The steps were for me a necessary thing to do and continue to do; without living their principles, I am certain I would not be as free as I am today and this book may not have found completion. While it is one man's journey, and that man is me, it is not only about any one thing or person or pathway mentioned and shared in its pages. It is mostly a story of possibility, human potential, and reaching beyond even this to find spiritual fulfillment. But more, it is a universal story of universal principles. It is a recounting of how I found that hidden treasure of real love buried deep within me, beyond all that I believed myself to be for too many agonizing years. It is also about what happened naturally when I found the peace that love brings: Sharing it with all else who seek it.

This brings me to the "God thing." I had to start somewhere. I do not put a single label on my spiritual orientation. I simply found a way that works for me, which grows and evolves with practice. Maybe naming it only diminishes it. Using words to try and describe what many call God always falls short, but let me have at it. My personal mission statement was much like a sling-shot for this. How I have come to know the Great Unknowable is still a giant mystery. It is through experience of divine bliss rather than through thinking about what it is or attempting to shove myself into a box of rules, that I get to experience living purpose and belonging. It was said to me along the way that contemplation is the highest form of prayer.

The more I focus my thoughts, feelings and actions upon the Source of Being, the more opportunities I am given to look for and find in others what I seek for myself. Through interaction with others are the new pathways and golden threads of all relations revealed. How I share in these pages and what ideas and practices were to me at the time have changed vastly, some having grown to immense proportions and others having become profoundly simple. Though many of the things written about may no longer be part of my walk today, all of it was necessary to get to this very point. We must take the low road to one day get to the high road, or so it seems. It is a truly mysterious and wonderful path. I know less than I did when I started, thank God.

What about you? What stirs in your heart? Can you feel it, or is it buried too deeply beneath what haunts you in this very moment? What do you truly wish to become, had you a choice? There is great purpose to your life, perhaps especially if you feel lost and alone and scared and hopeless. Fear, which so often masquerades as rage and anger, manifests in the kind of behavior you read about in these pages, in addition to so many other limiting behaviors that keep us subdued prisoners of our own minds. We can move through this. Are you willing to become what has always called from the essence of your being?

It is calling now

**

All my best,
Kevin Arthur Hart

Acknowledgments and Gratitude

A great many people, places and things corresponded to help me on the journey of awakening. It is as if the Universe opened up and poured upon me all its guidance and divine wisdom, in every imaginable form, not to be usurped and held, but to be allowed and shared. Much came through people, their notions, books, their intentions; it came through their life's work. Some are still alive in bodies, some are not. In many ways, the book you now hold in your hands is an opportunity for me to honor these precious teachers and way-showers.

When Tom died, I began to realize on a much deeper level what a blessing he was - and continues to be. At his memorial in the early summer of 2009, I felt him come through me. Strange as it may sound, some part of him is forever a part of me. I cherish him now more than ever. Every day his teachings and that to which he dedicated his life guides and helps me. Tom carried a small, hollowed bone in his pocket: "To remind me to be a channel and let Spirit flow through me."

And he was. He may not be in that body anymore, but he is still very much here. Extending what was freely given me to others has become my greatest joy. It has become my core intention. Something within opens, allowing a new vision. Ancient Ones are all around us, all the time, in human form and beyond.

When we allow ourselves to be taught, to become students, the teachings come in abundance. They do not stop, when we are willing to receive. The books and works and people listed below and shared throughout this book are some of the sources of these wisdom teachings. They are listed in no specific order. We realize these teachings are omnipotent and neither owned nor controlled by any one being; they are meant to be shared. They are eternal truths. I acknowledge and honor all beings who dedicate their lives to universal service.

Thank You.

***

Writing as a State of Conscious Dreaming – Robert Moss workshop

Mosswood Hollow Retreat Center

Secret Teachings of Plants: The Intelligence of the Heart in the Direct Perception of Nature - Stephen Harrod Buhner

A Course in Miracles

~ 257 ~

Yoga

The Secret - Rhonda Byrne

Secret History of Dreaming - Robert Moss

Seat of the Soul – Gary Zukav

The Prophet – Kahlil Gibran

The Seven Habits of Highly Effective People – Steven R. Covey

Patterns for Self-Unfoldment – Randolph and Leddy Schmelig

Ho'oponopono

Alcoholics Anonymous

Narcotics Anonymous

Landmark Education

Albert Einstein

Joseph Murphy

Neville

Louise Hay

Joseph Campbell

Wayne Dyer

Don Miguel Ruiz

Michael Beckwith

Joe Vitale

Dan Millman

Richard Bach

Phineas Quimby

Jesus, The Christ

Original Personal Mission Statement

PERSONAL MISSION STATEMENT

I AM ONE WITH MY HIGHER POWER, WE UNDERSTAND EACH OTHER, I DO HIS WILL, AND HE WILLS ME TO DO THE THINGS THAT ALLOW A HAPPY, PEACEFUL HARMONY. EVERY DAY I TAKE TIME TO MEDITATE, PRAY, AND REALIZE WHO I AM, WHERE I AM, HOW I GOT THERE, AND WHERE I WILL GO. I WILL LIVE IN THAT DAY, AND FOR THAT DAY, ONE DAY AT A TIME. HE IS MY MAKER, AND HE GUIDES ME WHERE HE WANTS ME. I FOLLOW, BECAUSE I TRUST HIM.

MY DISEASE IS NO LONGER ACTIVE BUT MY RECOVERY IS. I WORK ON IT EVERY DAY, SOMETIMES ALL DAY AND GOD HELPS ME. I AM HEALING AND AS I DO I BECOME STRONGER AND IT GETS FURTHER AWAY FROM AFFECTING MY LIFE. THE PEOPLE I HAVE IN MY LIFE HELP ME, AND I HELP THEM.

MY CHARACTER GROWS STRONGER EVERY DAY BECAUSE I AM HONEST, OPEN-MINDED AND WILLING. I CARE ABOUT PEOPLE AND I AM COMPASSIONATE, TOLERANT + PATIENT. MY INTEGRITY GROWS EVERY DAY, AND I GO OUT OF MY WAY TO HELP OTHERS BECAUSE I CARE ABOUT THE PEOPLE IN THIS WORLD, AND IT'S WELL BEING. I INSPIRE OTHERS AND IMPACT LIVES IN A POSITIVE WAY.

I DO NOT TRY AND CHANGE OTHERS, BUT I WILL CHANGE MYSELF WHEN NECESSARY. I WILL LISTEN TO OTHERS SO I MAY UNDERSTAND + LEARN, AND WILL BUILD STRONG + HEALTHY RELATIONSHIPS ALL WILL BENEFIT FROM.

I WILL PURSUE MY CHOSEN PATH WITH DILIGENCE AND HONOR AND SURROUND MYSELF WITH OTHERS WHO HAVE AMBITION + CHARACTER, AND WANT TO SUCCEED IN LIFE AS WELL.

I KEEP MYSELF IN EXCELLENT PHYSICAL CONDITION AS WELL AS EMOTIONAL + MENTAL, AND I KEEP MY APPEARANCE PRESENTABLE, SO I LOOK AS GOOD AS I FEEL.

I LOVE MY LIFE. IT IS PURPOSEFUL, MEANINGFUL AND I AM HAPPY. I AM THANKFUL FOR ALL THAT I HAVE.